EXPRESSIONS OF IDENTITY

Theory, Culture & Society

Theory, Culture & Society caters for the resurgence of interest in culture within contemporary social science and the humanities. Building on the heritage of classical social theory, the book series examines ways in which this tradition has been reshaped by a new generation of theorists. It will also publish theoretically informed analyses of everyday life, popular culture, and new intellectual movements.

EDITOR: Mike Featherstone, *Nottingham Trent University*

SERIES EDITORIAL BOARD
Roy Boyne, *University of Durham*
Mike Hepworth, *University of Aberdeen*
Scott Lash, *Lancaster University*
Roland Robertson, *University of Pittsburgh*
Bryan S. Turner, *Deakin University*

THE TCS CENTRE
The Theory, Culture & Society book series, the journals *Theory, Culture & Society* and *Body & Society*, and related conference, seminar and post-graduate programmes operate from the TCS Centre at Nottingham Trent University. For further details of the TCS Centre's activities please contact:

Centre Administrator
The TCS Centre, Room 175
Faculty of Humanities
Nottingham Trent University
Clifton Lane, Nottingham, NG11 8NS, UK e-mail: tcs@ntu.ac.uk

Recent volumes include:

Pierre Bourdieu and Cultural Theory
Critical Investigations
Bridget Fowler

Re-Forming the Body
Religion, Community and Modernity
Philip A. Mellor and Chris Shilling

The Shopping Experience
edited by Pasi Falk and Colin Campbell

Undoing Aesthetics
Wolfgang Welsch

Simmel on Culture: Selected Writings
edited by David Frisby and Mike Featherstone

The Consumer Society
Myths and Structures
Jean Baudrillard

EXPRESSIONS OF IDENTITY

Space, Performance, Politics

Kevin Hetherington

SAGE Publications
London • Thousand Oaks • New Delhi

First published 1998

Published in association with *Theory, Culture & Society*,
Nottingham Trent University

SAGE Publications Ltd
6 Bonhill Street
London EC2A 4PU

SAGE Publications Inc
2455 Teller Road
Thousand Oaks, California 91320

SAGE Publications India Pvt Ltd
32, M-Block Market
Greater Kailash – I
New Delhi 110 048

British Library Cataloguing in Publication data

A catalogue record for this book is
available from the British Library.

ISBN 0 8039 7876 6
ISBN 0 8039 7877 4 (pbk)

Library of Congress catalog card number 98-61015

Typeset by Photoprint, Torquay, Devon
Printed in Great Britain by The Cromwell Press Ltd, Trowbridge,
Wiltshire

CONTENTS

ACKNOWLEDGEMENTS

In the course of writing this book I have had discussions with many people. I have also used much of the material with students in classes on some of the various courses I have taught. I would like to thank all of these people, too numerous to name here. In particular, however, I would like to thank the following people: Nick Abercrombie, Paul Bagguley, Tom Cahill, Brian Docherty, Mike Featherstone, Joanne Hollows, John Law, Phil Macnaghten, Rolland Munro, Simon Naylor, Martin Parker, Rob Shields, Bron Szerszynski, John Urry, Alan Warde, and Pnina Werbner – all of whom have provided me with critical comments on all or part of the book or have contributed to discussions out of which some of the ideas for this book were formed. As is customary, I take sole responsibility for the contents of this book. I would also like to thank Stephen Barr, Vanessa Harwood, Chris Rojek and Robert Rojek at Sage for their patience and encouragement while I was writing this book.

An earlier version of Chapter 4 appeared as 'The Contemporary Significance of Schmalenbach's Concept of the Bund', *The Sociological Review*, 42 (1): 1–25. I would like to thank *The Sociological Review* for their kind permission in allowing me to reproduce it here.

INTRODUCTION

Imagine walking down the high street of any medium-sized town in Britain in the latter half of the 1990s. There would be the usual range of estate agents, banks and greetings card shops. There might be a small 1960s shopping arcade, revamped in the 1980s with atrium and glass roof to mimic the larger shopping malls that have become a major part of the retail scene in British cities since the mid-1980s. A few surviving traditional shops – bakers, butchers, grocers and so on – would be found. There would also, however, be other kinds of retailing outlets catering for what were once alternative or fringe interests, for example, a franchised branch of The Body Shop selling all manner of environmentally friendly, non-animal-tested cosmetics and bath foams, and a shop called something like 'Labyrinth' selling 'ethnic bric-a-brac', talismans and a range of authentic crafts such as hand-woven rugs, healing crystals, incense burners, handmade Indian jewellery, Peruvian earthenware pots, etc. You may also find a wholefood/ health food shop, perhaps a vegetarian cafe or restaurant and, in reasonably affluent towns, offices for chiropractors, reflexologists, homeopathists and other assorted complementary healers and counsellors (see Sharma, 1992). The term lifestyle shopping, that has become a part of the sociology of consumption, may be an apt means of describing the interests catered for by these latter enterprises and the customers they serve (see Shields, 1992a). Lifestyle shopping, however, has tended to be used to refer more specifically to consumption practices and lifestyles that are indicative of the playful and style conscious arena of identity performance and *bricolage* among urban, middle-class young shoppers interested in malls and designer labels rather than these more environmentally focused and ethnically identifying forms of shopping (Shields, 1989; 1992a; Tomlinson, 1990, Featherstone, 1991b; O'Connor and Wynne, 1996b; Taylor et al., 1996).

This fascination with the idea of a postmodern, consumer world among sociologists over the last decade has in many respects been a continuation of a long-standing interest in the urban, the hip and the cool. In some ways this contemporary interest in consumption and identity, and its association with broader ideas of postmodernism, developed out of earlier studies of youth subcultures and alternative lifestyles in the 1970s when they were indeed hip and at the cutting edge of youth styles (see Hall and Jefferson, 1976; Hebdige, 1979; more recently Thornton, 1995). While these can be seen to be the origin of many of the more alternative lifestyle interests that now have their place on the high street, that culture tends to be seen now as rather passé by those more interested in the cutting edge of street fashions and tastes during the 1980s and 1990s (for example, Thornton, 1995) – something, of course, that has also been reflected in most of the postmodern work on consumption.

These sorts of alternative lifestyles might have been of more interest among those involved particularly in analysing political rather than consumption practices. If consumption has been one of the leading indicators used to discuss the relationship between issues of identity and the changing character of society in a modern/postmodern world, so too have the related phenomena of new social movements, identity politics and the politics of difference and cultural hybridity often been seen in a similar light (see Lash and Urry, 1987; 1994; Rutherford, 1990; Featherstone, 1991b; Hall and du Gay, 1996; Sarup, 1996; Werbner and Modood, 1997). While this interest may be new, the issue is not one of newness in the simple sense. Such identity politics and the lifestyles with which they are associated have been a long-standing feature of modern societies (see Tucker, 1991; Calhoun, 1995). Feminist groupings and ideologies, for example, can be dated back to at least the eighteenth century. One can certainly also trace alternative lifestyles back to the Bohemian and Romantic identities of the nineteenth century (see Grana, 1964) as well as to religious and Utopian communities of earlier times. However, it is the 1960s that are often taken as a watershed for the development and proliferation of counter-cultures, alternative lifestyles and new social movements that have helped to shape this variety of identity and lifestyle examples that still exist today.

Some of this 'counter-culture' lifestyle can now be found in the high street; however, its more political forms, while less visible as a distinct oppositional culture than they were in the early 1970s, have never fully disappeared. Depending on who you read, they either remain as a subterranean cultural expression kept alive during the years of the Thatcher consumer-culture by New Age travellers, peace camps, and animal rights campaigners (McKay, 1996), or were transformed from an anti-structural moment of cultural resistance and opposition into a successful part of the cultural mainstream (Martin, 1981), or are a mixture of both (Heelas, 1996). Whichever is the case, such a body of lifestyle interests and identity politics are part of the current repertoire of examples that are drawn upon to illustrate the changing character of identity and indeed what that change might mean in terms of the changing character of society as a whole.

The type of lifestyle associated with this type of identity politics is, of course, about more than shopping. Indeed, one of the main features of the so-called counter-culture from which these lifestyle interests developed, was its anti-consumerism or more broadly anti-materialism (see Inglehart, 1977). Such 'post-material' lifestyles, while they do have their outlets in the high street, can still be found well away from the world of consumption, among the political activities of so-called new social movements. Those same towns in which this form of alternative lifestyle retailing can readily be seen are also likely to contain backstreets where one can find women's centres, alternative book shops, meeting places for environmentalist groups, whether they be mainstream groups like Friends of the Earth or more radical ones like Earth First!, animal rights networks, a few remnants of the once thriving peace movement, gay and lesbian pubs and clubs, and a host of tiny anarchist groups that still exist in just about every town in Britain (see Bondi, 1993; Bell and Valentine, 1995; McKay, 1996; Purkis, 1996; Ryan and Fitzpatrick, 1996). One might find small groups of New Age travellers parked up in a temporary encampment just outside the town in some quiet country lane (see Hetherington, 1992; 1996), or there may be a camp of anti-road protesters in tree-huts and down tunnels nearby on the proposed site of some bypass (see Docherty, 1996).

These groupings, especially those that do not go down an institution-alising route by transforming themselves into more formal non-government organisations, pressure groups and lobbyists, can often trace their histories back to the 1960s. As specific, identifiable groups, however, they are often individually short-lived, fluid in composition and rather ephemeral in a networked, dispersed sort of way (see Melucci, 1989). Interest ebbs and flows but earlier traces always seem to remain to be built upon at some later date by new generations of activists and supporters. There will always be a few remaining committed die-hards who have settled in the area who will carry on a tradition of activism that has persisted in these backstreets and student quarters. This in its turn will often be fuelled by young people, students and ex-students in particular, who can be found in the area or who remain in the area after finishing college or university. Groups emerge and develop as nodes within wider, more diffuse networks of supporters and become the source of a locally situated set of identity politics and lifestyle practices (see Melucci, 1989). All the same, it is difficult to continue to speak of this diffused and dispersed cultural assemblage in simple terms like counter-culture. While a certain degree of opposition to the values of society might remain, it is now less easy to identify what the mainstream is, especially in terms of questions of lifestyle where once radical alternatives have become part of what can be found in the high street. While most activists would shun such commercial outlets and what they represent, they are still part of the same phenomenon; they are part of a multiplicity of interests and activities that can loosely be said to be about alternative ways of living that place identity, identity politics, spatial politics and expressivism together.

This book is not specifically about consumption or politics as such but rather about the sorts of 'alternative' lifestyle interests that are associated with what I have called expressive identities. Just as there is little in the consumption literature on these sorts of expressive 'alternative' lifestyles, so too the literature on new social movements has been somewhat ambivalent towards these more cultural issues, often preferring to focus on more tra-ditional issues within political sociology such as mobilisation, organisation, and repertoires of action (for example, Zald and McCarthy, 1979; Tarrow, 1994), with the politics of social movements (Jenkins and Klandermans,

1995), or with the class background of members and its significance to the study of social movements (see Parkin, 1968; Bagguley, 1992). Attempts to focus on issues of identity and lifestyle can indeed be found in this new social movement literature (in particular Melucci, 1989; 1996; Pakulski, 1993; Rucht, 1990), but they often sit uneasily within studies of social movements in Britain and in North America. One gets the sense that many writing on social movements treat any focus on identity with some suspicion, seeing such concerns as a Continental import that might be better suited to cultural studies than to political science. Those who do write about issues of identity among new social movements are often called upon to justify their supposed lack of concern with the political actions of such movements (that is, what *really* matters). Rarely is it the other way around. Rarely are those who write about social movements as political phenomena called on to take questions of culture and identity as central rather than peripheral or marginal. The hope is that this book will challenge some of them to do so. One cannot separate politics from issues of identity and lifestyle.

This book is concerned with how we might come to look at the broad phenomena that make up such expressive identities, a view that takes in not only alternative lifestyles (see McKay, 1996) and the activists of the social movements and their identity politics, but also some forms of youth culture which overlap with these, certain New Age movements (see Heelas, 1996), green consumption, complementary healing practices and so on. This comprises a broad spectrum of interests, outlooks and activities for which terms like counter-culture, subculture, social movement, identity politics – even lifestyle – seem inadequate. Other terms have come to the fore in recent sociological writing that address the issue of lifestyle and collective identifications such as neo-tribes (Maffesoli, 1988a; 1996; Bauman, 1990; 1991), life-politics (Giddens, 1990; 1991) or sub-politics (Beck, 1992; 1996). These are worthy of consideration too, but the likelihood is that within this cultural spectrum that we are looking at there will be a range of distinct cultural practices that cannot be adequately explained with recourse to any one generic term or concept. Indeed, I will argue that it is important that we do not try and find one term or one concept to understand this set of phenomena but retain some sense of multiplicity of terms and concepts. Rather than look for a name that allows us to offer a neat definition, it would be a more worthwhile exercise to try and delineate some of the issues – cultural and political, as well as spatial and performative – that lie behind this range of activities that have come to influence not only those on the margins but those in the mainstream of many Western societies.

In Cahoots: expression and identity

An example which can be used to illustrate some of these issues is an alternative lifestyle publication, the Manchester-based *Cahoots*.[1] Manchester, a large city in north-west England whose composition is not dissimilar to many European cities of similar size, has all of the interests outlined above (see O'Connor and Wynne, 1996a; Taylor, et al., 1996). Partly these focus on the large student community and the ex-students who continue to live in the city, but also take in a broad range of people who live and work there as well. The magazine itself was established in the early 1980s primarily as a listings magazine for a variety of what it describes in its subheading as 'North West Alternatives'. As well as a range of articles on a variety of alternative lifestyle concerns, each issue contains a directory that lists an assortment of groups and activities that generically can be associated with the types of alternative lifestyle that are often described as emphasising the expressive realm of experience: New Age beliefs and spirituality, therapy and personal growth, minority rights campaigns, support and self-help groups, non-violent protests, complementary medicines, vegetarian and vegan organisations, and so on. From a study of ten issues of this magazine dated from 1985 to 1990, the following main features associated with the characteristics of these expressive identities can be identified:

1. The search for 'authentic experiences' and personal growth
2. Empathy and identification with the rights and freedoms of marginalised or oppressed others
3. Emphasis on the importance of establishing some distinct space for groups and networks of like-minded associates to meet, live or protest
4. Using these spaces as the basis for groupings that are held together by their emotional and moral solidarity
5. Seeing the body as a focus of well-being and an expressive source of communication and identification with others
6. Interest in knowledge rejected by the instrumentalism of modern science, medicine, religion, and politics.

These sorts of interests certainly have similarities with earlier counter-cultural activities and alternative lifestyles (see Roszak, 1970; Martin, 1981; Tipton, 1982; McKay, 1996), but many of them (all but 3 and 4) could just as easily illustrate a likely basis for the habits of the consumers who frequent the alternative shops as they might the motivation for many new social movement political activists. This ambivalence illustrates the mingling of fringe and mainstream activities, supporting Martin's contention that by the 1980s much of the once coherent 1960s counter-culture had started to become dispersed into mainstream culture (1981). We might add now the further point that it is just as difficult to locate the mainstream as it is the alternative to it (see also the introduction in Cohen and Taylor, 1992). It is not only that so-called alternatives become part of the mainstream but that alternatives draw on the mainstream as well; the use of information technology would be a case in point. With the Internet home pages we can see this blurring of boundaries. It is not clear where the boundary between the fringe, alternative origins of the home page culture that treats the Internet as a Utopian space for free expression, and the military and academic hardware and network linkage mainstream, lies.

Nor is it just about the blurring of the identity concerns of political activists with those of consumers. There are also many similarities here with the characteristics that have been used to describe the New Age movement with its emphasis on the processes of self-growth and spirituality. This too covers a spectrum of interests from the culturally oppositional to the highly commercial (see Heelas, 1996). As such, the terms lifestyle shopping, counter-culture or new social movement cannot adequately be taken as the terrain in which we will find this emphasis on developing an identity around expressive concerns and symbols. Instead, we have to accept that we are dealing with a range of cultural fields or a multiplicity of identity foci and practices that have some kind of elective affinity. That affinity has more to do with expressivism than with either consumption or politics.[2]

In this series of interests and outlooks, which may assume a consumerist medium or a more radical search for expressive alternatives, we find, therefore, an overriding relationship between issues of identity on the one hand and the affectual basis for wanting to belong on the other. Belonging is not a property of either the fringe or the mainstream, rather it travels between them (see Munro, 1998). This relationship between expressivism, belonging and identity is a major feature of the quest for identity that runs throughout modern societies, forming what would once quite simply have been seen as part of a romantic critique of the effects of the instrumental and alienating character of that type of society upon the creative individual (see Peckham, 1962; Gouldner, 1973). How we look at that without being drawn into the essentialising of issues of identity around ideas about human nature and its alienation remains to be seen. How we theorise such a diffuse and dispersed set of issues also requires some further thought.

Telling tall stories: identity play denotes social change

While the amount of detailed work, theoretical as well as empirical, on this constellation of expressive identity politics remains underdeveloped, the one way in which it has been extensively discussed is when it is taken as indicative of wider social changes associated with trying to define the current status of modernity. First, we have seen emerge within sociology from the mid-1980s the idea of a postmodernism: a term that moved from associations with art in particular used to describe the playful, ironic and pastiche character of certain styles of art and architecture (Jencks, 1986) to being one that is used to characterise the uncertain, stasis-defined, information and simulation rich social configuration, postmodernity (society now being seen as too much of a modernist term), that is thought to exist at the end of the twentieth century (see Jameson, 1984; 1991; Lyotard, 1984; Lash and Urry, 1987; *Theory Culture and Society*, 1988; Harvey, 1989; Bauman, 1987; 1991; Featherstone, 1991b).

The industry that has since grown up around this idea of postmoderni continues to thrive, yet we have also begun to see during the 1990s something of a backlash against the idea of postmodernity and the re-assertion of a belief in the current social condition as one still of modernity, albeit a different modernity: one less sure of itself, more uncertain, de-traditionalised, provisional and risk ridden – in general, more a reflexive modernity (see Giddens, 1990; 1991; Beck, 1992; Beck et al., 1994; Lash and Urry, 1994; Heelas et al., 1996). In both cases, a wide-ranging review of cultural, economic and political trends has been carried out in order to determine the character of the shift to this new type of society. While a major theme in this work has been that of the various processes associated with globalisation and the transformations of society across formerly neatly defined nation-state boundaries, the local has also been a part of this picture, notably through a focus on how the global translates into the local through new lifestyles and the politics of identity. While the lifestyles of the urban middle classes have been one means of illustrating these cultural changes (see Zukin, 1988; Featherstone, 1991b; Lash and Urry, 1994; O'Connor and Wynne, 1996b), the new social movements and alternative lifestyles – 'life politics' – have often been taken as another (see for instance Lash and Urry, 1987; 1994; Giddens, 1990).

A postmodern perspective has in large part focused on the urban cultural changes associated with shopping, consumerism and fashion, the declining salience of social class, and especially of class based social movements. Correlated with this has been the emergence of new social movements like feminism and environmentalism that have been equated with this post-modern shift (see Lash and Urry, 1987). In particular, the French sociologist Michel Maffesoli has followed this route in his argument that the decline of class and class identities has seen its replacement by different types of identifications: neo-tribes based around interests and outlooks not deter-mined by one's class background (1988a; 1988b; 1996). Similarly Zygmunt Bauman, in his own reading of the development of postmodernity as a society where class has become a memory (Bauman, 1982), has given neo-tribes a key place as the new form through which people identify with others (1990; 1991). The sorts of groupings identified above – new social move-ments, youth subcultures, alternative lifestylers – have been used to illustrate these neo-tribes as the main source of identification within the sociality of postmodernity.

Similarly, the critics of postmodernity and advocates of reflexive-modernity, whose work owes more to neo-functionalist German social theorists like Habermas and Luhmann than it does to the French post-structuralist ones who have come to be associated with the postmodern, also take these groupings – more recently described as a sub-politics (Giddens, 1990; Beck, 1992; 1996) – to illustrate the counter-argument to post-modernity. Modernity, and in particular the process of modernisation is no longer seen as defined by its differences from traditional, pre-modern societies as was formerly the case, but in relation to earlier understandings of the modern. Beck, for example, defines a reflexively modern society as one characterised by the modernisation of modernisation (1992). By this he means that the processes of modernisation have become reflexive processes that act upon their own conditions. While this process of reflexive modernisation is illustrated through a variety of areas of social change – in the labour market, through the generation of environmental risks brought about by science and industry, and in the ways that intimate relationships are becoming more reflexive (examples echoed in much of Giddens's recent work, such that both writers appear to be writing about the same issues simultaneously, see also Lash, 1993) – the new social movements and their lifestyles are also seen as illustrative of the unbinding of traditional forms of identity and politics in a reflexive modernity. The identity politics of these sorts of sub-political groups is, in this respect, taken as indicative of the emergence of a reflexively modern society and a process of *individualisation* that it unleashes, just as it is taken, in contrast, as indicative of a *de-individualising* process and neo-tribalism of a postmodern sociality in the work of Maffesoli (1996; see also Bauman, 1990; 1991).

As with almost any area of sociology, one can find earlier work on similar themes. In the 1970s it was not postmodernity that was the focus but postindustrialism. Modernity may not have been in question then as much as it has been recently, but it was still seen as crisis ridden and undergoing a change in character (see Bauman, 1987). At that time the leading social theorists argued that we were moving not from a modern to a post or reflexive modern society, but from an industrial to a postindustrial one where the axial principles of society were moving from the sphere of the economy to that of culture (see Bell, 1979). These concerns came to some sort of focus in the late 1970s around arguments that the social changes then developing were illustrative of the emergence of a culture of narcissism in which traditional forms of community and authority had been undermined by the new communitarianism and cult of the self brought about by the 1960s counter-culture (see Carroll, 1977; Sennett, 1977; 1986; Bell, 1979; Lasch, 1980; see also Bauman, 1987). Again, the counter-culture and the new social movements associated with it were taken as a key illustration of these cultural changes. Within these discussions of the counter-culture, issues of expressivism and identity were central. They have been a prominent part of the cultural terrain of contemporary societies. Before that Parsons identified an expressive revolution taking place in American society, the youth cultures, counter-cultures and social movement protests of the 1960s being used as illustrations. Before that, one can go back all the way to Max Weber and find in his famous lecture 'Science as a Vocation' his own worries about the expressivism and religiosity of an anti-scientific [counter] culture that was then strong in German society (1970a). Weber alludes to the German youth movement as an example of this. Clearly nothing is new here.

Whatever type of n-modern society we live in, there has been sociological interest in the direction of that society and scrutiny of those who try to offer some (Utopian) alternative to its main direction (see Mannheim, 1938). A link has often been made between expressivism, identity politics and either mass movements or mass cultural trends. The tension between established social forms and individual forms of expression that often challenge them, has consistently been seen by sociologists, preoccupied by issues of change and crisis, as one of the key indicators of social change.

There are two issues here that particularly concern me. The first is the relationship between expressivism and identity that can be found in all of these examples. The second is what this interest in it among sociologists reveals about the sociological gaze. We cannot write sociologically about a particular subject without also recognising what that sociology is doing in terms of its power effects. Of course, those effects will not always be obvious; authors do not make for good deconstructive readers of their own texts. All the same, what we are doing is an issue we have to take seriously when we write. And it is more than about being reflexive in style and self-consciousness as an author (see Law and Hetherington, 1998).

My concern with identifying and analysing aspects of the relationship between the expressive and identity practices is explicit in this book. The chapters that follow each take a particular theme associated with aspects of this expressive identity politics and lifestyle and discuss it in detail. Through the book I build up a theoretical account – a story of sorts, a narrative where one chapter builds upon the previous one – of this relationship between the expressive and identity. But it is a story that has no moment of closure. Each of the chapters cuts a different facet on identity politics. I aim to offer a series of ways of looking at it rather than to produce a whole picture; as with any faceted surface one cannot form a single picture, but a distortion and multiplicity of different, yet connected and overlapping images. But there is still a single image of a kind, albeit one that remains deliberately incomplete and ultimately uncertain. What I want to do is to refuse the sorts of approach I have identified above in both their postmodern and reflexive modern variations. The reader looking for my take on the final question, 'so are these expressive identities modern or postmodern?' will be disappointed. It is not so much that I try to dodge this question but that I think it is the wrong sort of thing to be asking. It is the wrong way to be approaching social theory and this book is as much about social theory as it is about the issue of expressive identities. Above all, my problem is the denotative problem: it is about the blindness that results from trying to get social theory to work holistically and represent the world as a single and simple picture (see Law and Hetherington, 1998). New social movement is a single and simple term. As such it defies its own multiplicity. My problem has to do, in particular, with the relationship between connotation and denotation in social theory (on this issue see Barthes, 1968; Bryson, 1983).[3] While it is sometimes difficult to avoid using such terms, the overall purpose of this book is to explode denotative terms like 'new social movements' and their Hegelian totalising heritage and to look instead at the fragments that make up the multiplicity that remains. The question I set out to address in this book through the example of expressive identities is: 'How might we think these new social movements, counter-cultures and alternative lifestyles otherwise?' 'Otherwise' to being 'new' would be a simple place to start. It is fairly easy to take issue with the idea of the newness of these 'movements' and argue that they are not all that new, that their origins can be traced back well into the nineteenth century where questions of identity were just as important within the labour movement, the women's suffrage movement, and the various peace movements as to the bohemian lifestyles of the past two hundred years. However, it is not the issue of newness that particularly worries me (except when it is associated with ideas of social conjuncture). Rather, my interest is in how we might think these expressive identities otherwise to being an indication of changes within society as a whole. In short, I want to argue that we not only have to drop the 'new' in new social movements but the 'social movements' as well.

It is this denotative move, indicated by the concept of social movement, that I want to challenge more than the actual theories themselves. The term social movement clearly has its origins in the Utopianism of Hegelian and Marxist understandings of society and agents of social change (von Stein, 1964). Such denotative social theory very quickly loses sight of specificity, multiplicity and locatedness of the identity practices that it wants to describe, seeking instead historical actors on the bigger stage. In other words, it loses sight of, or ignores, what this assemblage of cultural and political practices might connote in terms of the variety of identity politics, forms of collective identification, and situated symbolic and knowledge practices that are clearly apparent to anyone who has done research on new social movements and seen what is important in the lives of the individuals and groupings associated with this term. The connotative, while it does not dispense with narrative and theoretical work, challenges this attempt to represent the world as a single and simple picture rather than in its multiple state. Rather than think in terms of simple and singular pictures and operate theoretically through some sort of 'narrative Euclideanism', it is better to think in terms of matrices and sets and recognise that multiplicity, in totality, always escapes our grasp.

These identity practices and the politics that they are caught up in may well bring about change within society, and that change may be global but it is equally likely to be more local and plural and may also be just as much about both intended and unintended forms of social reproduction. To analyse expressive identities and identity politics as other than new social movements, revealing things that might otherwise either be overlooked or more likely be seen as unimportant, we have to move from trying to locate them in some linear sense of time. We need to cease locating them as points at which the line of society becomes hinged (a conjuncture) and moves off in another direction, and think instead in terms of more heterogeneous assemblages of political, cultural and individual factors that have no specific direction but that are significant and denotative in their own terms.

In this book I want to develop an approach that while it addresses a range of theoretical and conceptual issues in relation to this identity multiplicity can also be read as a critique of denotation as a strategy for social theory. One cannot altogether refuse to make denotative moves when constructing a theory; perhaps a degree of demoted denotation is always inevitable. However, I want to refuse the move to issues of bigger scale, in particular the move that says: 'expressive identities, lifestyles and politics denote the development of an *n-society*'. It is this that turns new social movements into a single picture rather than a multiple assemblage. This theoretical move makes the move from seeing what it studies in a multiplicity of connotative ways to a singular denotative way of describing what either is or ought to be going on within society as a whole.

The problem with the denotative move is one that is identified particularly well by feminists like Haraway, as in her argument for situated knowledges and multiple vision against ideas of science as having a singular objectivity (1991). The study of new social movements, lifestyle shopping, neo-tribes or sub-politics, as denoting the development of a new type of society, performs what Haraway, in her discussions of science, terms the 'god-trick'. It sees the world from no specific point, from a privileged position outside the frame, as a picture that can be viewed in total by the roving Cyclops eye of the theorist (see also Law and Hetherington, 1998). It then takes part of that picture and describes what is connoted in it. That connotation is then taken as denoting how we should interpret the picture as a whole. The question for me is how we might avoid the god-trick in our studies and its power effects, without becoming untheoretical and empiricist in our approach. For me the answer is to avoid the theorising that makes this move from connotation to denotation and its grand narrative form. We have to look at what expressive identities denote in themselves, in their own situated practices, rather than seeing them on another level as an indication of social changes that might come about through their activities. The commonalities that we might identify, in terms of orientation, symbolic practice, knowledge claims, group organisation and so on, do not denote anything outside of those situated practices. It is there that they are important. Outside they only connote. That is not, however, the same as saying they cannot have wider reaching effects. Rather, it is about not confusing the empirical with the analytical.

We cannot assume an independent position from which to use new social movements to interpret the world and give support to our theories of how it is changing. To try and theorise from such a position – a position that is both privileged and partial but blind to its own partiality – is to miss what is happening among the detail. This does not mean a move into empiricism in which no theoretical analysis is possible; it means theorising in terms of the constellation of situated practices, identities, politics, spaces and lifestyles that make up these interests in making expressive identities, while at the same time retaining that sense of assemblage and multiplicity. Of course, the problem here is that in saying this I too am in danger of making a denotative statement: that we focus our studies on the local, partial and contingent rather than the global. That denotation, however, does not rest on my analysis; it remains independent of my 'grand narrative' of local stories, multiple perspectives and partial truths. If we reject both the theoretical desire to denote and the alternative of an atheoretical empiricism, what we are left with is an adding process than never ends with an equals sign (see Deleuze and Parnet, 1987). The equals sign is implied in the process of adding rather than the end product. Each bit of the constellation or assemblage that we associate with this relationship between expressive forms and identity is equally significant. A social theory that only connotes is one which is opposed to holism. Its concepts are used in a rhizomic way, horizontally within a plane of immanence, rather than in a tree-like (arborescent) way and transcendentally (see Deleuze and Guattari, 1994). The bits may come together and be held in some tension with one another, there may be some sort of story that we can read, but they do not come together as a whole that denotes something more than their sum; which is why I have used the metaphor of the facet.[4] If there is a whole, the gem that our analysis seeks to capture, we can never see it except through a myriad of many distinct, if connected facets that refract and unsettle a total perspective.

One approach that challenges the denotative and holistic might be to take an overtly reflexive stance, to situate oneself within one's writing (and research) (see Clifford and Marcus, 1986). The danger, of course, is that denoting about society moves to denoting about the role of the researcher within the research process and becomes a preoccupation – a subjectivised occasionalism, for scrutiny of the self – of the author.[5] That too is something I want to avoid. I will, however, give a brief account of where I am positioned in relation to the identities and groupings analysed in this book so that the reader can see where my perspective is located. It is only right for me to acknowledge something of my own location (my formation, as some might say) that led me to write this text. It is not, however, something that I intend to dwell on in the rest of this book.

A space in a network

Between 1983 and 1986, while living in Glasgow, I worked in an 'alternative' or 'radical' bookshop. This not only sold a wide range of radical and small press books and magazines but also acted as a meeting place for a whole series of groups and organisations: feminist, anarchist, environmentalist and peace movement activists, self-help groups, and so on. In the basement, a printer had set up a small business printing much of the literature for these groups. The shop also served as a mail base for many of these and other more traditional far left groups. As such, I was located at a centre used by many groups and also on the fringes of a wide range of groupings that make up this arena of expressive identity politics. I was active in one or two but not all of these groups. Even though I was not conducting research at the time, I was able to see and experience something of their character in terms of group dynamics, membership composition, the web-like character of the networks in which individuals and groups were located, the moral codes of behaviour that operated, the charismatic figures, the use to which clothing and other forms of bodily adornment were put in the establishing of identities and identifications, the friendships and personal animosities that developed, and so on. I was also able to witness the many activities and political actions in which such groups were involved. Small-scale non-violent direct actions, involvement in protests organised by larger groups like the Campaign for Nuclear Disarmament (CND), the peace camp outside the nearby Trident Nuclear Submarine Base at Faslane, as well as some activities associated with the nearby Glasgow University were all a major part of activities of these diverse groups. But there was more to it than that. There was also reading, discussion, relationships, shared living arrangements, drinking and socialising, and all manner of equally important social as opposed to political practices. The network was a fluid one. Many groups were interconnected, others had connections with semi-active people from earlier generations. There was support and solidarity at both a group and an individual level but there were animosities and hostilities as well.

A key event during this period that crystallised many things was the 1984–85 miners' strike in Britain. For some, notably those who had become involved in these identity politics but who had formerly been involved in more conventional socialist and communist groups, this seemed to trigger certain feelings of guilt. While I did not witness a rush of people rejoining left wing political parties, many of these people were instrumental in setting up independent miners' support groups in order to raise money for striking miners and their families. Feminists became active and supportive of the many women's support groups that emerged within the mining communities. Some, notably pacifists in the peace movement, remained somewhat aloof from this trade union dispute and some, radical environmentalists in particular, found themselves torn between showing solidarity for people engaged in a political struggle while also remaining being critical of the environmental impact of the use of coal. However, one witnessed a coming together of many within this network of identity politics activists, and in some cases with representatives of the labour movement as well. Mainstreams and alternatives became blurred. After the defeat of that strike, many things fell apart. A major year-long impetus for action was gone: groups began to split apart; some, like myself, drifted away from this scene (in my case into university); a few remained as committed activists, to form the nucleus for new groups and networks that began to emerge a year or two later with different interests and different agendas.

Like many, I made a move from a certain degree of political activism into education, through the vehicle of social science. I soon noticed from some of my first year tutorials that universities appeared to be part of the identity politics network that I had already experienced before going there. One common route associated with identity politics seems to be from activism into education. Identity politics are, after all, an educational experience, based not only on personal experiences but also on required reading in order to establish and maintain one's credentials and political analysis.

While studying sociology had something of a depoliticising effect on me, debunking many of the beliefs I had held about society, individuals, power and so on, I retained an interest in the sort of groups and networks of which I had once been a member. I went on to undertake doctoral research on issues of space and identity, focusing on two case studies: the first on New Age travellers, and the second on a group of radical environmentalists, many of whom lived on canal boats in the north-west of England (see Hetherington, 1993). I had never been either a traveller or a radical environmentalist, but most of my observations and many of the issues brought up in interview seemed very familiar to my own experiences of a few years earlier. I have spent a considerable amount of time over the past four years turning this work into publications. Indeed, this book is a part of that work.

I do not intend to make any more of reflexively talking about myself in this book. No doubt I have left some things out. This is not a methodological book about the use of autobiography or about the role of the researcher within research. What this account aims to suggest is that my account is not an 'objective' one in the narrow sense that is often used within scientific discourse, but one that is born out of a variety of experiences within such groupings – both as a participant and then as an independent observer – that extends back over about fifteen years. The book is sociological and theoretical in tone rather than empirical or autobiographical. Perhaps that will not satisfy everyone. Maybe I am still performing my own version, a more limited and multiple version, of the god-trick. However, the themes the book addresses have developed as much out of my own life experiences as they have from study and research. That, therefore, is where the knowledge produced in this book is situated. It is an account that is situated in a mingling of personal experiences in the phenomena being discussed with academic training – a training that tells us to step outside and try and be objective. I prefer to write, if not an autobiographical and subjective account, one that at least recognises where it has come from and sees influences as being about more than a few key books that one has read.

Situating politics and identity

This book is divided into two parts. In Part I, identity, identification and expressive organisation, I look at a range of issues associated with identity politics and lifestyles within the cultural arena that I have described above and the sociological writing about it. This is not the only arena in which one finds identity taken as an important cultural and political issue. There are others, notably associated with questions of ethnicity and racism (see Rutherford, 1990; Gilroy, 1993; Bhabha, 1994; Sarup, 1996; Werbner and

Modood, 1997); with nationality and nationalism (see Anderson, 1983; Brubacker, 1996); with questions of religion and fundamentalism; with the virtual identities and communities found on the Internet (see Star, 1995; Turkle, 1995). While I do not discuss these issues specifically, looking instead at the alternative, expressive 'counter-cultural' identities, I do not seek to marginalise them and I recognise that they are equally significant areas in which identity politics can be found and an important source from which to draw ideas and apply them in a different context.

Identity is about both similarity and difference. It is about how subjects see themselves in representation, and about how they construct differences within that representation and between it and the representation of others. Identity is about both correspondence and dissimilarity. Principally, identity is articulated through the relationship between belonging, recognition or identification and difference. Any connotative reading of the issues associated with identity has to address these themes. There is a series of frameworks in which this might be done: philosophical, psychoanalytical, sociological, anthropological, political, and so on. My approach is a socio-logical one, although I do make some use of certain anthropological concepts as well. The book is not, however, about identity as such (for a recent general account see Jenkins, 1996), rather I look at issues associated with identity through the analysis of the field of expressive and elective identities associated with what mathematicians might call a 'set' of identity positions: alternative and counter-cultural lifestyles, some youth subcultures and new social movements. In doing so I want to be able to find a way of beginning to move away from having to use these arborescent and totalising terms. The emphasis here on expressive identities should not be read as an argument suggesting that we are moving into a new type of society where identities and the lifestyles associated with them are becoming more expressive. Instead, I have identified this expressivism as an important issue within the politics and lifestyles loosely associated with what are termed 'new social movements' and have tried to open up a number of ways of exploring elements of that expressivism in each of the chapters that follow.

In Chapter 1 I discuss what is signified by this set of identities. Through a discussion of some of the main analyses of new social movements, youth subcultures and alternative lifestyles, I show how one of the main identity questions within these groupings has to do with a politics of identification or recognition that is topologically complex in its composition. The politics of identity associated with these groupings is in some cases about challenging the ways in which some identities come to be marginalised or be given a non-identity status. When we come to other examples within this set of identities, however, marginalisation is less obviously the case. Youth sub-cultures may in some ways be about young people addressing their status, though some have argued, of course, that it is the status of their parent culture that is really at issue and that youth cultures seek magically to resolve that non-identity status (see Cohen, 1972; Hall and Jefferson, 1976).

But they are often just as much about assuming or creating a new identity, of embracing marginality, and being openly and provocatively different. These identities play with the idea of margins and marginalisation. Through a critical analysis of some of the ideas from the recent work on the sociology of modernity/postmodernity and identity, de-traditionalisation, neo-tribalism, and new social movements, I aim to unsettle some of the denotative claims being made about identity and identity politics within this body of work – and to do this through the idea of topological complexity. The space of these identity positions and what they signify is not Euclidean, smooth and homogeneous but folded, crumpled and uncertain. Much of the politics of recognition is about groups of people trying to deal with this complexity and the anxieties it can create. I look, in particular, at how forms of collective identification are established through an interplay between identity and identification. This play does not simply respond to lifeworld uncertainty and risk, nor is it an apolitical free play with signs and forms of symbolic creativity. Equally, it does not always generate large-scale mobilisation in the form of social movements. My argument is that the one thing that does characterise this diverse range of 'movements', groupings and lifestyles is their expressive or affectual character. The relationship between identity and identification is principally connoted by its affectual character.

Chapter 2 challenges the still very influential Weberian position that treats identity, and especially expressivism within identity, as a sign of individual weakness. From Weber's critique of the German youth movement (1970a), the debates in the late 1970s and early 1980s over narcissism (see Bell, 1979; Lasch, 1980; 1984; Sennett, 1986), to the current arguments about reflexive modernisation and de-traditionalisation, there has been a tendency to idealise the heroic puritan individual, the cultivator of a vocation as a calling, as the model for the development of a strong, inner-directed identity. Against this, I discuss the more anthropological and Durkheimian tradition, most notably conveyed in the recent work of Maffesoli (1988a; 1996) and suggest that this offers an alternative that sees collective identification and belonging as a means of developing individual identity rather than its dissolution into some vaguely conceived idea of a collective will.

Chapter 3 looks at the relationship between expressivism, forms of identity, and belonging. How one identifies with others and oneself in relation to others is considered through a critical discussion of Raymond Williams's concept of the structure of feeling (1965; 1977; 1979). I do not use the term structure of feeling in the Marxian language that Williams originally conceived it, nor in relation to his chosen focus on high cultural forms; rather, I suggest that this term might be used to help us understand the way that feelings and emotions influence identity positions in a much broader cultural sense.[6] Following from the *Cahoots* example discussed above, I argue that the compote of movements, groupings, political practices and identity positions I have been discussing might also be analysed in terms of the development of a distinct structure of feeling. I do not use this as a replacement term for new social movements but as another term – one that allows a slight shift of perspective which allows me to continue with my connotative move. I go on to argue that the distinguishing characteristic of the structure of feeling found among many in this identity area is the 'occasion' (see Schmitt, 1986). The event or events, both public and private within networks or groups are the loci of a play between identity and identification. It is in the occasion that we also find a strong link between the cultural and political aspects of such identities.

The creation of conditions of support, friendship, and solidarity are all important issues in understanding the role of a structure of feeling within processes of identity formation. A further question has to do, therefore, with the nature of solidarity, community and belonging that is established within this identity arena. In Chapter 4 I argue that the key issue is that of communion and the type of organisation that it generates. If one goes back through the contemporary expressive groupings such as peace campaigners (Liddington, 1989; Young, 1990; Roseneil, 1995), New Age travellers (Hetherington, 1992; 1996; 1997b; 1998), the commune movement of the 1960s and 1970s (Abrams and McCulloch, 1976), kibbutzim in the 1920s (Talmon, 1972; E. Cohen, 1983), the German youth movement of the 1890s (Becker, 1946), one finds a common feature among all of them, a feature central to their structure of feeling: that identity and identification are worked out through issues of belonging or exclusion within some form of elective communal association. Rather than use some neologism like neo-tribe to describe the seemingly contradictory idea of an elective or reflexive community, I return to Schmalenbach's writing from the 1920s on communion, using the German word 'Bund' as the key concept here (1961; 1977; see Hetherington, 1994). Originally derived as a sociological concept by Schmalenbach from his observations of the German youth movements in the early years of this century, and intended as an intermediary category between Tönnies's Gemeinschaft and Gesellschaft, a Bund was seen as a small-scale, transitory and elective social grouping based upon a shared emotional commitment to a particular set of values and beliefs, often, though not exclusively, focused around a charismatic leader (see Hetherington, 1994). Similar to Weber's conceptualisation (1970c) of a charismatic community, or Gemeinde, a Bund offers its adherents a form of expressive organisation through which a way of life can be sought among a group of fellow supporters, from whose emotional support a sense of solidarity and group identification can be attained.

Space, performance and identity

Part II of the book, Social space and the performance of identity, looks more specifically at the performative character of expressive identities. Identity formation as a process of identification is a spatially situated process. It is, however, about creating symbolic spaces rather than always adopting established ones. Identity is not only achieved through identification with groups of individuals who share a common outlook but also through recognisable performative repertoires that are expressive and embodied. Ritual processes, such as rites of passage and pilgrimages, through which new identities are created, stress the importance of the spatiality of performance in the process of identity formation and can be taken as a model for contemporary expressive identities. Recently this anthropological literature, notably that associated with liminality (Van Gennep, 1960; Turner, 1969; 1974), has been used within the broader interest with the significance of issues of transgression and marginality to the processes of identity formation within cultural studies, and in particular cultural geography (see Shields, 1989; 1991a; 1992b; Hetherington, 1992; 1996; 1997b; Ryan and Fitzpatrick, 1996). In the small-scale societies that much of the anthropological literature originally set out to describe, rituals involving transgressions can take place without endangering the order of those societies because the low level of social differentiation means that such transgressions, when organised through rites of passage in distinctly demarcated liminal zones, serve to reproduce the daily life of those societies rather than endanger it. Such spaces, 'heterotopia' as Foucault calls them (1986a), serve the purpose of providing a distinctive place in which social structures are challenged by the communitas of intensely affective forms of sociality in order that the structure of rules, norms and accepted social identities may be renewed and reproduced (Van Gennep 1960; Turner 1969; 1974). Identity spaces as well as being places for change or resistance are also, therefore, spaces that produce alternate social orderings (see Hetherington, 1997a).

Chapter 5 argues that the identity politics of this particular set of examples is also a spatial politics. This is not a new idea. Almost a hundred years of sociological writing on subcultures, gangs and political groups shows us that making a space for oneself – a turf – is a major source of identification within identity practices. Within this set of expressive identities, in which the occasion is paramount to understanding their cultural and political formations, the spaces of those occasions are highly significant. These heterotopic spaces, spaces that come to stand apart from the rest of society, are often significant. They have a social centrality for the production of identity (see Hetherington, 1990; 1992; 1996; Shields, 1989; 1991a; 1992b). Marginality in this context of expressive identities is often defined in terms of authenticity and of an alternative centrality and I discuss it in those terms.

I look at the whole issue of space and identity through a critical analysis of the idea of liminality (see Turner, 1969; 1974). The main issue here is that the space has a significant symbolic role in the production of identities (see Stallybrass and White, 1986; Shields, 1991a). Such spaces in complex industrialised societies, spaces that are chosen as sites for 'elective' rites of passage, however, are not generally integrated within the rituals of modern societies; they are out of the ordinary, out of place, uncertain and anomalous, heteroclite – like the identities themselves. The production of chosen identities takes place, I argue, through a series of performances, or occasions in which identity processes are played out.

Contrary to many of the claims made within cultural geography that these spatial politics are all about transgression and resistance, it is important to note that they are also about modes of ordering, most notably the ordering of identity. In Chapter 6 I suggest that the spaces involved come to represent an alternate mode of ordering identity (see Hetherington, 1997a). Those who seek to discover new meanings and establish a new identity are likely to be attracted to heterotopic places because of their perceived difference to the uncertain conditions of modernity. The structure of feeling shapes not only the parameters of a lifestyle and the types of identification and group solidarity but also an outlook on the world that includes its spatial and temporal dimensions. Places are seen through a structure of feeling (think of the Romantic poets like Wordsworth and their attitude towards the Lake District) and an affinity between the attributed meaning of a place and some of the meanings that are given to lifestyle practices. Such a process also involves the development of a distinct 'utopic' and I discuss what this means for those engaged in identity politics.

Finally, Chapter 7 considers the issue of performance directly. Drawing on the theatre studies analysis of identity formation, and Richard Schechner's work on restored behaviour in particular (1985), I show how the identities in question – ordered by a distinct structure of feeling that stresses the significance of the occasion and expressed in a particular spatiality – are held together and mobilised through distinct performance repertoires. Performance is, therefore, something else connoted within this field of identity politics and expressive lifestyle formation. It brings together affectual forms of belonging, the use of an expressive embodiment and its stylisation, and the events in which activists might be engaged. Performance, however, is as much about the routine lives of members as about their more visible politically motivated activities. One is always on stage, not just when one is performing in an overtly political sense as in some sort of action or protest.

There is a conclusion – 'Afterword' – that brings things together but given that my approach is about adding without an equals sign, a type of deliberate and overt conceptual stuttering, there is no denotative closure that says what this all adds up to. The epistemological challenge of the book is to say that we can do social theory without using the equals sign. It is about issues of situatedness but also the multiplicity of addition. There is always something else to add and so on. And so on.

Notes

1. The issues of *Cahoots* on which this ideal typical description of new social movement lifestyles is based are: Volume 14, Autumn 1985; Volume 15, Winter 1985; Volume 21, July, August, September 1987; Volume 24, April, May, June 1988; Volume 25, July, August, September 1988; Volume 26, October, November, December 1988; Volume 28, April, May, June 1989; Volume 32, April, May, June 1990; Volume 33, July, August, September 1990.

2. It is certainly the case that all identities can be described as expressive in character. When I use the term 'expressive identities' I am talking about those who place a special emphasis on creating a more expressive way of life, one that challenges much of the perceived instrumentalism of daily life. Expressivism becomes not just a feature of an identity but a source of identification that is itself expressed through distinctive identities.

3. I am particularly grateful to John Law for discussions on this issue of connotation and denotation (see also Law and Hetherington, 1998).

4. I am drawing here on Donna Haraway's ideas that knowledge is refracted and full of interference (1996).

5. The concept of subjectivised occasionalism comes from Carl Schmitt's analysis of political romanticism (1986; 1988). I use it here because it is a concept I go on to use to discuss expressive identities later in the book. The reflexive subject of much recent ethnographic writing might be taken as another example of an expressive identity, in many ways influenced by the politics and the structure of feeling under discussion in this book. The difference is that the space that it occupies is an academic-political one rather than a more conventionally political one.

6. I am very grateful to Joanne Hollows for discussions on this point: for her, structure of feeling is a way of thinking about different tastes in music and associated styles; for me it is about styles of politics and associated identities.

I IDENTITY, IDENTIFICATION AND EXPRESSIVE ORGANISATION

1

IDENTITY SPACES AND IDENTITY POLITICS

The complex topology of the politics of identity

It is difficult to escape the word identity in contemporary social science. Over the last decade or so it has come to prominence in more and more areas of inquiry. One area where it has had something of a mixed reception, however, has been in the study of new social movements and the lifestyles and identity politics associated with them. While North American studies of social movements have tended to emphasise the political dimensions of social movements – mobilisation, leadership, group dynamics and so-called repertoires of action (see Tarrow, 1994) – identity has been a major concern within predominantly European studies of social movements (see Habermas, 1981; Touraine, 1981; Eder, 1985; Melucci, 1985; 1989; 1996; Rucht, 1990; Pakulski, 1991).

More generally, however, identity has not just come to be seen as a key issue in describing the contemporary world. The denotative move has been to see identity as something of a problem (see Bauman, 1996). But perhaps it always was. Where once sociologists talked about uncertainty and identity in terms of identity crises, alienation or role conflict, now most commentators talk about the possibilities and forms of resistance opened up by fractured, hyphenated and multiple identities associated first with psychoanalytic, then structuralist and more recently with poststructuralist and feminist critiques of an essentialist subjectivity on which earlier sociological ideas about identity were founded (see Foucault, 1977; 1991; Hall, 1990; 1992; 1996; Rutherford, 1990; Bhabha, 1994; Sarup, 1996; Werbner and Modood, 1997). One of the main issues behind this interest in identity and in identity politics more generally has been the relationship between marginalisation and a politics of resistance, and affirmative, empowering choices of identity and a politics of difference.

In earlier work, the proliferation of elective identities and secondary groups within society, notably those that had a political tinge to them – what Louis Wirth once described as 'fictive kinship units' – led to worries about the decline in authority and the emergence of a world in which people might no longer act as responsible citizens, choosing instead to align themselves with mass political movements, gangs or forms of criminal behaviour (see Thrasher, 1927; Wirth, 1964). Marxist commentators too were quick to subscribe to a version of the mass society thesis, based on their fears of the fascist experience in Europe in the 1930s and the failure of the working class to recognise their real interests in their class identity (see Adorno and Horkheimer, 1979). Mass culture theory, in various political guises but invariably with an elitist stance, has always worried about the problem of identity in terms of issues of manipulation and alienation (see Swingewood, 1977). Behind such anxieties lies an idealised past, either seen as pre-modern or modern in character, in which identities were defined by stable gender roles, ethnic origin, occupation, life-stage, and especially class. While some may have had the opportunity to escape what they were born into through social mobility, education and through the many life-chances that modern societies present, it was hoped they would do so in a rational manner with stable identities intact rather than through expressive social movements that articulated some vague sense of unease over the instru-mentalism of modern life and the identities associated with it.

Now, however, the theoretical decentring of the subject developed in poststructuralist analysis, alongside the pluralising and fracturing or layering of identities that has developed out of the identity politics of new social movements over the past three decades, is often seen less as an indication of marginalisation and oppression than as the basis for a politics of difference in which marginal identities become a source of empowerment and resist-ance (see for example Spivak, 1988; Rutherford, 1990; Gilroy, 1993; Bhabha, 1994; Hall and du Gay, 1996; Sarup, 1996).

The emergence and proliferation of identity politics since the various social movements of the 1960s: civil rights, students' and women's move-ments on the one hand, and the replacement of the hegemony of Marxism with feminist and poststructuralist theory within social theory on the other, have, therefore, both influenced this changing perspective on identity. Identity politics is now celebrated as the arena of cultural and political resistance within society and is often viewed as indicative of a move to a new type of postmodern or late-modern society. This denotative move is often itself based on another type of move, taking new ways of thinking about the world, new theories and concepts, and then going on to suggest the world has changed; always the search for rupture and the new goes on. This way of thinking, a modernist way of thinking, that characterises both so-called modern and postmodern approaches, suggests to me that we are too quick to make this leap. We need to look in more detail at the conditions of possibility for changes in identity rather than see identity as an indicator for some sort of fundamental change.[1]

The conventional classical sociological story about identity within modernity did not exclude the idea of multiple identities and choices; it did, however, generally adhere to a belief that modern society created a life-script over which individuals had some degree of authorship, albeit within the context of certain structuring parameters like class. From birth to death individuals were called upon to construct a narrative of identity. This was a narrative, however, not predetermined by tradition and custom, but one which gave people the chance to write the script as they went along, even though some of the plot lines and sub-plots had been created within society. School, work, sexuality, political and religious affiliation, family – all of these were already scripted; individuals had the job not of writing the script from scratch but of understanding their life experiences through a larger script. But now new denotative stories have emerged that challenge this vision of modernity. The many accounts on postmodernity, late-modernity and reflexive modernity that have appeared recently all question the idea that we can see modernity as a fixed point in history beyond which nothing else is possible. When it comes to issues of identity, the structures of the life-script are seen to be less fixed and certain, the possibilities for producing conventional narratives about work, family, and locality are thought to be no longer possible.

The idea of subjects as authors of their own life-scripts requires that subjectivity be prior to and independent of identity. As in the perspectival-ism of Renaissance painting, it exists outside the picture in a privileged position in the viewing point. This distinct viewpoint has been challenged as either a discursive product of the Enlightenment (see Foucault, 1977; 1989b) or as a privileged position for some that is based on the exclusion of others (see Harding, 1986; Haraway, 1991). Rather than locate the subject in this viewing point or punctum outside of the picture, from which one can gain an overview and see one's own life experiences mapped out and used as the basis for making the assumption that all experience their subjectivity in the same way, now the subject is located in the picture itself. The subject exists within the frame rather than outside it. It exists within the panoptical apparatus that constitutes the very idea of a subject though positioning in an heterogeneous space that is folded and topologically complex, allowing only small glimpses rather than a full view (see Foucault, 1977; Deleuze, 1986). The position of identity – and of the lifestyle issues and identity politics associated with it – is one that is topologically complex. The space of identity is a heterogeneous, folded, paradoxical and crumpled space in which a distinct singular position is not possible (see Foucault, 1986a; Rose, 1993; Doel, 1996). That has perhaps always been a feature of modernity it is just that we have not seen it before.

This proliferation of scripts as subject positions may be presented as choices associated with lifestyle, sexuality, consumption or enthusiasms, or it may be presented as subaltern positions of marginality and resistance to marginalisation. However, these choices are not free choices and the marginality too is plural rather than singular, emerging as different groups have challenged the hegemonic hold of social class over identity politics. Everywhere can be both a centre and a margin. Identities exist within a paradoxical space in which there are no fixed centres and margins (see

Foucault, 1986a; Rose, 1993; Bhabha, 1994). In a world where identities cannot be attached to singular uncomplicated subject positions (authors or narrators outside of the story), identity becomes all about multiple location and perfomativity within that location. Under such conditions the main issue associated with such spatial uncertainty is identification. It is through identifications with others, identifications that can be multiple, overlapping or fractured, that identity – that sense of self-recognition and belonging with others – is achieved.

It is within the new social movements, counter-cultures and political protests of the 1960s that these issues have come to be seen most clearly. By raising awareness and consciousness about the unequal access to resources beyond issues of class, and by highlighting discrimination that blocks opportunities and the presence of patriarchal and racist ideologies, new social movements have challenged the liberal ideology that modernity brought universal freedoms and the break with traditional forms of authority.

Through the structuralist theories of Lacan and Althusser, in which it was argued that the subjectivity on which we based our identities was not something fixed or essential but located in language and ideology, subjectivity came to be seen as the product of an interpellating process in which individuals were seen to be located seemingly as free agents, but in reality are the products of the ideologies of capitalist societies (see Althusser, 1971). While the universalism and rigidities of structuralism have themselves been systematically challenged since their heyday in the 1970s, post-structuralist critics have continued with this anti-humanist, fracturing process which erases the essentialism that has lain behind the idea of human subjectivity and the identities it scripts. Subjectivity is, according to Foucault, constituted in discourse. The idea of the human subject as an essential thing that gives us autonomy as agents is a discursive construction of the human sciences that emerged at the beginning of the nineteenth century (Foucault, 1989a; 1989b). Discourses locate subject positions within a space of power–knowledge. All we can do, it is argued, is use the subject positions in which we are located to write, not life-scripts but little stories, poems, language games, in which we can rearrange our identities and our identifications with others in partial and contingent ways (see also de Certeau, 1984).

This topological space within which identities are distributed is all about play. Not play, however, in the narrow ludic sense, but play in the sense of shifts between being constrained and enabled in multiple ways. While the space of power–knowledge in which identities are constituted can be seen as all pervasive, this has led some to see it as a source of freedom in which anything and any type of identity is possible within a postmodern world. The rejection of an essentialist view of the subject has not led to the over-determination of identity by discourse but to arguments, in some quarters, about a new voluntarism and vitalism in which identity becomes a matter of choice and style (see Maffesoli, 1988a; 1996; Amirou, 1989; Shields, 1992a;

1992b). This is what has become known as identity in the postmodern world. It is a world in which there is no master life-script against which individuals might model their own. Whether people accept this view of the character of their social lives or not, it is around this issue that the current 'problem' of identity is located. This is the world of identity as difference and as recognition; dominant identities which defined themselves against a host of Others, whose Otherness was something dangerous and marginal, have lost their hegemony. Power and inequality still exist; they continue to be seen in areas of economic and cultural life, in social policy and state practices, and still proliferate in some of the racist, misogynist, homophobic stories of those who cling to an idea of essentialism (on this issue see Bauman, 1989; 1990; 1996; Rajchman, 1995; Werbner and Modood, 1997). However, difference does not just exist at the boundaries and beyond the city walls, it prevails and is everywhere, having become, if not hegemonic, then at least something that has to be taken into account: a powerful place from which the vestiges of the old but seriously weakening authority of essentialism is challenged (see Rutherford, 1990; Hall, 1992; Bhabha, 1994; Hall and du Gay, 1996; Sarup, 1996).

The interest in questions of identity and identity politics is one that has principally focused over the past few years, therefore, on issues associated with this topological complexity: dispersal, fragmentation, uncertainty, difference, contingency, hybridity, ambivalence and multiplicity (see for instance Said, 1979; Hall, 1990; Rutherford, 1990; Featherstone, 1991b; 1996; Lash and Friedman, 1992; Marcus, 1992; Bhabha, 1994; Hall and du Gay, 1996; Sarup, 1996). This approach to identity rests principally on a challenge to realist and essentialist views of identity that see it as something fixed and ordered and mobilises new social movements and the politics of difference to illustrate the alternatives (see Rutherford, 1990).

To speak of identity at all in non-essentialist terms, while not impossible, is somewhat problematic. If it is not a quality that derives from our human being or from fixed social structures and relations, then it can only 'exist' in a space between, in relation to something else, across an uncertain gap between identity and non-identity and in the recognition of that gap. This can take the simple 'us and them' form, defining identity in relation to its (often marginal and oppressed) 'other' (see Said, 1979; Hall, 1990; Todorov, 1995) or between positions of identity and non-identity within an identity. In this case identity is performed through bricolage (see Levi-Strauss, 1966; Hebdige, 1979).

Hall, for example, has illustrated this latter process by arguing that non-essentialist conceptions of identity develop around a play of difference within identity positions which are articulated through a dialogue between their constituent parts (1990). He has shown, for example, that a Black cultural identity is constituted through the different positions of: présence Africaine, présence Européenne, and présence Americaine (1990: 230) and this difference is used to create a unity and sense of shared identity. Topology is about bricolage and about identification (see Levi-Strauss,

1966). Identity involves combination and the mixing of things at hand, and an ordering associated with that process of mixing. This performance produces an ordering in the form of an homology. While there can be some form of homology that gives a coherent sense of ordering to the bricolage within certain identity positions and the play of difference with which they are involved, this is not always as clearly the case as in Hall's example of Black identity. If one focuses on issues within race or gender or class or sexual orientation, it is possible to see homologies between constituent parts that give a sense to this difference within an identity. When, however, these categories are brought together it becomes clear that the homology does not easily operate across positions and that identities sometimes dissolve back into a contestatory identity politics and an essentialism that often accompanies it.

Difference, therefore, is not always an uncomplicated location (see Bhabha, 1994). It does not neatly define what is central and what is marginal; rather it operates through a shifting similitude of different locations from which identities – or bits of identities – emerge, often in tension and partial connection with others (see Strathern, 1991). It is not just those who have been placed on the margins of society who occupy identities defined by difference; difference is a condition in which everyone has some experience. While many of the positions we occupy as subjects may be privileged in some ways – as men, as middle class and White; as Westerners, as young, and so on – it is also possible to occupy marginal positions at the same time. A young, White, affluent, Western man might still be marginal in terms of his sexual orientation or in terms of some disability that he may have. The converse is also true. Those whose identities are located on the margins: working class Black men, for example, may still occupy some positions less marginal than others – Black women for example. However, we cannot know this for certain. There is no stable classificatory scheme by which degrees of difference and marginality can be measured and ranked. Who, for example, is the more marginalised in society, an unsighted, White, working class man or a fully sighted, Black, middle class woman? Any judgement can never be finally arrived at. It has to be local and specific. To make some universal judgement would be to call upon either an essentialist idea of subjectivity underlying identity or, equally likely, an essentialising of centres and margins. Topology and difference both resist essentialism and operate together. Any provisional judgement has to relate to the criteria associated with the specificities of marginality being referred to in a particular instance.

It is in a confusing and uncertain space, therefore, that the politics of identity and identity politics have developed (see Rutherford, 1990; Bhabha, 1994; Hetherington, 1996; 1997b). Among many activists associated with these forms of identity politics, internal debates – often hostile in character – have raged over issues of centrality and marginality. For example, Black feminists have accused White feminists of excluding issues that relate to their lives, just as many lesbian and gay groupings have worried over whether to admit bisexuals into their meetings and clubs. Issues of race, class, gender, sexual orientation, ability and disability, nationality, occupation and so on do not produce subject positions and identities that can always be neatly hyphenated and classified; they can generate identity issues that are often confused, plural, contradictory and uncertain. Difference does not always produce an easy reference for recognition. The bricolage of identity politics does not always produce a simple homology. This identity politics, which emerges from the plurality of subject positions in which individuals come to be located and interpellated, can often lead – for example, through some forms of discourse associated with anti-racism or anti-sexism – to a search for a new essentialism, an essentialism that wants to have clearly demarcated centres and margins in which friends and enemies, resisters and oppressors can be easily located (see Werbner and Modood, 1997). The fragmentation and plurality of identities and their shifting correspondence with subject positions create as many internal political contests over identity within the arena of identity politics as sources of empowerment and resistance to those who stand outside, in the space of the older essentialisms and their forms of discrimination.

This uncertainty with difference and its inability always to establish a harmonious identity politics is equally clear when one moves from talking about the constraints of marginalisation and subaltern positions to identities associated with the choice of marginality. Being marginal is generally seen as being about where one is put by society and most of the research that has been carried out on identity politics has addressed issues of marginalisation in this way. Identity politics, however, can also be about choosing to be marginal: what would once have been described as 'dropping out' or adopting an alternative lifestyle on the fringes of society (see Young, 1990; Hetherington, 1996). While one might quite reasonably respond by saying 'well at least they have a choice about becoming hippies/peace camp activists, I did not choose my gender/ethnicity', the logic of a non-essentialist view of identity, and the politics associated with it, is that we are all making choices about identity, even within the oppressive conditions of marginality, just as there are always constraints involved when we make those choices.

Subject positions associated with race, class, gender, sexual orientation, disability and so on do not generally focus on questions of choice. These are seen as discursive locations around which inequalities persist but through which opportunities for new identities associated with resistance can also emerge. Acts of resistance are choices, whether they be choices about fighting racist violence born out of one's own experiences or about trying to live a life in which one is responsible towards the environment and tries to encourage others to be so as well. Alongside these expressions of identity politics associated with such issues as race, class and gender, we also see, therefore, an identity politics around issues of the environment, animal rights, vegetarianism and veganism, anti-nuclear and anti-militarist stances, and the adoption of nomadic lifestyles or communal forms of living. It is not a question of making a judgement whether one is more real or authentic than the other but about recognising that the politics of identity is broader than issues of class, gender and ethnicity; it also involves a range of lifestyle issues and identity choices that often generate their own opponents and require forms of resistance.

This is not to argue, however, that identity politics is about playing games with fragmented identities in a world simply defined by shopping and style, where there are no unequal positions of power or opportunity. Instead it is to suggest that one way of addressing issues of identity and marginality, that tries to avoid lapsing into an essentialism, is to ask questions about identification, its forms, locations and ways in which it is performed. The weakness of clearly defined subject positions associated with class, gender and ethnicity as the basis for identity does not necessarily lead to a complete dissociation between these factors and identity, but, more often, to a politics of identity through which people try to renegotiate their identities (see Mercer, 1990; Hall, 1992). Race, class and gender are all significant sites in the topology of identity but so too are lifestyle choices, alternative and experimental ways of living. The topology of identity is one where there are local positions of centrality and marginality but no clear centres and margins.

Much of the politics of identity addresses this issue of complex topology indirectly. For many, even those who accept and valorise a position of difference, it is a worrying position to be in. As a consequence, the local processes of identity negotiation do not always produce clear homologous identity positions. Identity is about bricolage, identification is about homology. The identity politics and the alternative ways of living we see all around us are connotative of the interplay between bricolage and homology, or between the playful tactics of identity and the ordering strategies of identification and recognition. In many cases the (radical) politics of identity associated with new social movements and the constellation of other groupings that are partially connected to them can be about difference for the sake of difference, and an endless search for alternatives and new forms of authenticity and expression, but it can also be about stability, belonging, and fixing identity boundaries.

We can also say none of this is about newness. Politics just as much as culture reflects an experience of eternal recurrence. Things change, subtle shifts take place, but issues of speed, scale and topology are never that simple. Society, as Michel Serres points out using examples drawn from physical geography to illustrate, moves at different speeds – dramatic earthquakes on the surface are caused by slower movements of continental plates which are brought about by chaotic, yet subtle movements within the mantle of the earth, which in turn are caused by the very slow cooling of the earth's molten core (Serres and Latour; 1995: 139; see also Lee, 1997). The French Revolution, just as much as the Enlightenment, has a lot to answer for in terms of simplifying our ideas about change, agency and political identity. Denotation has always got excited about rupture and newness alongside (big) issues of scale. It has also often tried to express its certainty not only through essentialism but Euclidean symmetries and simple geometric arrangements. The assembly during the French Revolution divided a political spectrum into left and right and we have had to live with that labour of division ever since.[2]

Ever since then new groups, usually seen to be located on the outer fringes of this left or right, have sought to change things from either within or without. Social movements, as they came to be called since Lorenz Von Stein in the early nineteenth century (1964), have been associated with a political identity defined by a Euclidean geometry of master and slave – a geometry of opposing sides, opposing classes, opposing genders, opposing skin hues, opposing sexualities and so on. The marginalised have often adopted this geometry as well; as is said, it takes two to tango. To adopt a connotative approach means not only challenging the simplicities of denoting but also the simplicities of Euclidean thought. Topology, with its folds, tears, and crumples, creates multiple locations; it is a space where the excluded third (neither friend nor enemy) can exist in many forms (see Serres, 1995). In many respects, the shift in attention that began in the 1960s and 1970s away from the Euclideanism of capital and labour on to other forms of politics – feminism, civil rights, environmentalism, peace campaigning – might have challenged this way of thinking about politics. Rather, however, a new Euclideanism has set in and it began with the earliest studies of new social movement theorists looking for a new historical agent (Touraine, 1981), a new source of rationality (Habermas, 1981), or a new form of identity politics and collective action.

New social movements as identity politics

The point in question, therefore, is how we might think about these issues of identity within the identity politics of new social movements without resorting to the denotative and the Euclidean. To begin, the term new social movement is a problematic one. I have already argued in the Introduction that it is too narrow when we want to look at all of the groupings associated with the move to expressive lifestyles and the identities associated with them. It is also a denotative term, Hegelian in origin (see Von Stein, 1964), that sees collective action as a movement that aims to change the course of history. As a term, 'social movement' essentialises the activities associated with cultural and political forms of expression within historical agency. To think about the identity politics of new social movements without wishing to make this move means that we must also question the very term in doing so.

A simple place to start might be to question the 'newness' of these social movements. It would be fairly simple to take issue with the idea of newness as indeed some have, arguing how new social movements as movements concerned with issues of identity are not all that new, that their origins can be traced back well into the nineteenth century where questions of identity were just as important within the early labour movement (see Tucker, 1991; Calhoun, 1995), indeed right back to the time when Lorenz Von Stein first coined the term social movement, referring to the labourers in France in particular (1964). Feminism, environmentalism, peace movements, anti-racist campaigns, animal rights movements and so on are not new; they have existed for at least two centuries within Western societies. Women sought access to the public sphere of male power in the eighteenth century (see Jacob, 1991), a century before the Suffragette Movement in Britain and almost two centuries before the so-called second wave of feminism in the 1960s. The nineteenth century was witness to anti-slavery campaigns, anti-vivisection protests, pacifism and anti-militarism as well as to many experiments in alternative ways of living (see for example Webb, 1974; Hinton, 1989; Liddington, 1989; Walkowitz, 1992). All the same, we are unlikely to get very far if challenging the issue of novelty is all we are interested in. Recognising, however, that the newness of 'new' social movements as they are often conceived does not simply imply the emergence of new types of movements but, more broadly, new configurations of social movements around issues of identity and the politics of identity might be more significant.

When commentators use the term new social movements, a term usually associated with European traditions in the study of social movements (for example Habermas, 1981; Touraine, 1981; Eder, 1985; Melucci, 1985; 1989; 1996), they invariably refer to the variety of politically motivated actions, groupings and ideologies that have (re)emerged and come to prominence since the 1960s, mainly in western Europe, North America and Australasia – movements such as feminism, environmentalism, student protests and so on. This emergence has often been correlated with the declining significance of old social movements, notably the labour movement – if not from exactly the same time, then certainly soon after.

What makes this 'European' approach distinctive is the importance it gives to issues of identity, identity politics and the lifeworld in trying to understand these social movements, their dynamics and their agency within society. While theoretical analysis within this body of work has not ignored issues such as the character of political actions, cycles of protest, repertoires of action, group mobilisation over resources and group organisation, the latter have more generally been the concern of North American studies of social movements which have more generally been interested in questions of collective behaviour, rational choice and resource mobilisation (see for example Smelser, 1963; Zald and McCarthy, 1979; Tarrow, 1994). The ongoing debates among theorists of new social movements being carried out in Europe, North America and Australia (but less so in Britain, see Bagguley, 1997) have begun to focus on whether identity should be so central and whether its centrality detracts from more traditional questions about the politics of such social movements.

The issue for social movement theorists who do give central place to identity is not, therefore, one of newness in the sense of never having been seen before, but more an issue of the newness of the social conjuncture that makes these questions of identity significant. The 'new' in new social movements is a denotative statement rather than a connotative one. Advocates of the idea of new social movements (notably Habermas, 1981; Touraine, 1981; Melucci, 1985; 1989; 1996) argue that it is structural changes in the character of society since the 1960s and the colonising impact of systemic factors upon everyday life or the lifeworld – the terrain of identity – that give these social movements their importance as agents (Habermas, 1981; Melucci, 1989). While approaches may vary in their theoretical sources, new social movement theory retains a broadly Hegelian idea of a movement as collective agent, located within a master–slave dialectic, albeit no longer a single movement defined by the labour process with single historical purpose. It sees these social movements as attempting to bring about change in society, operating not only at the point of historical conjuncture but also at that between civil society and the State if seen in a narrow political sense, or system and lifeworld if broader cultural processes and issues of identity are considered as part of the terrain upon which new social movements operate (see Habermas, 1981; Eder, 1985; Melucci, 1989; 1996). New social movements are used as a denotative instance of broader social, cultural and political changes within Western capitalist societies that are usually dated as beginning in the 1960s. Where it differs from the study of older social movements is in saying that issues of identity are more important and relevant to the current social conjuncture than those of equality and justice.

Whereas the old social movements, like the labour movement, were thought to be a vehicle of change because of their location around structural inequalities within society, the new social movements are mobilised around societal risks and the lifeworld uncertainties that these risks bring. Identity in this work, generally conceived as self-identity and operating through practices that are reflexive as well as rational (Giddens, 1991), sees individuals confronting the uncertainties and disembedding processes of modernity in their own lives and seeking some form of expression and identification with others.[3]

This denotative move loses sight of the specificities and locatedness of new social movements. In other words it loses sight of, or ignores, what they might connote. In particular, it either over-looks or marginalises the expressive dimension to identity and identification, focusing much more on (Hegelian) questions of rationality, especially value-rationality and reflexivity, or it tries to fit new social movements into the stories it wants to tell about modernity. This means that some issues are privileged while others get ignored. Most significantly, it is the idea of new social movements as moral communities involved in rational critiques of societal development that is privileged, while their more expressive, affectual, and lifestyle features are ignored or seen as trivial. To begin to think new social movements otherwise means, for me, starting otherwise than from this denotative approach that wants to see new social movements as an indication of something big that lies elsewhere. It means we have to drop the social 'movement' from new social movement. That leaves us with 'new'; but the 'new' is part of this denoting strategy. This leaves us with a blankness, with zero. Zero, however, is not nothing; it is a point from which ordering processes begin (see Rotman, 1993). To think new social movements otherwise is not to deny the existence of feminism, environmentalism, the peace movement, and a whole host of other loosely defined, single issue political, identity and lifestyle concerns, nor is it indeed to say that they are not important or significant in terms of questions of rationality and reflexivity. It is, however, to think them otherwise in diffuse, situated and plural ways, in connotative ways – otherwise than as an indication of social and historical processes of change, rationality and moral critiques of the development of society. Identity politics is connotative of all sorts of things associated with the lives of those who are in some way drawn into its ambit. It exists within a topologically complex space in which this diversity of perspective is important.

Identity in new social movements

Among writers on new social movements, then, the interest in identity as a significant component of social movements' activities and interests is brought to the fore. The problem for me is what is then done with this move, most notably the downgrading of its connotative significance. A major example is the expressive aspect of identity politics that does not always sit easily with the search for more global significance associated with political agency and rationality.[4] In general, the starting point is to take identity and the politics of identity within new social movements as indicative of wider social or systemic processes. The expressive in particular is ceded a very small place in this sort of approach, as we can see in the work of some of the leading writers on identity and new social movements (notably Habermas, 1981; Melucci, 1989; 1996; Pakulski, 1991).

Habermas's major work offers a general theory of modernity and not just one of new social movements (1984; 1987); he does, however, see new social movements as a politics that addresses issues of the lifeworld and, as such, as an important aspect of contemporary modern societies and their dynamics (1981). According to Habermas, modern politics developed in a bourgeois public sphere that first appeared in Europe in the eighteenth century as a realm between civil society and the state (1989). This public sphere was, Habermas argues, the public sphere of civil society, reflecting bourgeois – we should add mainly male – interests in a realm of private autonomy from the state. A major concern was one of justice and the protection of private economic interests (Habermas, 1989: 54). Over the course of the nineteenth and twentieth centuries, this public sphere changed from one in which people were involved as agents to one which became colonised by the media, a process in which, according to Habermas, individuals were stripped of their critical abilities and opportunities to participate in that public sphere as autonomous agents.

In his more recent writings, Habermas has used these arguments in his analysis of the state in welfare capitalism. Here the institutionalisation of the public sphere – the conflict and debate that constitute the political-administrative system – is seen as having developed to such an extent as to impinge upon the lifeworlds (Lebenswelt) of individuals. New social movements, for Habermas, are an outcome that responds to the systemic colonisation of the lifeworld by rationalising economic and administrative processes (1981). New social movement lifestyles and their political activities are responses to such a process, responses that seek to challenge instrumental rationality within everyday life through value-rational and expressive or affectual means. For Habermas, however, this contains an ambiguous message in that he sees new social movements reflecting both a retreat from modernity in its expressive forms and a source of emancipatory potential within modernity when it takes a more rational stance (1981; see also Eder 1993). This ambiguity, as he sees it, emerges because he wants to be able to see new social movements as denoting a new form of communicative rationality that has rational and emancipatory potential to change society. Any trace of the expressive has to be challenged in his account. Denotation requires a Euclidean space in which the geometry of position is known rather than a topologically complex 'geometry' more suited to a more connotative approach. In some respects new social movements do stress the importance of value rational action in their own conduct and in that of others, but in other more affectual and expressive ways associated with identity and lifestyle, they do not easily fit with Habermas's idealisation of communicative rationality (1984; 1987).

Habermas argues that the main concerns of social movements are those which arise from conflicts over 'grammar of forms of life' (1981: 33), which I take to mean questions of lifestyle and identity. The issues that Habermas identifies with new social movements are: quality of life; equality; individual self-realisation; human rights; and democratic participation (1981: 33). Habermas criticises social movements when they take what he sees as a retreatist, anti-modern stance. In other words, he criticises them when they associate themselves with the expressive, the romantic and the local rather than with the communicative and value-rational. It is only those movements, especially feminism for Habermas, that have the ability to denote the emancipatory potential of communicative rationality that should be taken seriously as social movements (1981: 34). In particular, Habermas emphasises the positive elements of movements which adopt a value-rational, intersubjective, communicatively rational approach, an approach which Habermas sees as the way to re-ground modernity and restore its rational and emancipatory potential (Habermas, 1984; 1987). In his overt fear of the affectual and expressive, however, Habermas has a tendency to ignore much of what is involved in new social movements, notably their situatedness and entanglement in the intricacies of everyday life in which communication does not necessarily take some abstract rational form. Issues of feeling and emotion – in particular, issues that have been very important within feminism we might add – and in relation to them issues of collective identification and its symbolism, are problematic for Habermas but they are significant and visible features of the identity politics of many new social movement activists. In Habermas's approach these are the mere connotations of the systemic colonisation of the lifeworld but do not have within them the potential to denote an alternative, or a way out of that instrumental colonisation through communicative rationality.

A second writer who appears to take this expressive realm more seriously is the Italian sociologist Alberto Melucci (1989; 1996). Melucci, however, is still mainly concerned with the denotative potential of the collective actions of new social movements and of retaining some aspects of the more traditional approach to understanding social movements (1989: chapter 2; and even more in his recent book, 1996). Melucci begins by seeing new social movements as embedded in everyday life in a similar way to Habermas. He also, following Touraine (1981), sees new social movements as forms of collective action that emerge at social conjunctures within complex 'information' societies, societies that are no longer defined in class terms (1996). The difference when comparing Melucci to Habermas is that he gives more credence to affectual issues associated with cultural forms of self-expression and identity formation within new social movements that do not necessarily take an obviously communicatively rational form (1989: 66ff.). Melucci stresses, therefore, the significance of symbolism and meaning involved in the organisations, and the interactions and networks associated with the production of collective identities from which the politics of these movements is generated. With his focus on symbolism, Melucci sees new social movements as carriers of new knowledge, not world-historical knowledge, but knowledge applied more locally to the politically sensitive issue of difference and expression associated with identity formation.

In other important respects, however, Melucci shies away from this connotative position, notably in his most recent work when addressing more directly the issues of collective action and its relation to the systemic character of society (1996). However, he still in large part retains the focus on how new social movements construct themselves in terms of personal issues associated with lifestyle and identity that he developed in his earlier work (1989). Melucci argues, in contrast to Habermas, that new social movements be considered within the private as much as the public sphere. As he suggests:

> Today's social movements contain marginal counter-cultures and small sects whose goal is the development of the expressive solidarity of the group, but there is also a deeper commitment to the recognition that personal needs are the path to changing the world and to seeking meaningful alternatives. (1989: 49)

What it is important to emphasise here is the diversity of forms of identity creation and re-creation that new social movements perform and the embeddedness of their politics within those processes. The denotative move, however, comes in when Melucci locates the identity characteristics of new social movements in a more general theory of collective action within what he describes as complex societies (1989; 1996). In a version of the post-modern thesis, albeit one that does not use the word postmodern explicitly, Melucci sees contemporary societies as having undergone a process that makes them more (informationally) complex such that they can no longer be analysed through simple Hegelian inspired theories of social change in which the end can be predicted. He places particular emphasis on major transformations based upon the role played by information technology and communication that tends to undermine the productivist basis to class politics. The politics of identity, for Melucci, is located in issues of information and knowledge. From their embeddedness in the expressive realm of everyday life and identity, new social movements generate new forms of knowledge about the world and new identities that match this.

Given that information is a less materially tangible thing than other resources, systemic changes and conflicts within society largely take place, according to Melucci, in a distinctly symbolic manner. By focusing on what he calls the submerged and latent features of new social movements, which then act from everyday life against new symbolic orders being created, Melucci has both shifted and deepened the understanding of new social movements – a term which, as he recognises, begins to have little meaning (1989: 40ff.). But the denotative move remains. Melucci, like Habermas, wants to retain the god-eye that can say something, through social move-ments, about society as a whole and its leading dynamics. He wants to go on to analyse collective action as an agent that brings about systemic contra-dictions within society. In making this move, he is in danger of losing sight of the multiplicity of issues in which new social movements are entangled, and on which he is such a perceptive observer, in favour of locating them in the one big perspective on contemporary society. New social movements, in Melucci's approach, denote one form of collective action that resonates with the latent possibilities of bringing about systemic contradictions and social change. In the final instance in Melucci's account they come to assume an indicative rather than an implicative role within the analysis of a type of society and the means by which change is brought about. To reiterate, I am not suggesting that new social movements do not bring about change, indeed that is often their explicit goal, but it is also just one effect among many, the many others being about issues of identity, identification, how one conducts one's life, and how one relates to others in the process. If we take topology seriously we cannot privilege any one aspect of what they are about – we cannot know what their impact will be nor in what ways they will be important within society.

For another leading writer on new social movements Jan Pakulski, who also sees the significance of the expressive issues of issues of identity and lifestyle, denoting takes the form of emphasising the importance of the value-rational outlook of new social movements and the effects that it has. Pakulski, like Habermas and Melucci, is another writer on new social movements who looks at the issue of identity. He claims, following Melucci, that social movements are cultural as well as anti-systematic political phenomena. For Pakulski, the way to address the issue of identity politics within new social movements is through the Weberian distinction between formal and substantive rationality around which he sees new social movements develop as moral communities (Pakulski, 1991: chapter 1; see also Brubacker, 1984). In another version of the system-lifeworld argument found in Habermas (1981), Pakulski argues that social movements are value-rational critiques of the instrumental or formal rationality of the political-administrative systems of modernity – through their adherence to post-materialist values that emphasise quality and equality of life outside of material gain (see Inglehart, 1977).

Bureaucracy, technocracy, partocracy and democracy are identified as four ideal typical modes of co-ordination that make up these systems, with each, it is argued, having its own social movement opposition. For Pakulski, it is the rationality of each political administrative system and its organisational mode that is the source of social movement opposition, which centres around a number of ultimate values. Each social movement, in opposing a mode of co-ordination, is seen as having a directionality towards one or two of the other modes of co-ordination (1991: 63ff.). Thus, according to Pakulski, anti-bureaucratic movements and anti-technocratic movements each have directionality towards partocracy and democracy, anti-partocratic movements have directionality towards democracy, and anti-democratic movements have directionality towards partocracy.

The main problem with Pakulski's account is its singularity that derives from his use of a Weberian ideal type methodology. Pakulski's treatment of social movements solely as value-rational moral communities again leaves little room for the more expressive aspects of their identity politics. The 'ideal-type' is another Euclidean style of thought that seeks to abstract a denotative position out of the mess of connotations that it recognises exist. Rather than just accept them and find them interesting, it wants to smooth things out and simplify them. In doing so, certain things are privileged while other issues are ignored or marginalised.

While there is certainly strong evidence offered to support the claims about moral communities, the real weakness in Pakulski's account lies in its subsumption of what Weber describes as affectual social action within value-rational action.[5] Although often found together, the two are also quite distinct in that one derives from feelings and emotions that may be ethically expressed (see Bauman, 1995), while the other derives from an identification with a normative code. The two types of social action are commonly found together, in that a value-rational stance is often based on an affectual empathy with others (see Scheler, 1954). New social movements, I would argue, are not just moral communities but also what Maffesoli describes as

emotional communities (1988a: 146), in that their concern for oi
involves forms of empathy for those perceived to be oppressed as the b
for their own expression of tribal identification. If this is correct, thei
would be wrong to see new social movements, as Pakulski does, as primaɪ ꞇy
organised around ultimate values in their critique of the administrative
forms which embody the instrumental rationality of modern societies. As
emotional communities, the cultural aspects of new social movements are
equally significant as their more obvious political features; indeed there is
likely to be a strong link between the two.[6] Feeling and morality are not
separate; caring for others, wanting to take responsibility for them is as
much based on a sense of emotional solidarity as it is on abstract moral
precepts (see Bauman, 1995). This link is at the very heart of questions
of identification found within identity politics and the lifestyles that it
generates.

New social movements and their wider lifestyle linkages offer not only a
means of challenging powerful administrative systems morally, but also
provide a form of affectual solidarity which allows – through the creation of
distinct lifestyles, shared symbols and solidarity – a process of identity
formation that seeks to develop a politics of difference and resistance
through expressive means and forms of communication. It is not just the
rationality of administrative systems, therefore, that is opposed by social
movements, but also the supposedly inauthentic, disenchanted instrumental-
ity of interpersonal relations embedded in a routinised, often unjust, everyday life. Where Pakulski's approach to social movements is particularly
useful is in the way that he identifies their rejection of formal rationality,
offering instead new forms of value-rational beliefs or knowledge. This
needs to be coupled, however, with affectual criteria that lie behind the
process of identification and a recognition that its effects are more plural,
local and dispersed. Just as Foucault argued that power was not just located
in the heart of society but ran through even the tiniest capillaries, so too do
social movements have a dispersed, fluid capillary action not always directed
solely at the immoral heart of society.

All of these theorists make the move from seeing new social movements
in a multiplicity of connotative ways to a singular denotative way of
describing what either is or ought to be going on within society as a whole.
We can now see the problem with the term new social movement more
clearly. The term 'new' is there so that something can be denoted as a
potential new agent of change within a different social conjuncture. However, the term social movement is also there so that once that newness has
been explored it can be brought to a singular focus which can then be used,
like a mirror, to denote something else and something bigger. The very term
new social movement, or indeed collective action, implies the desire to move
from an analysis of the diverse character of new social movements to one
that takes them as indicative of something else. The question for me is how
we might avoid this god-trick in the study of new social movements (see
Haraway, 1991). The commonalities that we might identify – in terms of

orientation, symbolic practice, knowledge claims, group organisation and so on, things that Melucci in particular is very effective in describing – do not necessarily have to be taken as denoting anything outside of those situated practices.

The study of new social movements involves analysing the interplay between the particular instance and the commonalities that exist across a variety of instances. This shows what is connoted by the existence of new social movements. What is denoted for the activists is what they get out of what they are doing; what is denoted for the sociologist is separate from that analysis, it has more to do with the approach to theory that I take than from the subject matter of my studies.[7]

The politics of identification

New social movements, in all their overlapping and networked diversity, have a multiplicity of concerns with issues associated with the politics of identity. These can take the form of challenging social identities and the ways that they are used as labels to denote something, for example, woman, Black, ethnic, disabled and so on; or the ways that what is positively connoted by those terms is often ignored by society; or they can challenge new and unwelcome connotations that are thought to exist. New social movements can be associated with a politics of identity that is also a politics of identification. If we were to look at the variety of ways in which many new social movements, like feminists, have challenged stereotypical attitudes and what they both denote and connote about women this becomes apparent. This can mean challenging the stereotypes using diverse tactics that both use the existing political and legal apparatus and step outside of it as well. Alternatively, it can mean living up to some parts of the stereotype in order to deliberately make something seen as a negative come to be revalorised as something positive. Or again, it might mean adopting completely new identities, by becoming playful bricoleurs in order to explore new ways of living and identifying with others. Such issues of identity immediately raise important questions about achieving forms of identification and recognition: something that in the language of the old social movements would have been easily identifiable and have been characterised as issues of consciousness and solidarity.

The key to thinking about issues of identity within new social movements, therefore, is that it does not lead to it overriding other issues such as political action, mobilisation, group organisation and so on, or being overridden in its turn by the search for some global historical relevance. How we might avoid this involves an analytical approach that makes use of ideas of both multiplicity and assemblage. We can think of assemblage in terms of analysing new social movement multiplicities in ways so that these activities can be grouped and theorised, albeit in an immanent or connotative way. The interplay of multiplicity – identity, identification, centres, margins, difference, resistance – is connoted by the identity politics of 'new social movements'. To argue this means that we have to erase the term new social movements as we do so and look instead at the partially connected forms of political and cultural activity that are associated with the expressive politics of identity.

If we refuse both the theoretical desire to denote and the alternative of an atheoretical empiricism, what we are left with is an adding process that never ends with an equals sign, theorising by 'stuttering and and and' rather than looking for 'a beyond' or an overarching concept (see Deleuze and Parnet, 1987). The equals sign is implied in the process of adding rather than the end product. Using terms like expressive identity, identity politics and identifications (and I shall add others in later chapters) allows us to theorise 'new social movements' as an heterogeneous, multiple and diverse assemblage of practices. These concepts help us to make sense on one level but they do not lead on to greater things. The topology that 'new social movements' are located in is a complex one. They are local yet interconnected standpoints that allow us partial, multiple, yet connected perspectives on what we choose to study. I have argued for the importance of connecting issues of identity to political actions in the study of new social movements, and have tried to suggest ways in which such phenomena might be considered in their own right rather than as an illustration of wider political and social processes. In Chapter 2 I look in more detail at the issue of identification and the ways in which identity politics develops through expressive forms.

Notes

1. It is for this reason that I write here a form of macro-sociology rather than a micro-sociological or ethnographic account (although see Hetherington, 1999). The question has to do with effects of scale (see Law, 1999). Connotations fit much more easily into micro-sociological work than they do into macro-sociological ones. Connotation usually implies small-scale effects and local, subtle conditions, whereas denotation is seen to fit better at the grand scale. If this book has an unusual feel to it, it is likely to be because I have not followed all of the denotative moves in my macro account of identity politics. There is a subtext to this book about topology. Social theory makes a whole range of often unacknowledged spatial assumptions: about regionalism, direction, scale, volume, density, and so on. Generally social theory performs this repertoire of spatial assumptions in a Euclidean way: rigid, fixed, geometric and knowable. My attempt is to try and think the world as more topologically complex, folded, uncertain and fluid. To connote, to use concepts in some sort of horizontal relation to each other seems more fitting to these conditions of possibility.

2. On the labour of division (see Hetherington and Munro, 1997).

3. A major problem with Giddens's work on self-identity is its dyadic character; focusing as it does on the psychoanalytic understanding of self-identity (1991) and intimacy conceived in the realm of intimate relationships between couples (1992).

4. I am grateful to John Law for his insights on the necessity of considering both connotation and denotation within social theory.

5. I discuss this issue in more detail in Chapter 2.

6. The relationship between issues of expressivism and political action is developed further in Chapter 3 where I discuss them in relation to the structure of feeling associated with expressive identities and identifications.

7. One approach might be to write a reflexive account, either drawing on autobiographical material of one's own involvement in social movement activity or commenting on one's own position within one's fieldwork. This is not, however, an unproblematic strategy as it too makes certain denotative moves away from the subject matter and towards the identity of the researcher. An alternative approach, and one adopted here, is to develop a theoretical account of certain issues of identity, based on connotative interpretations of the denotative moves made within new social movements themselves.

2
TRIBAL VIBES: EXPRESSIVISM AND IDENTIFICATION

It is not just the sociology of new social movements that downplays the significance of the expressive and affectual. Feeling and emotion have often been dealt with somewhat critically by sociology in general, especially when they are identified as the basis of a cultural trend. There are, of course, some major exceptions, notably the work of Elias (1978), feminist and other writers on emotion, sexuality and impression management in work (see Hochschild, 1983; Wouters, 1989; Adkins, 1995), as well as the ever growing literature on the sociology of the body which has become an important issue within sociology in recent years (see Turner, 1984; Featherstone et al., 1991; Shilling, 1993; 1997; Mellor and Shilling, 1997). All of this, however, has in no small part developed as a critique of the absence of issues of affect and emotion in classical sociology (although see Scheler, 1954). When it comes to more specific questions as to the affectual relations within identity politics, alternative lifestyles and social movements, this absence becomes even clearer. Writing in his famous lecture 'Science as a Vocation', Weber speaks in derogatory terms of the expressiveness of youth that has set the tone for future generations of sociologists:

> Redemption from the rationalism and intellectualism of science is the fundamental presupposition of living in union with the divine. This, or something similar in meaning is one of the fundamental watchwords one hears among German youth, whose feelings are attuned to religious experience. They crave not only religious experience but experience as such. (1970a: 143)

He goes on to say:

> Today the routines of everyday life challenge religion. Many old gods ascend from their graves; they are disenchanted and hence take the form of impersonal forces. They strive to gain power over our lives and again resume their eternal struggle with one another. What is hard for modern man, and especially for the younger generation, is to measure up to *workaday* existence. The ubiquitous chase for 'experience' stems from this weakness; for it is weakness not to be able to countenance the stern seriousness of our fateful times. (1970a: 149)

The German youth movement to which Weber is alluding, and its hostility to a scientific and rational outlook in favour of a more expressive and religious one, is treated in dismissive terms here. Its search for experience, often associated with mystical symbolism and pagan beliefs, has some similarities with the current expressive lifestyle concerns of today (see Becker, 1946; Lacquer, 1962; Mitterauer, 1992). We tend to look critically now on the

German youth movement, notably because of its associations with the Hitler Youth of the 1930s who shared many of the earlier ideas and symbols of the more egalitarian, anti-capitalist, yet pagan inspired Wandervogel of the 1890s. Groupings and lifestyles that are strongly associated with feeling and emotion tend to be feared as leading to massification and a herd mentality. From Nietzsch, Le Bon (1967) to Adorno and Horkheimer (1979) and Habermas (1981; 1984), it is anxieties of the apolitical and potentially amoral stance of the expressive that has been the major source of anxiety for those who have wanted to question what the people, sometimes conceived of as a mass, are up to.

The Nietzschean influence on Weber (see Hennies, 1987) no doubt influenced him in his critical view. His stress on the rational outlook, and a commitment to the idea of a vocation that valued an ascetic, committed, hard-working and rational attitude was modelled on an idealised vision of the modern person as self-assured, self-confident and motivated by rational goals. This is a vision of a puritan individual that Weber identified in his best known work, *The Protestant Ethic and the Spirit of Capitalism*. In it he gives us a description of the formation and character of the puritan and later bourgeois subject (1985).[1] This self-assured reasoning subject is also the subject of critical theory, able to make individual critical judgements on the world (Adorno and Horkheimer, 1979; Habermas, 1989). Its supposed decline and the 'retreat' into the romantic and the expressive have been a persistent theme in twentieth-century Weberian-inspired sociology and beyond.

This fear of the expressive and the reduction of the affectual to a supposedly irrational realm of manipulatable drives and desires is a common theme within sociology. The fear of a mass society of individuals unable to think and act on their own behalf has coloured the view of the modernising vision sociology has had of itself during the twentieth century. The fear of cultural alienation and massification (Le Bon, 1967), of secondary associations leading to the breakdown of social order (Wirth, 1964), of the personality shifts from the inner-directed to the other-directed (Riesman, 1950), or more recently the supposed emergence of conditions of narcissism (Carroll, 1977; Sennett, 1977; 1986; Bell, 1979; Lasch, 1980), all illustrate a celebration by sociology of a bourgeois subject whose individuality is self-defining, rationally motivated and reflexively assured (most recently see Giddens, 1991; Beck, 1992). The same is true of views within society as a whole, where such things as religious cults, extreme political groups and their like are perceived to brainwash or dupe their supporters into a slavish obedience to alien doctrines or charismatic manipulators.

If Weber can be seen as standing behind this celebration of the heroic bourgeois subject (see Featherstone, 1996), then it is Durkheim, notably his work on religion, who stands behind the smaller group who have tended to put forward the opposite view (1971). The importance of affect within collective sentiment, emotional groupings and forms of identification can be seen in the work of a number of sociologists and anthropologists who take their lead from Durkheim. Georges Bataille (1994), Victor Turner (1969; 1974), René Girard (1979) and most recently Michel Maffesoli (1988a; 1996) have all written on the emotional character of groupings in ways that valorise the significance of affect, rather than treat it as in some way irrational and a detraction from the reasoning and judging capabilities of the bourgeois, individual subject.

I have argued that analysis of the identity processes, which are found within the many forms of identity politics and lifestyles that form a significant part of the cultural scene in many Western nations, has to recognise the importance of the expressive and the forms of multiplicity of identification it generates. This means addressing both those whose work challenges such a view as well as those who have gone some way to developing this point of view. In this chapter I look at the work of those since Weber who have developed a critique of the expressive and the collective forms it takes. I go on to develop my own argument in relation to those who have offered an alternative view. This is not always a straightforward process. It is not my intention here to establish a debate between Weberian and Durkheimian traditions in sociology. Neither do I want to adopt the denotative theoretical stance that can be found in both positions. All the same, it will be clear that my own position owes more to those like Turner and Maffesoli than it does to Weber, Bell, Giddens and others for whom the individual rather than the collective is the main focus of attention when discussing issues of identity.

Life orders: narcissism and the inner-directed personality

This Weberian critique of the expressive is an important and influential one that requires further investigation. The sociological tradition that takes his views about identity as its starting point has tended to use the idea of the heroic, inner-directed individual as its model (see Hennies, 1987; Scaff, 1989; Owen, 1991; Featherstone, 1996). Such individuals are perceived as moral subjects, able to act reasonably on the basis of rational thought. Such individuals, heroic in make-up in the sense that they are self-directed subjects capable of moral judgement independent of external pressures, have, it is argued, been undermined throughout the development of modern societies. The reasons for this undermining have been variously attributed to the influences of romanticism, hedonism, consumerism, the decline of the family, the rise of mass movements, the manipulative powers of the culture industry and the blurring of moral issues by changing cultural values that devalue individual responsibility and critical judgement.

The starting point for most of these arguments is a perceived weakening of the Protestant ethic and the puritan personality within modern society in light of the rise of a hedonistic counter-culture. The Weberian 'puritan', often taken as characteristic of the modern personality type, has been associated with the constitution of self-identity through commitment to a vocation leading to personal achievement, self-denial of spontaneity, ascetic commitment to goals, and deferred gratification. The puritan places a value on the effects of suffering, with the redemptive aim of transforming self-identity through rational, reflexive and self-critical effort (see Weber, 1985; Hennies, 1987; Goldman, 1988; Scaff, 1989).

The subjectivity of the puritan has been one that is constituted through an affectual dyadic relationship with an absent Other (God) who shows no response to the subject. A consequence of the lack of tangible response has been that affectual gratification with tangible human others comes to be denied by individuals, who seek instead to concentrate on perfecting the self through a reflexive or inner-directed renunciation of pleasure and an emphasis on God's calling, work and worship as signs of election. Weber dismisses the importance of the communitarian tradition in Protestantism as the basis for his analysis of the modern personality when he chooses to use Calvinism rather than Lutheranism as his model for its genesis. In the Lutheran tradition, the possibility of communion with God through a mystical union with Christ is of major importance (see Liebersohn, 1988: 105). That idea of union allows for value to be placed on an affective communion with one's fellow Lutherans. In Calvinism, however, that communion is not permitted. Expressive relations were rather with an unknowable God, meaning that solitary reflection and commitment to one's calling as a sign of election replaced the affectual and communitarian tradition found in Lutheranism. Weber, following Kant, found in this ideal typical puritan outlook a model for solving the problems of identity established within modernity (see Goldman, 1988). That modernity is funda-mentally individuated in Weber's understanding of society (Liebersohn, 1988). In Weber, as can be seen in his famous typology of social action, the affectual, along with the traditional modes of social action are both seen as collective and irrational in motivation, and contrasted to the value-rational and the instrumentally rational as the sole forms of rational social action (1968: 1–28).

More recently, there have been arguments that have suggested that this type of personality, once associated with the spirit of capitalism, has been undermined by capitalism itself. This type of individuality, articulated through a discourse of individualism, is now seen as problematic for capital-ism (Abercrombie et al., 1986). Developments within the work process and in consumerism have led, it is argued, to promoting depersonalisation and the death of the puritan (Bauman, 1987: 149–154). The new type of personality which is supposed to have emerged, with an elective affinity with late-modern capitalism, has variously been described as narcissistic, hedonistic or remissive (Steiner, 1971; Carroll, 1977; Bell, 1979; Lasch, 1980; Sennett, 1986). Such work reflects a worry, asserted also by members of the Frankfurt School for instance, with the problematic status of the puritan personality and the future of capacities for critical judgement by individuals, and the fear of the development of an authoritarian personality (Adorno and Horkheimer, 1979; Adorno, 1991; see also Jay, 1973; 1984; Held, 1980). Weber already believed this to be the case in his day, but these anxieties have lived on after him. Debates in the late-1970s that associated cultural crisis and the decline of moral responsibility with a condition of narcissism are a case in point (see Lasch, 1980; 1984).

Arguments about a culture of narcissism began to emerge in response to the move from a highly politicised counter-culture found in many Western societies in the late-1960s to one that became much more interested in issues of hedonism, personal growth and New Age spirituality from the 1970s (see also Tipton, 1982; Heelas, 1996). A critique of this move was made by a number of commentators, most notably Christopher Lasch, Richard Sennett and Daniel Bell. While their work differs in that each can be located at a different point along the political spectrum, they are all critical of the narcissism and hedonism of the counter-culture and the identity politics associated with it.

Lasch's arguments, which formed the focus for many of these issues, were largely concerned with locating changing personality types with broader cultural changes, most notably associated with what he saw as the failure of 1960s radicals to transform society and their subsequent activities (Lasch, 1980). He argues that progressive reforms, emergent from the values of the counter-culture, undermine individual autonomy producing narcissism as both a cultural and personal phenomenon. He goes on to suggest that people have lost faith in the future and are now living in fear of impending disaster and uncertainty (1984). The result, according to Lasch, is that people become self-absorbed, and make a virtue out of self-growth therapies and a reliance on experts in their search for meaning and security rather than drawing on their own ego for this sense of self-worth. For Lasch, narcissism is characterised by weak ego-formation, which is seen as a result of the loss of the paternal authority of the father in the patriarchal family (1980: chapter 10). This has been replaced, Lasch argues, by a therapeutic state which encourages progressive education, permissiveness, a cult of authenticity, and general fear of emotional involvement and dependence.

Sennett, another leading commentator on narcissism, has offered a some-what different view as to the origins of this narcissism, albeit one that is equally critical. He sees its emergence as a consequence of the successes of the puritan personality itself, rather than coming from outside in the form of hedonism. Sennett's key concepts in respect of narcissism are those of destructive Gemeinschaft and the protean self (1977; 1986). Modern Gemeinschaft, for Sennett, is seen as a celebration of intersubjectivity as a moral condition. Whereas the bourgeois individuals excluded emotional criteria from public life and sought to cultivate their emotional life in the private sphere of the home, the present sees, according to Sennett, the erosion of the boundaries between public and private, allowing narcissists to seek emotional satisfaction in public arenas as well as in private ones. The loss in self-confidence and the belief in an ever-changing, malleable or protean self, lead, Sennett observes, to the need for a new Gemeinschaft. Such a Gemeinschaft is destructive, according to Sennett, because it makes impossible demands on intersubjectivity. Self-disclosure to others' good faith underestimates, Sennett argues, the way people can become dependent on the estimation of others, denying their own genuine needs and leaving themselves open to the possibility of manipulation and exploitation.

These anxieties about narcissism transcend the normal political boundaries. If Lasch's arguments about narcissism can be associated with the left tradition of critical theory and Sennett's with a more liberal political position that idealises the eighteenth-century bourgeois public sphere as a space for the development of individual identity, then a third contributor to these debates, Daniel Bell, raises similar anxieties from a neo-conservative perspective. Bell has also criticised narcissism in contemporary Western capitalist societies which he sees as emerging out of the modernist cultural tradition (1979). Modernism, for Bell, responds to what he describes as the disjuncture of the three realms of society: techno-economic, the polity and culture, brought about by capitalism (1979: 14). The axial principle of modernism, according to Bell, is an emphasis on the remaking of the self. This principle has the tendency to make the realm of culture paramount, which has led to an emphasis on hedonism as opposed to the work ethic that was behind earlier bourgeois culture:

> The character structure inherited from the nineteenth century, with its emphasis on self-discipline, delayed gratification, and restraint is still relevant to the demands of the techno-economic structure; but it clashes sharply with the culture, where such bourgeois values have been completely rejected – in part, paradoxically, because of the workings of the capitalist economic system itself. (1979: 37)

The 1960s counter-culture is seen by Bell as symptomatic of the anti-bourgeois modernist culture of the self, with hedonism set in motion by the modernist emphasis on the centrality of culture within society. Bell sees this culture as having failed to provide individuals with values and moral precepts that enable them to live together happily. The counter-culture, for Bell, is a decadent culture which fails to meet the aspirations of people as individuals within society.

What all of these writers have in common is a fear that the other-directedness and expressiveness of contemporary lifestyles undermines individuality, ethical codes and the ability to make critical judgements. For all of them the heroic bourgeois *Persönlichkeit*, self-reflexive and motivated by commitment to the rigours of a self-disciplining vocation, is taken as an ideal personality able to meet these individualistic and somewhat elitist demands. Reliance on others is taken as a sign of weakness – a herd-like mentality, in which people deny their individuality. While all of these writers offer perceptive comments on contemporary culture and personality formation, their arguments are based on a somewhat idealised and nostalgic vision of bourgeois individualism. Whatever the origin of this supposed condition of narcissism, all of these writers agree that the basis of identity in the expressive world of feeling and sentiment, inherently other-directed, is a sign of individual weakness and a source of cultural and moral decline. Expressive identities, and their associated lifestyles with their emphasis on feelings for others as the basis of identification, are seen as often deeply romantic in their quest for authenticity in experiences, relationships and identity.

Most recently, this Weberian approach to personality has influenced work on self-identity and the so-called reflexive and de-traditionalising conditions of modernity said to characterise the current period (see Giddens, 1990; 1991; Beck, 1992; Beck et al., 1994; Heelas et al., 1996). The reflexive modernisation thesis argues that only now are the 'feudal', ascriptive elements in modern societies – such as those associated with social class and gender relations – disappearing as a source of identity and lifestyle, making us truly modern individuals able to choose identities increasingly free from the constraints of class, gender roles, locality, religion and occupation. Modernisation, according to Beck, has itself become the subject of modernising forces (Beck, 1992; Beck et al., 1994). Individual identity, which had existed as a project since at least the eighteenth century, he argues, has now become a reflexive project, one in which individuals are consciously aware of and able to monitor or change their own identities (Beck, 1992; Giddens, 1991). Not only is the lifeworld exposed, therefore, to the aesthetic conditions of a consumer culture and the choices it offers for the construction of self-identity (Lash, 1993; Lash and Urry, 1994), but to the instrumentalism of a risk society in which mediating cultural institutions are seen as having failed to filter out social uncertainty or indeed to have even caused it (Beck, 1992).

They suggest that now, with the decline of pre-modern ascriptive traditions, the full effects of modern individualisation, in a period of high modernity, are being realised (Giddens, 1990). According to writers such as Beck and Giddens, changes in the division of labour, the family and within gender relations have led to the de-traditionalisation of social roles such that individuals are able to bracket off possible consequences of modern life by trusting in expert systems on the one hand (Giddens, 1990), and experiencing the consequences as risks through which self-identity has to be managed (Beck, 1992). The consequences are often problematic at the level of identity, leading to a politicising of daily life and new forms of life politics that lead to forms of self-reflexive identity formation (Giddens, 1991). One indication of the condition of high or reflexive modernity, these writers argue, is the emergence of the 'life-politics' of new social movements (see Giddens, 1990; Beck, 1995; 1996). Following a broadly Habermasian and therefore also Weberian view on new social movements, advocates of the reflexive modernisation argument have come to see these movements in highly individualised terms, a politics of the lifeworld that responds to systemic processes of disembedding from traditional social relations and the uncertainties and risks generated by institutions such as science, industry and medicine.

As with the Habermasian view on new social movements, while issues of identity are seen as problematic within this type of society, the subject is not. The idea of modernity producing subjects as authors of their own life-scripts is not seen as being undermined by the conditions of reflexive modernisation but heightened by it. For Beck, a reflexive modernity is a society of increased individualisation. Rather than a society where uncertainty produces expressive collectivities and romantic rejections of this intensification of the modern, it is seen as generating greater individual autonomy and individualised responses to risk and change (1992). New social movements, or sub-politics as Beck prefers to call them (1996), are little more than collectives of atomised individuals responding to the systemic challenges to their own individualised lifeworlds.

We have already seen in Habermas's analysis of the relationship of new social movements to the lifeworld (1981) that expression and affect is allowed little place in it in his quest for a denotative example of communicative rationality. This uncertainty over the expressive remains the case in those writing on reflexive modernisation. Where they have been concerned with issues of feeling, intimacy and emotion, this has remained at an individualised level, focused especially on intimate, sexual relations between couples, romantic love, and relations within the family (see Giddens, 1992). While Giddens does concede that what he calls life-politics has an emotional dimension, he still treats emotion in terms of the dyadic relations of communication between individuals rather than in terms of collective identifications and sentiments (1992: 196–203).

From Weber, through the debates about narcissism during the 1970s, to the current arguments about a high or reflexive modernity lurks a nasty, peculiar and very singular ideal type of the modern individual against which all other types of individuality are to be judged and found wanting. This ideal type is of an autonomous, bourgeois, male subject that exists outside the frame of social process in a privileged position as author and spectator of social process. Attempts to bring this subject into the frame – so-called postmodern approaches to subjectivity – are resisted theoretically by these writers, all of whom still adhere to a theoretical humanism in defining their version of the subject. Equally, they resist what they see as the social challenges to that subject which has no position. They either do this through a critique of the expressive culture and social movements in which such a challenge to that subjectivity is made, as in the case of Weber and the critics of narcissism, or they theorise those changes in terms of this autonomous subject, as in the case of Beck and Giddens, and give those groupings the slant that fits with their own vision of the modern world.

To question such a view, to offer an alternative that does not accept this singular subjectivity but one which recognises its privileged position, social construction and its partialness, means that we have to look to other writers on identity. Within sociology, this means looking in particular at a more Durkheimian tradition, indeed a more anthropological tradition, that sees subjectivity and identity caught up in *collective* processes of identification.

Neo-tribalism and the politics of identification

Those who have taken the opposite view and stressed the importance of collective processes of identity formation have usually started from Durkheim (see Turner, 1969; Maffesoli, 1988a; 1996; Bataille, 1985; 1991). Whereas Weber saw a solution to the challenges modern societies created for individuals in the idea of a personal vocation (which he saw originating in ascetic Protestantism), an idea which in the most recent work on reflexive modernisation has translated personal vocation into reflexive life-project, Durkheim's well-known solution to the problems of what he and others like Guyau called 'anomie' was the creation of a new type of social solidarity – organic solidarity – in the form of corporations which, he believed, rather than undermining individual autonomy and responsibility would create the conditions of moral individualism that would facilitate both personal development and social harmony (Durkheim, 1964).

In this approach to questions of identity, the main theme has been to focus on the relationship between identity and identification. In doing so, the whole terrain of the affectual and expressive has been given its rightful place within analysis of identity. To analyse the relationship between identity and identification means looking at a range of issues including the relationship between choices and constraints, the forms through which identities are constituted, the means of establishing collective identifications and groupings, and the performances through which these identifications are developed.

The identities that form part of the expressive outlook and lifestyles have been described as being principally elective, affectual and tribal in character (see Maffesoli, 1988a; 1996; Amirou, 1989; Bauman, 1990; 1991; Shields, 1991a; 1992b) The terms 'elective' (meaning chosen) and 'affectual' (meaning derived from feelings), in the context of such identities, can be used together without too much cause for concern. Religious identities associated with sects and cults provide the model case for such a statement. Indeed, Weber as much as Durkheim has provided many of the original starting points for the analysis of such religious communities (Weber, 1965). The tribal element among these three terms, however, is perhaps less immediately obvious. While tribes in small-scale societies (a term now rarely used because of its earlier derogatory connotations associated with the primitive and the simple) may be described as affectual in terms of the identifications between members that they establish, there is an apparent inconsistency between the terms elective and tribal. In classical sociology and social anthropology, tribes would normally be said to be ascribed and not elective or achieved. They would be seen as part of the dense sociability of small-scale societies where one's lifestyle and identity would be established at birth by ascriptive categories of culture such as caste, kinship, religious customs and beliefs.

Elective tribes that have an affectual basis for their existence and reproduction are not, therefore, the tribes of pre-modern small-scale societies.

Instead they are what Maffesoli, and following him Bauman, called 'neo-tribes' (Maffesoli, 1988b: 145; Bauman, 1992: 136–137). These neo-tribes are what Scheler might have called 'communities of feeling' (1954: 12–13) which provide the basis for chosen lifestyles derived from emotional, empathic identification with like-minded others (1954: 18ff.).

The term community as used here is clearly not the idea of community as established within the sociological tradition by Tönnies's notion of a Gemeinschaft, organised around an organic will and offering a traditional basis for a person's lifestyle and identity (1955). Instead, these communities of feeling are achieved as intentional 'communities', that can be seen as both moral communities or emotional communities (Moss-Kanter, 1976; Weber, 1968). Community as a concept, however, is invariably fraught with problems, not least because it has invariably been invoked as a basis for an essentialist understanding of identity and belonging. If in our world of multiple and fractured identities, however, we seek to belong, this may take the form of the search for some lost, authentic and essential community – something which we have witnessed all too vividly in the nationalist struggles in many parts of the world, notably in eastern Europe since the end of Communism. It can, however, just as readily be seen as a more para-doxical search, a search for community in choice, whose sense of belonging and authenticity may not be attached to issues of nation or ethnicity but to other symbols: spiritual harmony, belonging with the earth, communion with the cultures of native peoples, or simply a shared solidarity around political goals or the desire to express oneself through a particular style of living.[2] Whether we choose to use the term community or not, some way of addressing the expressive basis to the forms of collective identification and belonging associated with the many forms of identity politics and lifestyle has to be found.

Those writing on neo-tribes and emotional communities, drawing on Durkheim's sociology of religion, have sought to separate out the expres-sive, the realm of feeling and emotion, from the irrational and treat it as something distinctive. Maffesoli has been at the centre of this work over the past decade, but it is a sociological tradition that has a long history, albeit one not as dominant in Anglo-American sociology as the Weberian approach discussed above (see for example Gurvitch, 1941; Scheler, 1954; Schmalenbach, 1977; Bataille, 1994; as well as more recently Maffesoli, 1988b; 1996; Shields, 1992a; Evans, 1997).[3] Studies which emphasise issues of choice when talking about community, friendship, belonging, love and feelings of what is real or authentic in social life all share this approach.

This sociological and anthropological tradition is not just concerned with the various counter-cultures of the twentieth century. The value that has been placed on the expressive as both an ethical concern and an aesthetic one can be traced back from contemporary lifestyle concerns through early twentieth-century youth movements, nineteenth-century bohemians (see Grana, 1964), to the Romantic movement of the late-eighteenth and nine-teenth century (see Campbell, 1987), and indeed to the Protestant cults from which arose its opposite – a rational, calculating outlook that shuns worldly pleasures for inner reflection, hard work and an ascetic renunciation of immediate gratification. Many of these early Protestant sects were not just inner-directed sets of autonomous individuals, they did not simply cultivate an inner self through rational self-reflection, they also moved and shook in a collective and emotionally charged setting. Alongside the cultivation of a heroic, self-contained, self-sufficient person there were groups that facilitated an intense communion and sense of belonging. The rational is not the antithesis of the affectual or the expressive; the two have to be seen as originating together. Both have come to define what it is to be modern and both have shaped the identities that have come to be associated with modernity.

It is perhaps the privileging of the faculties of reason by the Enlightenment and the alignment of the expressive with the world of unreason that have led to this marginalisation of the expressive as a source of identity within sociological analysis. The elevation of the world of science and rational thought above everything else, notably religious experience, within modern society, has seen the marginalisation of the expressive and has turned it into the arena of critique and a counter-modern stance. That critique has at different times gone under the label of romantic anti-capitalism, the counter-culture, and the New Age, all of which have one thing in common: in each the subjective world of experience is put at the centre of its identity practices and politics (see Peckham, 1962; Berman, 1982).

The whole edifice of counter-modern critique, whether from the political left or right, has been based on an elevation of the expressive over the rational; revolutionary action, solidarity and comradeship, the symbolism of revolt, and so on all call upon the feelings of people and seek to ground a sense of moral right and wrong in that realm of feeling and expression rather than in reason alone. To have an identity is to find ways of expressing oneself through identifying with others, and that identification is based in the expressive world of feeling and emotion and forms of collective sentiment.

While sociology has told us a good deal over the years about the alienating and disenchanting experiences of modernity, it has tended to look down on the solutions that individuals have tried to come up with to counter these experiences: they are not rational enough; they do not turn themselves into a rigorous, scientifically based social critique; they exhibit weak character formation and an over-reliance on manipulative charismatic leaders; and so on. Recent analyses of neo-tribes have tended to reject earlier fears of 'mass societies', seeing in processes of tribal de-individualisation and the adoption of group identities by individuals a source of individual strength and self-expression. Tribes may be collective phenomena but one chooses which, if any, one wants to belong to and can also choose when to leave. The massification of postmodern consumer society, according to this theory, does not lead to irrational, mass cultural forms as in previous analyses of collective behaviour (see Smelser, 1963), but to localised, spatially situated neo-tribes, derived from a 'totemic consciousness' and shared vitalistic 'puissance' that leads to the development of an empathic sociality (Maffesoli, 1996). In other words, the decline of the category of the modern individual, so loved by Weber and who feared its tragic demise, is not replaced by uniformity in personality but diversity, polyculturalism and much more disparate forms of identification that support the condition of de-individualisation.

Maffesoli's claims about neo-tribalism are worthy of further analysis. His approach is one, however, that still carries certain modernist assumptions with it (see Evans, 1997): not least, the issue of whether such groupings be seen as indicative of the move to a postmodern society is a theoretical move in which denoting takes precedence over connoting.

By performing a certain twist on Durkheim's ideas about the relationship between different types of society and their forms of social solidarity (1964), Maffesoli argues that modern societies (in contrast to the more familiar Durkheimian argument about pre-modern societies) are characterised by a mechanical solidarity, while postmodern societies become the societies organised around an organic solidarity. This is in many respects quite similar to the argument that modernity has been de-traditionalised by conditions of reflexivity (see Giddens, 1990; Heelas et al., 1996). A consequence of this move is that neo-tribes are devalued in themselves at the same time that their value rises as an indication of the bigger modernity/postmodernity issue (see Bauman, 1991; Shields, 1992b; Evans, 1997; Mellor and Shilling, 1997).

In Maffesoli's analysis of neo-tribes, as opposed to his suggestions about postmodernity, we have the beginnings of a way of thinking about identity, identity politics and issues of identification, and positions that are sug-gestive, notably because of the ways in which associations are analysed in terms of issues of election and emotion, and the symbolic and performative expressions of identity through which they are organised. This is what neo-tribes connote. To use them to denote, to promote them to the big stage of history (or allow others to challenge their existence at that level), is to devalue all else that might be said about expressive groupings and their relationship to questions of identity. For me, the important thing to recognise is that this concept of a neo-tribe, and the groupings and identifications it is used to describe, is associated not with rationality and its modes of identification and organisation but with sentiment, feeling and shared experience – with affectual forms of sociation. I am not interested in the modernist issue of what this indicates about the current status of society/ modernity and the social theorist god-trick that it performs.

For Maffesoli the conditions of modernity were still ascriptive ones, with social roles determined by factors such as class, gender or ethnicity, whereas only in postmodern 'societies', it is argued, do social roles become a matter of preference and individual choice.[4] Maffesoli's claim rather over-generalised with regard to his presupposition of a complete rupture with modernity and the implication that everyone becomes involved in neo-tribes. The important thing to recognise, however, is that this type of tribe – which is now with us and can be seen quite clearly in what otherwise have been described as new social movements – is based upon sentiment, feeling and shared experience. A neo-tribe is an affectual form of sociation through which both individual and collective ideas of identity are expressed.

The emphasis by those who have followed Durkheim has been on the identity shaping conditions of collective sentiment, performance and the importance of communitas (see Turner, 1974). The expressive, in the form of shared feeling, emotion, love, solidarity, loyalty, belonging and ritual processes of identity transformation, is of central importance to this understanding of identity. The consequences, however, are not without conflict. The loosening of such structural constraints de-centres identities and makes a sense of self problematic. While this may offer new freedoms for people to define who they are, it also creates new and often troubling uncertainties. It is a form of sociation that reflects the topological complexity of identity politics rather than one that smooths things out. Performance as a perspective is a way in which we can address the issue of individual identity and collective identification without losing sight of either.[5]

The main virtue of the Maffesoli approach is that he centres his analysis of contemporary cultural life in the expressive realm of feeling and emotion, something that reflexive-modernisation theorists do not do, preferring to use the Weberian model of the rational, self-reflexive self instead. The main weakness in Maffesoli, however, is that he ignores power relations, constraints and uncertainties placed on identity choices when he indicates that such factors as class, gender and ethnicity are no longer relevant in establishing styles of life. Maffesoli's approach continues to think in the Euclideanism of 'before and after' and associated contrasts about moves from one type of society to another. It is arguable that the pluralising of elective lifestyle opportunities does not lead solely to a playful and transgressive enjoyment of being Other, but, perhaps more significantly, also leads to the emergence of lifestyle responses to the problematising of identity. The plurality of choices available creates uncertainty and conflict as much as playfulness and inventiveness. The unbinding of class, gender and ethnicity as the basis for identity does not necessarily lead to a complete dissociation between these structural factors and identity but, more often, to a troubled politics of identity in which people try to renegotiate their identities – as say women, Black, gay, disabled or somehow different (see Mercer, 1990; Rutherford, 1990; Hall, 1992; 1996; Sarup, 1996). To hyphenate identities with an and-and-and is in many ways an attempt to negotiate a position of singularity in identification (definitely to belong) more than it is to avoid a singular identity. All the same, we can still talk about class, gender and ethnicity alongside neo-tribes. Contrary to Maffesoli's own suggestions, the latter is not the form of identification that replaces the former; to speak in topological rather than Euclidean terms means that we can accept their co-existence. Neither class nor gender determines all that we do in our lives but they still have some hold over us. Their efforts are real enough. Equally we do not have complete freedom of choice in terms of the tribes we can choose to join, but we do have some

consumerism / capitalism – makes it hard 4 some tribes.

choice independent of issues such as class and gender. To say this is not to fudge the issue. Rather, it is to recognise the plural and folded nature of the society we live in; it is to recognise that social space is not uniform and homogeneous, that time and space do not always map onto each other, that different parts of society can move at different speeds and with variable effects upon different groups (see Lee, 1997), and that the orderings that make up society are always provisional, plural and revisable (see Law, 1994).

In many respects such a process of identity formation does not reflect, in a playful or ironic manner, the pleasures of the many choices available, but instead, a politicised quest for an authentic sense of self amidst the uncertainty that is the conditionality of the topology of the social terrain in which we live. What is significant, I argue, is that neo-tribes often use this uncertainty in order to attempt to create new certainty rather than retreat into the safety of routine. Of considerable significance within this neo-tribal outlook, therefore, is the emphasis that is placed on the creation of group identifications in dealing with the uncertainties of the world – identifications among consociates that emphasise the importance of the affectual and the expressive in their quest for new meaning, authentic experience and a sense of belonging. There are a number of ways in which this is achieved: a shared outlook on the world and through forms of grouping are two of the most significant (these are the subjects of Chapter 3 and Chapter 4). Another is through means of identification; we know, if not from the study of new social movements then certainly from the analysis of youth subcultures, that one of the key issues here is that of style (see Hall and Jefferson, 1976; Clarke et al., 1976; Willis, 1978; Hebdige, 1979; 1988).

Identifications, affect and style

We are more familiar with the analysis of style within youth subcultures (see Hebdige, 1979) than we are within the wider realm of expressive identities that often, although not always, transcend issues of generation and life stage. The subcultural analysis of style by members of the Centre for Contemporary Cultural Studies (CCCS) at Birmingham in the 1970s have been most influential in this area (Clarke et al., 1976; Hebdige, 1976; 1979). Adopting a neo-Marxist position, notably associated with Gramsci's theory of hegemony, and adding to it elements from French structuralism – notably Levi-Strauss's analysis of bricolage and homology developed in his study *The Savage Mind* (1966) and Barthes's work on signifying practice (1968; 1973) – they wanted to suggest that the styles created by youth subcultures were skilled semiotic accomplishments by young bricoleurs that challenged the dominant culture, often through inversion of stylistic messages associated with fashion and dress codes, notably those of their parent culture.

Hebdige, who developed this analysis of style to its most complete form, argued using the example of punk that they were bricoleurs – young people who used a heterogeneous mixture of things to hand to create a collage effect that then became the basis of a distinct and homologous style (1979; 1988). The collection of things together produced an ordering of those things into an homology; items of clothing, jewellery and so on, organised in an homology, became signs within this system of an homologous meaning – one that, for Hebdige, was then used to challenge the dominant culture.

The accepted position within studies of youth subcultures at the time was that young people, located within the contradictions of class position – between a dominant culture and their own, often working class parent culture – were led into seeking a magical resolution of class antagonisms (see P. Cohen, 1972) through subcultural opposition to society, expressed most clearly through the use of style. While this approach has had a lasting impact on the analysis of style and subcultures, it has also been subject to numerous criticisms (see Thornton, 1995). Subcultural analysis has focused on the spectacular rather than the mundane in youth culture, it has tended to focus exclusively on class at the expense of issues of ethnicity and gender (McRobbie, 1991), it has been accused of imposing meanings onto styles that never existed among the practitioners of those styles – a criticism of overinterpretation (see S. Cohen, 1980). Subcultural analysis may appear to work well for teddy boys, skinheads and punks, but does not work so well for the more recent and less oppositional subcultures such as the new romantics of the early 1980s or the rave culture of the 1990s. The over-emphasis on issues of class, more so of class consciousness than the class membership of subcultures, is now apparent. Similarly, the rather overly simple dualistic view of a dominant culture being opposed by counter-hegemonic subcultures appears obvious now in ways that it perhaps was not at the time in which this work was being developed. One might also add that Hebdige is rather loose in his reading of structuralist theory, notably that of Levi-Strauss. For Levi-Strauss, the bricoleur makes do with things that are to hand and uses them to create myths. The issue is one of randomness and the derivation of an homology from that randomness. Homology is about an ordering of things into a system of meaning, not an ordering of things and values together.[6] Hebdige tends to interpret the style of the subculture through its expressed values; he starts with the homology and then looks for the bricolage. His reading of meaning into a style is one result of his move from connotative interpretation of signifying practices within a style to denoting a form of class politics. Because he starts with values taken as indicative of a nascent form of class struggle, he sees style not so much as an expressive and symbolic form of communication but as a bigger sign of working class alienation and resistance. The attempted fusion between Gramscian Marxism and the structuralism of Levi-Strauss is one that is not particularly interested in the connotations within a style but what that style denotes in terms of broader issues of class and class politics. Hebdige's analysis of style is at its best when it does not make this denotative gaze but sticks to the sideways glancing of connotation, such as in his reading of the scooter in the mod subculture (1988).

A further problem with subcultural analysis is its emphasis on hegemonic and counter-hegemonic cultures. The boundaries are too static, Euclidean and one-dimensional. It is increasingly difficult to identify what the dominant culture is (see Martin, 1981). The boundaries of nation states, the multiplicity of flows of information, the breakdown of distinctions between high and low, do not sustain any view of a canonical culture – whether that be a culture in terms of high culture or in terms of lifestyles associated with class cultures. This is not to suggest that culture does not produce areas of dominance and areas of subculture that are counter-hegemonic, but these are mobile, partial and porous boundaries that vary within different cultural fields and within different societies. Equally, while social class may still influence lifestyle in some areas and in some ways, it is not all-inclusive in determining a lifestyle or membership of a particular subculture. The expressive lifestyles and identity politics that are the subject of this book are multiple: overlapping in some areas, yet exclusive in others. In some ways, issues of class, gender, ethnicity, and sexual orientation may influence types of lifestyle; in other ways, not at all. If we are to understand them we cannot begin from a neo-Marxist analysis of subcultures in which class is a dominant issue. If we have to speak of class at all, then we should see it as something that for every individual – just as for groups of individuals, class fractions and whole classes – is negotiated differentially across different areas of cultural and economic life, and mobile in space and time. We have to use concepts that can show pattern and order where it exists, but also account for the fluidity, difference and mobility where they too are found.

Style, however, is still an important issue when we look at the issues associated with elective and affectual identification; it is one of the means through which identity markers and indications of belonging are expressed. An identity is constituted, in the neo-tribal context, through what Maffesoli refers to in the title of one of his papers, as 'Games with Masks' (1988a). The link between identity and neo-tribalism is made through the persona, or mask, that is performed in part through style. The construction of a persona involves, I argue, a combination of bodily dispositions, situated perform-ances and identification with others that use stylistic effects. The emotional communities that constitute neo-tribes for Maffesoli, offer the empathic support for those who want to try on new masks and become someone different. Like others working in areas like that of marginal groups and subcultures, Maffesoli is interested in the practices or tactics of daily life, and the bricolage through which identities are constituted (see Levi-Strauss, 1966; Hebdige, 1979; de Certeau, 1984). However, we should not rush too readily to find a single explanation for any pattern or homology that emerges out of this sign-work. Identity for Maffesoli is not so much about ideologies as about practices associated with emotional links with others and the elective groupings that emerge, the totemic symbolism and use of style to convey a shared sense of identification, and the senses of belonging – not located in essentialised categories – through which identities are performed.

These issues are both more diverse and less clear-cut than those of homologous pattern but they are equally important.

It is such contact with others, as Maffesoli recognises, that provides the basis for the neo-tribe (1988b: 142). Examples of neo-tribal lifestyles include: youth subcultures; sporting allegiances; gangs; new social movements; new religious movements; cults; and self-growth group therapies. All of these neo-tribal identifications involve shared identifications of some sort. The significance of a neo-tribe is associated, I argue, with a perceived ideal identification with others, as a direct and expressive form of 'Thou' like identification (see Buber, 1958). How this is performed and maintained is the subject of this book. It is not an issue that can be reduced simply to questions of style but they are certainly an important part of the modality of identification through which both identity and its politics are expressed.

All of the cultural, political and religious enthusiasms that can be associated with neo-tribalism are elective in that individuals make choices as to whether they want to become involved. This does not mean, however, that one's social class, gender, ethnicity or locality are of no significance. While these structural categories do not inevitably lead to neo-tribal involvement, it can be established that involvement in particular neo-tribes is related to such factors. It is well established, for example, that the membership of new social movements often comprises people from middle-class backgrounds (see Parkin, 1968; Scott, 1990; Bagguley, 1992). Equally, there are class and age patterns of involvement in youth subcultures (Clarke et al., 1976). However, not all members of the middle class or youth become engaged in such activities. If they do become active, they choose to do so. Similarly, this does not explain membership by those from other classes who can also be found involved in such groupings.

Maffesoli wrongly ignores power relations, constraints and uncertainties placed on identity choices when he claims that such factors as class, gender and ethnicity are no longer relevant in establishing styles of life. The plurality of choices available creates uncertainty and conflict as much as playfulness and inventiveness. Neo-tribalism, I argue, owes more to the ideas of romanticism than it does to those of postmodernism. What is significant, I reiterate, is that neo-tribes often use this uncertainty in order to attempt to create new certainty rather than retreat into the safety of routine.

Expression, collective sentiment and the politics of identity

In an article written some years ago on counter-cultural movements, an argument was expressed that an understanding of counter-cultural politics had to take account of the religiosity used to counter the secular and instrumental aspects of contemporary societies,

> 'Post-modern' individuals . . . seek to 'recentralize' their world through adherence to one of the symbolic-moral universes enveloping a host of competing 'elective

centres' such as those proposed by the new cults and religions, new life styles and communal movements, as well as by radical movements. Each of these typically embodies a vision of some ultimate salvational goal and proposes a 'salvation path' . . . The 'post-modern' individuals, facing this wide choice of goals of the new salvationism and lacking stable criteria for judgement and discrimination, tend either to move from one elective centre to another in a continuous quest . . . or to jump from total alienation to absolute and indiscriminate allegiance to one of those elective centres, only, in most cases, to fall away again after the thrill of the new experience lost its grip. (E. Cohen et al., 1987: 375)

It has been said that new social movements are not new (Tucker, 1991); this is of course true. First wave feminism, anti-vivisection movements, anti-war protests, communal living, concerns for nature and environmental destruction, along with religious and spiritual experimentations were all part of a thriving 'counter-culture' in nineteenth-century Victorian Britain (see Webb, 1974). Indeed, as we have seen, Weber himself makes a number of disparaging remarks about the 'expressiveness of the Youth' in his 'Science as a Vocation' lecture which might suggest the development of similar lifestyles in the early part of the twentieth century in Germany (1970a: 143). New religious movements, the New Age movement, the identity politics associated with new social movements and some youth subcultures, as well as the less clearly defined consumer practices outlined in the Introduction to this book, are all manifestations of this expressivism. All, despite their different characterisations, have in common a focus on the expressive as a source of identity formation, which is articulated through their ways of life.

Such expressivism can be located within the well established romantic rejection of modernity. It is concerned with feeling, emotion and belonging as a source of symbolic and spiritual creativity and with the eclectic use of totemic identifications often associated with the Otherness of non-modern lifestyles. I would argue that romanticism is important to this discussion of the sociological literature on identity and expression. In Chapter 3 I look at this issue of outlook on the world underlying many of the current forms of identity politics by developing Williams's concept of a structure of feeling, to help understand the particular outlook that has developed within these expressive lifestyles.

In this chapter I have argued against those who have criticised these expressive movements or who see them in individualised, non-affectual terms. They either offer a one-dimensional, ahistorical view of the subject underlying the politics of identity or ignore issues of collective sentiment, expressivism and identification. While analyses of neo-tribes and style within subcultures offer important alternatives to these approaches, they do not in themselves address all of the issues of identification within identity politics. In the two chapters that follow, I address in particular the issues of outlook and group dynamics in more detail, through the concepts of structure of feeling in the first case and Bund or communion in the second.

Notes

1. Hennies has recently argued that the search for this vocation is central to understanding his sociology of modernity. Its use as the basis for a new type of person was the main purpose of Weber's life work (1987).

2. Belonging is not, however, the sole preserve of expressive identities that take this anti-materialist, New Age form. As Munro has pointed out, it can equally well be adapted to the market and to the firm (1998). Conversely, those who seek to escape from the materialism of modern societies do not always do so in an unambiguous way. My own analysis of free festivals among New Age travellers in Britain – a group who take a staunchly anti-materialist stance on life – has shown that on occasions like that of the festival they can still find their sense of belonging in acts of consumption and consumerism (Hetherington, 1992).

3. Some of this earlier work, notably Schmalenbach's on the Bund form of sociation (1961; 1977 [1922]), is discussed in more detail in Chapter 4.

4. It should be said, however, that such an argument is already suggested, albeit more implicitly, by Goffman in his discussions of the ways that people create and manage their identities through the presentation of self, face work and impression management (1971a).

5. The issue of performance, in particular the spatiality of identity performance, is the main theme of Part II of this book.

6. I am grateful to Pnina Werbner for discussions on these issues of homology.

3

SITUATIONS AND OCCASIONS:
THE STRUCTURE OF FEELING
AND EVERYDAY LIFE

Identity and everyday life

In order to understand the importance of expressivism within processes of identity formation and identity politics, I have argued we need to move away from a critique of the expressive based on some idealised model of the individual derived from the ascetic and rational personality to be found in the Weberian tradition. I further argue that the issue is not so much one of self-identity *per se*, as is assumed within this approach, but of the role in which expressive forms of collective identification facilitate the development of self-identity. Without wishing to suggest that we have to return to Durkheim, and all the methodological problems that that might entail, to find an alternative approach with which to address these issues, those such as Maffesoli who have taken Durkheim rather than Weber as their starting point have opened up ways in which the collective process of identity formation can be analysed effectively. To reiterate, a more anthropological approach to identity formation, associated with performativity, symbolism and indeed expression, provides us with a useful framework with which to begin (see Turner, 1969).[1]

In this chapter I want to develop this argument to show how the expressive dimension of identity might be analysed in the context of the set of identity positions associated with the current alternative lifestyles, New Age and new social movement assemblage. There are a number of important issues that have been raised about this, notably by Maffesoli in his recent accounts of neo-tribalism and in association with what he has called the ethics of aesthetics (1988a; 1991; 1996). His approach, which I outlined in Chapter 2, fuses together elements from the Durkheimian tradition on the analysis of forms of collective life with an understanding of social forms, sociations in particular from Simmel, into what can be described as a vitalist approach to understanding the importance of how people express themselves through collective identifications within their everyday lives. Expressivism involves, for Maffesoli, a combination of the ethical with the aesthetic (1991); as such, style as a means of communication is an important aspect of expressive identifications. This focus on style as we have seen has been encountered before in the analysis of subcultures (see Clarke, et al., 1976; Hebdige, 1979). However, for Maffesoli, it is not tied to the issue of class identity but to a wider range of social identifications.

It is not British subcultural theory, however, that is the starting point for Maffesoli. Rather, his analysis stands in a long tradition in France in which everyday life is seen as the arena of both cultural creativity and social revolt. Like the Surrealists (see Nadeau, 1987), Situationists (see Home, 1988; Plant, 1992), and individual writers like Lefebvre (1971; 1991) and de Certeau (1984), Maffesoli focuses on the aesthetic and expressive as forms of resistance and communication found in the hidden spaces of everyday life. His focus on the local, the proximate and the intimate maps out the terrain of these expressive identities, something also made clear in Melucci's analysis of the embeddedness of new social movements in the locales of everyday life (1989; 1996). While the issue of the spatiality of identity performance is one that I look at in detail in Part II of this book, at this point it is useful to discuss some of the issues associated with the space of everyday life to help us understand some of the characteristics of expressive identities.

Having recognised the importance of everyday life and spatiality to the expression of identity, I go on in this chapter to ask how we might characterise the principles behind the range of expressive lifestyles I identified in the Introduction. I return to the list of key identity issues listed there (p. 5) and discuss these in more detail. In particular, I use Raymond Williams's analysis of a structure of feeling to do this (1965; 1977; 1979). Creating a differential model of structures of feeling, one that does not rely on some notion of a dominant culture or on high cultural forms, allows us to look at how culture is experienced and how it expresses itself in distinct lifestyle forms. The similarities with Maffesoli are apparent. Where Williams speaks of practical consciousness and the structure of feeling, Maffesoli talks of puissance (see Shields, 1996: 3). Both locate this expressive dimension of identification within the interstices of everyday life. The main features that go into characterising the outlook of those who opt for the expressive as a basis for identity can be identified as a distinct structure of feeling.

Based on what happens at the boundary between the alternative lifestyles, youth subcultures and new social movements that make up the identity set under consideration here, I describe this as a romantic structure of feeling. Following Schmitt, the main feature of (political) romanticism is one of subjectivised occasionalism (1986; 1988): creating events and situations (often in spatially symbolic locations) for the cultivation of an identity that sees itself as morally elect. In this we can see links between identity and identification, identity politics and a type of structure of feeling that is characterised by a practical consciousness which adopts an ethic of aesthetics.

Expressive lifestyles and everyday life

Identity is more than about self-reflection, understanding and the development of a life-project based on the idea of a calling. It is fundamentally about issues of belonging, expression, performance, identification and communication with others. To begin to analyse these claims requires that we take a closer look at what is implied by this.[2] Given the links I have already discussed between identity and identification (see also Shields, 1992b), an important place to start is Maffesoli's analysis of the emotional community on which much of his analysis of neo-tribalism is based (1996: 9–30).

For Maffesoli, the key to understanding contemporary lifestyles, what he calls neo-tribes, is the idea of an affectual sociality. The sense of belonging derived from fellowship or communion – what Maffesoli, following Durkheim, calls the social 'divine' (1996: 10) – is, for him, the impetus behind collective lifestyle identifications. People want to belong, they want to have some way of showing their empathy with like-minded people (see also Scheler, 1954); they want a form of solidarity based on shared ethical and aesthetic values. Even though the idea of an emotional community is one developed by Weber, the moves Maffesoli makes in his use of the term are not particularly Weberian. Unlike Weber, Maffesoli does not associate affectual social action with the irrational world of tradition and custom but, to continue with Weber's terms, with value-rationality. Furthermore, value-rationality is no longer seen as the preserve of isolated puritan individuals reflecting on their calling but expressing values through a collective, proximate, emotional solidarity with others. This is more akin to a Lutheran ideal of religious affiliation and identity, perhaps, than a Calvinist one. What we can say is that emotional communities are also often moral communities. This is a point often missed in new social movement analysis that tends to focus on the idea of a moral community and its political effects rather than its relation to more affectual and expressive forms (see Pakulski, 1991). For Maffesoli, however, ethical beliefs are not expressed discursively simply through speech and text but through the aesthetic marks, or masks, of group identification. Feeling and emotion, the expressive realm, is a realm of belief and value that expresses itself through stylistic forms of communication and signification.

I have already argued in Chapter 2 that we do not have to follow Maffesoli's denotative direction when he argues that the old structures, such as that of class, have disappeared to be replaced by neo-tribes, and then go on to advocate the shift to a postmodern society. It is clear that the old structures have not gone; and we are still moderns (see Hetherington, 1997a). However, we should accept the argument that we cannot rely on concepts like class alone to explain contemporary lifestyles and group affiliations.[3] The issue of style and of signs as forms of communication are important but not necessarily as indicators of class consciousness. For Maffesoli, style operates in a different way to that suggested in subcultural theory (Hebdige, 1979; Thornton, 1995); it forms part of an ethic of aesthetics (Maffesoli, 1991; Shields, 1996; 1992b). Like Habermas (1981) and Melucci (1989; 1996), Maffesoli suggests that the lifeworld, associated with everyday life, is an important arena for the development of new forms of cultural expression often at odds with the social world of institutions. Unlike Habermas but still in line with Melucci, however, it is the expressive and the emotional within this lifeworld rather than the rational and discursive that he sees as the source of new styles and new ethics (see also Bauman, 1990; 1991). The lifeworld of people within any particular period, Maffesoli argues, produces an ethos. In some periods, this ethos is determined by the institutions of society and is inscribed in moral codes (1991: 7). These moral codes then become the basis of identity. This seems to be similar to the sort of thing that Weber is arguing for in his vocation lectures (1970a; 1970b). During other times, however, Maffesoli argues, the ethos is defined within the lifeworld of the people rather than in social institutions, and expresses itself in ethical practices rather than moral laws. Whereas morals are the basis of identity, for Maffesoli ethics are derived more from identifications. The current ethos which Maffesoli argues is defined within this lifeworld and sometimes associated with the idea of a postmodernity, he describes as an ethic of aesthetics (1991; see also Bauman, 1991).

Maffesoli sees aesthetics as a popular, expressive mode of communication; as such, he is more concerned with issues of lifestyle than with art. Maffesoli's position can be summarised as follows: a collective, shared lifeworld that is denied its expressive outlets within the institutions of modern society, floods out through the sociality of everyday life in the combination of ethical and aesthetic forms of communication (1996). For Maffesoli, everyday life is the source of new forms of social solidarity that are manifest in a collective will that takes on distinct tribal forms as groups of individuals seek to express their particular concerns and feelings through this ethos of identification (1996). For Maffesoli this everyday sociality, found in the form of neo-tribes, derives from the expressive life of individuals in a form which he calls an underground puissance or 'will to live' (1996: 31–55). While Maffesoli invokes the Bergsonian language of vitalism to explain this collective sentiment and its neo-tribal expression, he is also working within a well-established tradition in French social and political thought, a tradition that sees everyday life as a site of both alienation and resistance that can be traced not so much to Bergsonian vitalism as to the Surrealists and Situationists and to the work of Henri Lefebvre and Michel de Certeau (see Lefebvre, 1971; 1991; Debord, 1981a; 1983; Vaniegem, 1983; de Certeau, 1984). In this world, everyday life is seen as something colonised and alienating in its effects that has to be resisted at the local level. Often that everyday life has been seen through the prism of the modern city and its rationally planned urbanism. Everyday life becomes a spatialised arena of resistance, and resistance a spatial politics of identity. In Maffesoli this becomes an issue not only of public space but also of proximity or proxemics.

For surrealists like Andre Breton or Louis Aragon the everyday, often routine and banal in character, hid within it the imaginary world of wonder. Like Freud's unconscious, this imaginary realm was able to influence the routine and structured world of consciousness. In places it burst forth and expressed its resistance to repression. For the surrealists, it was not only the human mind that had this unconscious layer, the city had its own unconscious hidden away in the forgotten spaces, in the arcades, the gardens at night, as well, of course, as in the back rooms of the Parisian cafés. Within the city, the imaginary would always be found just below the surface waiting to be uncovered (see Breton, 1961; Benjamin, 1973; 1979; Aragon, 1987). Within dreams and desires, this puissance would exert itself. This is a very nostalgic view of the city, harking back to the nineteenth-century city – Paris in particular – of barricades, bohemian districts, the Commune, and public space such as those of the French Revolution like the Palais Royal (see Hetherington, 1997a). One could go back to others who lived and wrote about such spaces in the eighteenth and nineteenth centuries: to Rimbaud, Baudelaire, Retif de la Breton or Blanqui, who all shared similar views on the importance of space to the people and their lives in struggle (see Grana, 1964; Bradshaw, 1978; Billington, 1980). This surrealist/bohemian outlook on the city and on everyday life in the more general sense was one also shared by the situationists in post-war France. They, along with Henri Lefebvre, did much to carry on this tradition of locating resistance in the everyday life of the city:

> All cities are geological; you cannot take three steps without encountering ghosts bearing all the prestige of their legends. We move within a closed landscape whose landmarks constantly draw us toward the past. Certain shifting angles, certain receding perspectives, allow us to glimpse original conceptions of space, but this vision remains fragmentary. (Chtcheglov, 1981: 1–2)

Writing in 1953, Chtcheglov's 'Formulary for a New Urbanism', working within this surrealist tradition, itself firmly set in Paris, saw the contemporary city as a banal, boring and oppressive place. It was the capitalist city whose dominant representation of space was that of the spectacle:

> Capitalist production has unified space, which is no longer bounded by external societies. This unification is at the same time an extensive and intensive process of banalization . . . Urbanism is capitalism's seizure of the natural and human environment; developing logically into absolute domination, capitalism can and must now remake the totality of space into its own setting. (1981: 165–6)

For the situationists (of whom Chtcheglov was an associate) whose work on the banal world of the everyday takes up many of the themes begun by the surrealists before them (see Knabb, 1981; Home, 1988; Plant, 1992), acts of resistance took the form of seeking out forgotten or unappropriated felicitous spaces or by the re-appropriation of urbanised space, through the creation of situations, which were defined as 'the concrete construction of momentary ambiences of life and their transformation into a superior passional quality' (Debord, 1981b: 22).

The method behind such a form of resistance called for a 'psycho-geographie' which consisted of, 'the study of the precise laws and special effects of the geographical environment, consciously organised or not, on the emotions and behaviour of individuals' (Debord, 1981a: 5). The principal means of conducting such an experiment was through the 'derive' (drifting), which consisted of traversing the city in small groups in an aimless and random manner so that chance encounters, reverie, unexpected

es and encountered places would provide a new ambience of the
an enlivening of everyday life against the city. Such a process
the recovery of an expressive experience of space that challenges
sentation of space produced within the social relations of capitalism
ebvre, 1991). The deriver, like the flaneur before, aims to provide a
new way of seeing that transgresses the power relations of institutions as
they affect a person's everyday life. For the situationists, however, although
the tradition of the flaneur is apparently influential, it was the ideal of
schizophrenic experiences that was seen to provide the new way of seeing.
Drawing on Gabel's analysis of false consciousness, the main characteristic
of schizophrenia that they wished to use was that of the spatialising of time
(1967).[4] The schizophrenic was seen to be a person without memory who
experiences all events in a continuous now, unable to distinguish between
before and after. The idea behind such a practice is not simply that it should
make routine occasions unfamiliar, but that in doing so, relations of power –
notably spectacular power and its representation – would be made visible
and open to contestation.

We remember this obscure little avant-garde group (see Home, 1988)
partly because of Debord's seminal analysis of spectacle within consumer-
capitalist societies (1983) but more because of the (often exaggerated)
influence they have been seen to have had on the student and worker
uprisings in France during May 1968. There, in the situationist-inspired
posters and slogans that the students used, was resistance to the banalities of
a bureaucratised everyday life exemplified by the instrumentalities of the
French university system at the time. The streets of Paris became, in
Maffesoli's terms, the spaces of a puissance that expressed itself in a revolt
against the values that that education system came to represent. The shock
effect of those times was felt not only by the de Gaulle administration but by
all left of centre academics who were, by and large, caught by surprise.

If any academic might be said to have anticipated the events it was Henri
Lefebvre. Despite his lifelong love–hate relationship with the French Communist Party and commitment to a rather heterodox form of Marxism, his
analysis of everyday life, which shared many of the themes to be found in
the writings of the situationists, might be said to have provided some sort of
theory for the '1968 events' before they actually happened. For Lefebvre,
the dominant social relations of capitalism are not met simply by working
class resistance within the workplace but through the heterogeneity of
opportunities for resistance that exist within everyday life as a field of
political struggle (1971). For Lefebvre, capitalist societies produce a space
through a triadic process, which consists of the three related elements:
'Spatial Practice', 'Representations of Space', and 'Representational Spaces'
(1991: 33).

According to Lefebvre, spatial practice is associated with the production
of a distinct space by social relations associated with capitalist production
and reproduction. Representations of space are the types of ideological
representation and semiotic codes associated with how that space is under-

stood within society – in a way, like a dominant ideology of
Lefebvre's belief that within the capitalist social formation, s[
dered invisible as abstract space, obscuring the social relations c
which it is produced. In other words, space can be said to be fetisl
same way that Marx argues that the commodity is fetishised (Ma
For Lefebvre, resistance to the dominant social relations must i
abstract space visible, in order to make the social relations of spatiaı practice
visible. This resistance takes place through what Lefebvre calls representational spaces. Such spaces Lefebvre describes as, 'embodying complex
symbolisms, sometimes coded, sometimes not, linked to the clandestine or
underground side of social life, as also to art' (1991: 33). Lefebvre goes on
to suggest that representational spaces are:

> space as directly lived through its associated images and symbols, and hence the
> space of 'inhabitants' and 'users', but also of some artists and perhaps of those,
> such as a few writers and philosophers, who describe and aspire to do no more
> than describe. This is the dominated – and hence passively experienced – space
> which the imagination seeks to change and appropriate. It overlays physical
> space, making symbolic use of its objects. (1991: 39)

Such spaces, therefore, are defined by the heterogeneity of the lived reality
of everyday life where it displays forms of resistance to the capitalist and
bureaucratic institutions of modern societies. These representational spaces
have their origins in the realities of everyday life and in particular, through
the realm of the imagination not immediate to the natural attitude, in
resistance to the mundane and alienating features of everyday existence.
Representational spaces involve making use of sites within everyday life that
have been left behind by modern society.

A further continuation of this tradition, that sees everyday life as the focus
for a politics of identity and resistance, is found in de Certeau's arguments
about strategies and tactics (1984). For de Certeau, strategies are the power
games and truth claims made by the institutions of society. Tactics, however,
are the practices carried out by the people in their routine everyday lives that
can come to resist the strategies of society (1984). Rather than a Foucauldian
micro-physics of power (1977; 1980), we have here the belief that everyday
life can be the source of a micro-physics of resistance. This does not usually
take the form of building barricades but of a creative set of practices that do
not conform to the norms and institutionalised practices of society. In other
words, a tactics of resistance is also a tactics of identity. That tactics of
identity is expressive in character and is developed through forms of
identification with others, and the political forms of action that groups and
networks of activists and their supporters might then engage in.

The spatiality of everyday life and the expressive ethos it produces is
localised for Maffesoli. He uses the metaphor of the black hole, one also
developed by Deleuze and Guattari (1988), to describe the spatiality of
this new ethos he sees emerging within this everyday life (1996: 46). For
Maffesoli, the institutional world of politics (also religion and culture
generally) becomes disassociated from this puissance of the everyday lives

of the majority of the people. As the ethos of society collapses in on itself, the creativity of the masses in their everyday lives, Maffesoli believes, gives birth to new forms of cultural expression that resist the institutional ethos and power of society.

As with both Habermas and Melucci, as well as with this surrealist tradition, everyday life is contrasted with the world of institutions and indeed the institution of identity. Identities defined in terms of citizenship, political rights and obligations, workplace employment, institutionalised religion, and other forms of codified logic of belonging and community are challenged by this expressive resistance that emanates from within everyday life. For Maffesoli, the logic of identity gives way to what he calls the logic of identification (1991: 16). Identification, neo-tribal in form and totemic in character, is an expression of the puissance that resists within everyday life through its multiplicity of tactics. This is not always an overtly political form of resistance; this is why most of the writing on new social movements fails to capture much of the significance of 'social movements': it still largely speaks the language of identity, of liberal political science, of macro-politics rather than the language of the micro-politics of identification and localised resistance. In the context of expressive identities, politics and identity are the same thing. They are inseparable from one another. A political act, of direct action for example, is also a performance of identity and vice versa.

If we are to understand the expressive lifestyles, New Age beliefs and the cultural politics of (at least) the past three decades, we need to draw on our understanding not only of social movements and of the sociology of consumer lifestyles, but also a range of ideas about feeling and emotion. The virtue of Maffesoli's approach is that – despite its occasionally florid style, the conceptual vagueness of his vitalism, and annoying tendencies to over-generalise and use examples from the whole of Western history back to the Greeks rather than sticking with the present – it does just that! It cuts across the intra-disciplinary boundaries and specialisms within sociology to try and explain in a way which does not adopt the elitism of a sociological approach that looks down on the expressive lives and ambitions of people.

Authenticity, identity and the 'other'

If we return to the *Cahoots* example I used as an illustrative case in the Introduction (p. 5), we can now look in more detail at the type of issues that lie behind this expressive identity politics. I identified six themes that touched on the issues of experience, identification, location, solidarity, communication and knowledge. These issues inform the ethic of aesthetics of the expressive identity set that can be seen as an example of one of Maffesoli's neo-tribes. It is around these issues that identities developed and the identity politics of our set of interests are expressed.

Experience: the search for authenticity

The issue of authenticity is one that has had a long-standing link with sociological analysis associated with the alienation of modern societies and the romantic critiques of modernity (see for instance Gouldner, 1973). In these instances we can see it as part of the expressive identity processes associated with the identification with cultural expressions that either identify with supposedly authentic alternatives or develop through syncretist new forms of 'authentic' expression. This is a major theme of the New Age movement as well as one found within new social movements (see Heelas, 1996).

Heelas has recently offered a detailed description of the multitude of New Age religions and forms of spirituality that now abound, covering a diverse array of forms that range from counter-cultural practices to the managerial practices of New Age capitalists, a description that conveys the importance of the expressive across a wide field of activities (1996). He sees the main cultural themes that are associated with the New Age as: the sacralisation of the self; authenticity; self-actualisation; expressivism; self-healing and personal growth. These themes are taken up and developed by Heelas by relating the character of the New Age movement to both the certainties and the uncertainties of modernity. Instead of seeing the New Age as anti-modern or counter-modern, he argues that it is a significant feature of modernity and is one of the major sources of cultural expression focused around a matrix of religious and humanist perspectives on the sacralisation of the self. For Heelas, the New Age is a form of spirituality that seeks to sacralise some of the core values of modernity (1996: 169); it is seen as both a radicalised form of modernity and a reaction to its conventional main-stream.[5] This desire for authenticity and the expressivism found in the New Age movement, but also in 'new social movements' and other forms of identity politics that do not necessarily have a strong spiritual component, is a major theme within the focus on the expressive and the identities associated with it. This is in many ways a familiar theme, and not one introduced solely by the current writings on de-traditionalisation. It is a central theme in classical sociology, the problem that focuses the minds of writers like Tönnies, Weber and Durkheim. This quest for authenticity is generally taken as a consequence of the routinisation and rationalisation of everyday life and the separation of value spheres like religion, politics, law, and culture by systemic or institutional processes. Everyday life becomes de-centred by such processes – stretched and fragmented so that it is impossible to have a single location called everyday life. The disenchantment of the world, as Weber famously put it, leads to a search for new forms of experience and identification, often located around issues of identity within everyday life. We have seen in the previous chapter how Weber and those who followed him have tended to argue against this quest for authenticity and identity in cultural and political expression and group identifications in favour of identification with an inner calling and its expression in a vocation.

Bringing everyday life back together as a unity through forms of identity politics is a significant part of this quest for authenticity. It often takes the form of identifying with other cultures, in many cases through an adoption of symbolic expressions of ethnicity and locality, the lifestyles of aboriginal peoples, idealisations of pre-modern community, craft working practices and artefacts; the consumption of organic products which are locally and simply produced, the development of lifestyles that involve a high degree of communal activity, and the development of skills associated if not with total self-sufficiency, then at least with a high degree of self-provisioning.[6] Authenticity is associated with issues of identification and belonging, and takes the connected forms of symbolic identification and forms of perform-ativity that allow a life to be created in which a sense of control and autonomy over how one wants to live can be achieved.

It is important to note that the relationship between authenticity and experience, while it may often be expressed in terms of the symbolism of community and belonging to some sort of whole, is at the same time associated with a highly individualised outlook on the world and one's place within it. As Heelas's analysis of the New Age rightly shows, and as Melucci has demonstrated in the case of new social movements, the practices of identity associated with issues of authenticity are means by which a sense of individual self-expression is achieved; they achieve this through collective rather than individualised forms of communication and grouping. People choose to involve themselves in new social movement politics, alternative lifestyle experiments, and all the other related activities associated with therapy, self-help and active campaigning. While the expres-sive forms that identifications might take will often be achieved through some form of emotional community which appears from the outside to have a strong hold upon individuals, the decision to join and the purpose of belonging as a source of self-expression and identity should not be under-estimated.

Identification: empathy and identification with the rights and freedoms of marginalised others

If one of the main issues associated with expressive identities is the idea that the contemporary world does not allow sufficient room for self-expression and development in the context of some form of supposedly authentic communal belonging, then a second issue of equal importance is that of free-dom and justice. While in their more organised form the non-government organisations (NGOs) and social movement organisations that have emerged out of a 'new social movement' milieu, such as Greenpeace or Friends of the Earth or the legal campaigning by feminist groups over issues to do with women's rights, have often adopted institutional and legalistic forms of campaigning and representation to address issues of rights and freedoms, these can also carry a heavy symbolic load within the terrain of everyday life as well.

Expressive identities are not only associated with the formalistic issues of the minority rights of activists or others that they wish to represent, but with the idea of the Other as a symbol of identification around which their own identities are expressed. First nation peoples, oppressed minority and ethnic groups, those which cannot have a voice – such as animals or parts of the natural world that are subject to the uncaring instrumentalist practices of industry, science and agri-business – are all a source of identification through which these identities are expressed.[7] Identifying with the Other does not just mean acting on behalf of that other; even though that is often an important political form through which some activists become involved in the political process, it is also clearly a vehicle for self-expression. One becomes authentic, has an identity that is real and valuable, by identifying with that (or who) which is marginalised within society. The politics of difference is not only a politics where those in a subaltern position begin to speak for themselves and challenge the way they are represented as the other within society, it is also a politics of metonymy in which those not in a subaltern position identify with one or more such positions as a means of valorising their own identity as real and significant.

I am not suggesting here that the interest in issues of freedom and rights involves those in a privileged position feeling guilty, and subsequently taking the side of the oppressed and seeking to undermine their own privileges; the world is not divided up into simple minority/majority positions. The complex topology of identity positions, as I discussed it in Chapter 1, does not allow for a straightforward centre–margin distinction. The case is that the idea of margins, the idea of ethnicity and the idea of Otherness become important symbolic resources for those seeking to express their own identities in a world in which they do not feel at home. The main ways in which this identification is achieved are through the use of style and through the political practices in which various groups may become involved.

The issue of ethnic identity is not, however, insignificant. The nature of these lifestyles and the related process of identification are highly eclectic, creating an elective and pastiche ethnicity, drawing on sources as diverse as: youth cultures such as hippy and punk, eastern mysticism, first nation American traditions, environmental and pacifist beliefs, anarchism, gypsy lifestyles, communal living, Celtic paganism, and earth mysteries beliefs. The main characteristic of such a series of tribal identities is their syncretism, within which a process of differentiation occurs as a means of establishing smaller identifications around ever shifting and hybridising boundaries.

Location: the importance of network and personal space

Belonging, community and identification are key terms within expressive identities. Where one belongs is an important related issue. Over the years,

in many community experiments, dating back to religious and artist communities of the nineteenth century, through kibbutzim (Talmon, 1972;
E. Cohen, 1983) and the communes of the present century (Abrams and
McCulloch, 1976; Pepper, 1991), being part of a separate and distinct
community has been an important means of establishing forms of identification with others. As well as belonging to some form of grouping, however,
this sense of community and location has also carried with it symbolic
attachments to particular places. These might indeed be communal living
spaces, homes of one sort or another, in which identification with others is
invested in a sense of home, or they may be places invested with other sorts
of meaning – gathering places, places of pilgrimage, safe places, places of
meditation and rest, sites of play and festival – or places that have some sort
of significance for a particular group because of some historic event. Spaces,
sometimes deliberately, other times more arbitrarily chosen, come to have
symbolic attachments to them that give them a social centrality for a
particular group. A sense of belonging and community may come to be
ordered around the social centrality of particular places (see Shields, 1992b;
Hetherington, 1996).[8]

Solidarity: spaces of expression

The centrality of particular places is not only significant to the establishment
of a sense of belonging, it can also take on direct political significance.
Much work has been done in cultural geography in recent years to show the
significance of 'marginal' space to outsider or marginal groups (see Shields,
1991a; Keith and Pile, 1993; Rose, 1993; Cresswell, 1996; Hetherington,
1996). Margins are places, it is argued, where the marginal can find a space
in which they can articulate themselves and be heard. For some this has
meant living visibly on the margins, as did the women at the peace camp
outside the USAF base at Greenham Common (near Newbury in southern
England) during the 1980s (see Liddington, 1989; Young, 1990; Roseneil,
1995) or as New Age travellers, people who choose a nomadic existence
organised around free festivals, have done since the mid-1970s in Britain
(see Hetherington, 1991; 1992; 1996; 1997b). For others, sites of social
centrality become sites of resistance (see Keith and Pile, 1993). Not only
marginal sites, but also spaces that come to symbolise the socially central
values of a society are often challenged through symbolic protests, marches,
rallies and direct actions at those particular sites. In all these cases, spaces of
belonging and spaces of action and resistance become spaces for the
performance of identity. Spaces that have some form of symbolic attachment
for a particular group become spaces for the occasion of adopting and
expressing an identity, and for developing identification and solidarity with
others of a similar mind.

Communication: the body, style and expressive communication

The body also plays an important part in this process of identification. The
stylistic use of the body associated with expressive identifications is one in

which identity is represented as otherness. In many cases this means adopting a style for the body that can be described as other in one of two senses: the 'authentic' body; or 'grotesque' body, both of which are likely to be related to distinctive groupings. In the first, the authentic, a person might wear brightly coloured clothes drawn from a variety of ethnic sources. Such a bodily means of identification might also be expressed through various so-called 'ethnic' styles of clothing and jewellery, along with New Age accoutrements such as talismans and crystals expressing a concern with spiritual healing and bodily well-being. There is here a strong identification with the dispossessed and marginal peoples of the world and their cultures, notably native Americans or first nation peoples.

A second significant style of embodiment is that of the grotesque. This embodiment can be summed up by the idea of 'resistance through dirt'. Taking the punk anti-aesthetic to extremes, such people are likely to dress in old combat fatigues and boots and perhaps have long, matted dreadlocks. Such an identification is a celebration of matter out of place, that which transgresses the boundaries of respectability (Douglas, 1984). Marginal identities, it may be suggested, are in part produced by the adoption of a marginal body outside of the placing of conventional standards, as is shown through associations with either the circus or dirt – both of which, of course, are central to the idea of a transgressing, boundary-defying, carnivalesque body (Bakhtin, 1984: chapter 5).

This desire for a coherent identity often derives from a wish for a sense of belonging with the group or groups one identifies with. But this ordered identity, in the singular, is in fact a representation of a combination of identity positions whose meaning in total is derived from a play of differences around a series of identity positions which are brought together through an ordering that is associated with the performance of identity. We may, therefore, describe such identities as *heteroclite identities*, meaning monstrous, freakish and anomalous. While this is a somewhat archaic term, associated with Francis Bacon and his desires to study the freaks and monsters of nature (Bacon, 1974), it does convey quite well the sense of making an identity out of an heterogeneous bricolage of things to hand. Also, we should not forget that one of the terms that 1960s counter-culturalists used to describe themselves was 'freaks'.

Rejected knowledge

Knowledge and values form another distinct aspect of this expressive identifying and belonging process. The recent work of Eyerman and Jamison on social movements as forms of cognitive praxis that generate new forms of knowledge within society has begun to look at this issue in some detail (1991). Most notably, they have done this through their recognition that new social movements often challenge the existing parameters of knowledge, most notably scientific knowledge (1991: 4; see also Yearley, 1991).

For Eyerman and Jamison, social movements produce 'movement intellectuals' who become bearers of new ideas as part of a learning process within society. According to Eyerman and Jamison:

> The collective articulation of movement identity can be likened to a process of social learning in which movement organisations act as structuring forces, opening a space in which creative interaction between individuals can take place. (1991: 55)

New forms of knowledge production and the questioning of technocratic and instrumental rationality are features of such movements as the peace movement and the green movement.[9] The sort of knowledge that Eyerman and Jamison identify is that associated with successful social movement organisations, institutionalised into the political system. They are much less successful in accounting for the knowledge which underpins new social movement lifestyles and questions about identity within which such new social movement politics is embedded.

If expressive identities – and here my focus is wider than social movement organisations – are producers of knowledge, the sort of knowledge that they identify with is not so much a proposed counter-hegemonic set of new beliefs to a supposed dominant ideology, but more often what Webb has described as 'rejected knowledge' (1974: 191; see also Wallis, 1979). The critique of instrumentally rational activities and forms of knowledge that are predominant within society leads many engaged in developing expressive identities to seek forms of knowledge derived from more expressive or spiritual sources, forms that have often been socially constructed as marginal within society. Beliefs rejected by modern, Western science and deriving from much earlier gnostic, hermetic and neo-platonic forms are what Webb has in mind when he uses the term rejected knowledge (1974: 194).

For associates who take up a position within the set of expressive identities, these forms of knowledge, it can be argued, offer a critique of the particularism of scientific knowledge in favour of holistic, spiritual and expressive forms of understanding derived more from feelings than rational calculation. Nature religions, Eastern mysticism, forms of self-discovery, the beliefs of pre-modern or oppressed peoples, along with mystical, cabbalistic, astrological and anti-techné attitudes, are types of knowledge that are likely to be promoted by new social movements through the lifestyles they adopt. In terms of rejected political theory as a source of knowledge, it is most likely to be anarchism that many new social movement activists will sympathise with. This is so because its anti-authoritarian, anti-hierarchical, pro-spontaneity stances are in keeping with the beliefs and practices of many new social movement groups.[10]

Structures of feeling and the ethics of aesthetics

If this description characterises the issues that underlie the ethics of aesthetics of expressive identities, the issue that remains to be answered here is how we might begin to bring this range of issues associated with identification, communication and belonging together. I want to propose that a way to do it is not through Maffesoli's sometimes rather vague vitalism but through an adapted version of Raymond Williams's concept of the structure of feeling (1965; 1977; 1979).

Raymond Williams's use of the term 'structure of feeling' has an important place within cultural studies but it has mainly been associated with the reception of high culture rather than with lifestyles in general. Williams's main interest was in trying to understand what characterised the cultural outlook of a particular period and how that outlook changed over time. In any period, he argued, a distinct 'pattern of culture' prevails (1965: 63–64). This pattern of culture consisted of a selection and configuration of interests and activities, and a particular valuation of them, producing a distinct organisation: a 'way of life' (1965: 64). Williams's aim was to address directly not how people enjoyed a type of cultural activity because of their structural location within society but how they experienced it. This experiential approach, with its focus on the communication and inter-subjectivity of feeling, has much in common with that of Maffesoli (see Shields, 1991b: 3) and is useful when looking at the whole realm of the expressive within contemporary culture. There are, however, a number of limitations to Williams's approach that need to be addressed before this can be done.

Williams's model is informed by the view that culture, within any period, it is shaped by a dominant position and challenged by a new culture rising from within the consciousness of a new generation (1977: 130ff.). The model would appear at first glance to be clearly a Marxist one, focusing on a hegemonic dominant ideology shaping the structure of feeling, then being challenged at particular points of conjuncture by a counter-hegemonic structure of feeling that arises from the practical consciousness of particular groups of the younger generation. Where Williams diverges from the Marxist position is over the central issue of class. For Williams, a change within a structure of feeling is brought about by successive generations rather than by specific social classes. While Williams does try to address the issue of the relationship between structure of feeling and class (1977: 134–135), he recognises that he does not do so adequately (1979: 158). For me this is not a failure but a strength, allowing us to make use of the concept without having to adopt a class analysis of culture or the structure of feeling. Williams's view suggests that a structure of feeling, the culture and values of a particular society at a particular time, is hegemonic within a society. The structure of feeling is the outlook on culture that prevails and, for Williams, can be seen in (high) cultural forms such as drama and literature. In taking the canon of high culture as his model, Williams overly limits the usefulness of a concept like the structure of feeling. He assumes that there is a cultural unity at a particular point in time and that conflict and the emergence of a new structure of feeling is a generational thing. It is too simplistic to suggest that there is a unity of taste within the cultural field. Not only can culture mean different things to different people, it can also apply in different fields.

Indeed, what type of culture people like, their tastes, and moving beyond culture in the narrow sense to lifestyle as a whole, are far more differentiated than a simple generational model allows.

Any use of the term 'structure of feeling' must start by recognising that there are a plurality of structures of feeling at any one time within a particular society. In the language of strategies and tactics, society produces more than one strategy and there are a range of tactical responses. The importance of structure of feeling is that it allows us to look at the whole arena of feeling and emotion beyond the personal level to a much broader one. Distinct identities and their associated collective identifications are the expression of particular and distinct structures of feeling.

We cannot talk in simple terms of periods being defined by one structure of feeling and one generation (unless perhaps modernity be taken as our period), nor can we limit ourselves to high cultural forms as our model. Where structure of feeling as a term is of use is in looking at the broad range of cultural experiences that are lived by people. Williams's basic model, on which his concept of a structure of feeling was based, is still of use if drawn from the wider cultural life of individuals rather than being restricted to their experience of high cultural forms. For Williams, people experience the world through a practical consciousness. That practical consciousness – a person's lived experiences – comes up against formal cultural expressions that are alien to it and confront it as something external. In attempting to overcome cultural forms, the processual, fluid world of practical consciousness generates new styles (for Williams these were literary styles but we can use style in the wider sense) that aim to express the lived meanings, values and sentiments.

It is, in effect, this practical consciousness that Maffesoli is talking about when he speaks in terms of puissance or the vitalism of the expression of the people within everyday life (1996). For me the constellation of terms like counter-culture, alternative lifestyle, identity politics, new social movements, expressive individualism, and other-directed personality – terms which express themselves in the lifestyle concerns that I have discussed above – suggest a distinct structure of feeling. For want of a better term I will call this a 'romantic structure of feeling'. It contrasts with, say, a rationalist structure of feeling of the kind valued by Weber (perhaps we should call it a puritan structure of feeling) and the host of sociologists who have followed him in their worries about the arena of feeling and emotion in social life, notably when associated with politics of one kind or another. It may well be possible to identify further structures of feeling within a society and any given time period; here, however, I will limit myself to a discussion of what I have called the romantic structure of feeling.

The romantic structure of feeling

Leaving aside the extensive work in the arts (see Abrams, 1971; Honour, 1979; Peckham, 1962), Romanticism is a theme that comes and goes within sociology and political science (Gouldner, 1973; Berman, 1971; 1982; Schmitt, 1986; Koselleck, 1988). In recent times it is an issue that has had to sit on the sidelines while sociologists re-evaluate that other great influence on modern ways of thinking, the classicism of the Enlightenment, in light of the postmodern and post-structuralist critiques of its totalising vision of order and control. It is not my intention here to provide a detailed account of romanticism, rather there are a number of key features that define a romantic outlook that I want to consider. These are: the quest for experience and authenticity, the meaning of selves, and the occasionalism of self-creation. It is in Romanticism that we find an importance placed on the expressive as an alternative to the cognitive as a mode of apprehending both self and others which is clearly associated with the classicism of the Enlightenment (see Gouldner, 1973).

The great theme of the romantic critique of modern societies is that of alienation. One's self within a romantic perspective becomes an alien and inauthentic product of an artificial world, no longer capable of experiencing things directly. The individual is placed at the centre of an understanding of the world rather than humanity or society and critical reflection on its condition is brought into effect. Romanticism offers an aesthetic outlook on the world rather than one defined by science and rationality (Gouldner, 1973) and is often oriented towards the past rather than the future. The focus is on issues of creating conditions of authentic lived experience, a sense of belonging within an organic community, and conditions of harmony with others and with nature. It differs from Conservatism in that the latter seeks to restore an idealised past whereas Romanticism, while it might share a nostalgic outlook on the past, seeks to create these things in new form in the future. At the centre of Romanticism is a condition that the German legal theorist Carl Schmitt has described as subjectivised occasionalism (1986).

Drawing on Schmitt's work, even if critically as here, leaves a bad taste in the mouth. His elitist, anti-democratic theory that led him to become an apologist for Nazism during the 1930s leaves room for nothing but critique.[11] Leaving aside his attack on Romanticism and on its links with democracy as a basis for his defence of a Hobbesian view of the strong state, his analysis of Romanticism's key theme is, however, still analytically useful. In Schmitt's view Romanticism focuses on the issues of individual experience and 'the occasion'. Through political activity, the romantic seeks to express him or herself as a moral agent. In the romantic world-view, events (we might say situations, protests or direct actions) are the means through which this moral authority, based in individual agents, is expressed. This, for Schmitt, derives from a romantic view of the self as an independent agent of morality which is expressed through what Schmitt calls sub-jectivised occasionalism (1986: 16). The romantic subject who challenges the authority of the subject or King, treats the world, according to Schmitt, '[A]s an occasion and opportunity for his romantic productivity' (1986: 17). He goes on to add, 'Instead of God, however, the romantic subject occupies the central position and makes the world and everything that occurs in it into a mere occasion [for himself]' (1986: 17). Furthermore, according to Schmitt, this occasionalism is used by members of the bourgeoisie to try and produce new forms of social cohesion and order (see also Koselleck, 1988).

Schmitt's position was a decisionist one, in the sense that he believed that social order should derive from the ability of the Sovereign to make decisions unimpaired by any other authority (1988). As a supporter of the Hobbesian position, he believed in the absolute authority of the sovereign as the embodiment of the State and criticised the bourgeoisie, with its Romanticism, for its inability to produce social order out of the subjectivised occasionalism (which would include such things as democratic processes associated with discussion and decision making by consensus) that came to be associated with state formation in Europe from the seventeenth century onwards. Schmitt is hostile to the Utopianism and Romanticism of the bourgeoisie generally because he believed that it would fail to produce the order that a sovereign with absolute authority might. There is, of course, no evidence whatsoever to suggest an absolutist state is any more politically effective in making decisions and maintaining social order than a democratic process which places more emphasis on the 'occasionalism' of open discussion and consensus politics. But it is true that the centre of the romantic outlook is shaped by the view that expressing oneself in the public arena and using that activity politically is the basis of shaping one's identity. *It is above all through the occasion that identity and politics become linked and are inseparable.* Another term for subjectivised occasionalism can be seen in the feminist slogan that has now become the slogan of most new social movements and indeed of most who adopt an expressive lifestyle: 'the personal is political'. It is through this subjectivised occasionalism that an ethics of aesthetics is performed. The sense of one's morally elect position comes from the drama of the occasion and the aesthetics of identity performance it facilitates.

The romantic structure of feeling is one that is organised around ideas of experience, authenticity and identity that derive from the idea of participating in changing the self through engagement with others in forms of localised 'resistance' to the symbols of inauthenticity and instrumentalism. These can all be characterised as examples of the romantic structure of feeling. The six focal themes I identified from the magazine *Cahoots* – associated with experience, identification, location, solidarity, communication and knowledge – are the occasions through which this romantic structure of feeling expresses itself. Everyday life is the source of this structure of feeling. It seeks to express what is felt to be missing within the lifeworld of individuals. The host of groupings such as those associated with new social movements, youth cultures and religious cults can be taken as examples of forms that this structure of feeling leads to. There are also wider cultural forms, less clearly defined by particular groups but significant within society as a whole, that are also expressions of this romantic structure of feeling such as: complementary health and therapy, New Age spirituality

(Heelas, 1996), identification with the (authentic) cultures of first nation peoples, interest in astrology and pagan myth or earth mysteries, and participation in certain types of tourism and travel to experience other cultures (see E. Cohen, 1973; 1979; Urry, 1990).

There is a spectrum of involvement in which individuals can engage to express this structure of feeling; this spectrum ranges from political activism and the adoption of a total lifestyle at one end, to occasional use of complementary medicines or shopping for natural products at the other. Structures of feeling express a shared practical consciousness but not necessarily a shared outlook on all aspects of life. They can result in seemingly odd political alliances over particular issues, can facilitate an attitude that is anti-materialist and hostile to consumer societies, or find expression through forms of consumption. The outcomes of a structure of feeling may be close-knit groups or more diffuse networks (see Melucci, 1996). In all their outcomes, expressive lifestyles are messy, contradictory, diverse and heterogeneous. What these expressive lifestyles share is a structure of feeling and that alone: not politics, not religious beliefs, not dress codes, not occupations, not even degrees of commitment. There may well be distinct groupings and there will certainly be identifiable preferences, but overall there is diversity that has this one thread running through it holding things together – a structure of feeling.

Conclusion

By interweaving the work of Maffesoli (1996) with that of Williams (1965) and to a more limited and qualified extent Schmitt (1986; 1988), I have tried to offer some account of both why and how the expressive is an issue of fundamental importance when considering the processes of expressive identity formation and identity politics. How experiences and shared identifications are expressed is the key to understanding this creative process. That process is not an arbitrary one left to the individual as an autonomous agent to create as a product of their self-reflection but is one that is expressed by individuals through the commonality of a structure of feeling. Structures of feeling are located within everyday life, within the routine practices of ordinary people. Everyday life, the local and the particular afford some opportunities for resistance that are not often possible to many through the institutionalised worlds of politics or culture. This is not to suggest a distinct separation of society and everyday life, they are indeed interwoven and draw upon one another. There is a danger, one that can be glimpsed in Maffesoli and others writing before him on everyday life and resistance, in making this separation. However, if we recognise that there is a plurality of structures of feeling and that some are more established than others, we can accept this synergy while still recognising everyday life as a source of creativity and resistance and the development of particular preferences for types of identification and types of lifestyle.

The main point about structures of feeling is they offer a structured outlook on how one experiences the world and how one seeks to express that experience or what might be felt to be lacking from it. It is the various combinations of any number of these themes that lead to the lifestyle characteristics that derive from this romantic structure of feeling. In the following chapter I look at the issue of expressive organisation in relation to the romantic structure of feeling. Much of the literature on new social movements is about organisation, largely because most of it knows only how to speak the language of rational choice and liberal political science, associated with membership, leadership, activism, free riders and so on. In doing this it often misses one of the most important aspects of organisation. Emotional communities are developed through forms of expressive organisation–emotion. To help me look at the relationship between a structure of feeling and what I call expressive organisation, I return to work undertaken by a German sociologist, Herman Schmalenbach, in the 1920s and his analysis sparked off by an interest in the German youth movement, the Wandervogel, and their favoured form of expressive organization, a Bund.

Notes

1. I look at Victor Turner's work in detail in Part II of this book, notably his work on liminality and liminal space and the ways in which this is related to the idea of identity performance.

2. I look at the whole issue of performances of identity in detail in Chapter 7 below.

3. Those who do so, Bourdieu and his supporters for example, find it difficult to account for factors like gender, ethnicity, lifestage and so on in their argument that a class-based habitus, and its association with volumes of different types of capital, determines lifestyle choices (Bourdieu, 1984).

4. I am grateful to Mike Peters for pointing this out to me.

5. Heelas tries to deal with this obvious ambiguity through the concept of detraditionalisation (see also Heelas et al., 1996). In doing so he becomes another who wants to make the 'x indicates the move to a new type of society' type of move. This is a shame as in many other ways his work offers some very suggestive readings of the issues associated with expressive identities. However, in wanting to preserve the New Age as a religious phenomenon, he rules out its overlapping with other more social phenomena. This is too purist a move to make. It may have some use for analytical purposes but the very nature of the New Age spirituality is one of hybridity. It may have a religious core but its ability to trail off into more cultural or political forms (which Heelas ignores) just as much as into economic ones (which he does not ignore) surely cannot go unrecognised.

6. Most of the shops selling ethnic lifestyle artefacts have a distinct way of conveying this authenticity. It is often found in the form of use of natural materials: wood, stone, crystals, cotton and so on; glass and metal are used far less and plastic hardly ever.

7. In the sense that they care for and want to let an inanimate other speak through their actions, those who adopt an expressive identity and its associated lifestyle might be described as the first moderns (see Latour, 1993). At the very least, these identity positions often have as wide a vision of the agency of things as actor–network theorists.

8. This issue of social centrality is a theme that I discuss in more detail in Chapter 5.

9. There is often a tension over the use of scientific knowledge within new social movements: while many oppose the instrumentally rational approach associated with science,

they will often use that same sort of science to justify their claims in order to make themselves appear more respectable and authoritative (see Yearley, 1991).

10. This recognition of the importance of rejected knowledge to new social movements is based upon reading new social movement magazines and periodicals over the last ten years. It is reflected not only in an identification with rejected political knowledge, but also in mysticism, fantasy writing and the beliefs and practices of aboriginal peoples. Such an interest in rejected knowledge can be seen as part of what Mannheim describes as a 'utopian mentality' (1938: chapter 4). New social movement magazines that I have consulted during the course of this study are: *Greenline* – radical green magazine; *Ethical Consumer* – magazine devoted to ethical consumption; *Trouble and Strife* – radical feminist magazine; *Archangel* – Animal Rights magazine; *Sanity* – Campaign for Nuclear Disarmament (CND) magazine; *Green Anarchist* – Anarchist magazine with environmentalist slant; *Vision Seeker Sharer* – pagan, environmentalist magazine; *Cahoots* – north west alternatives listings magazine.

11. There are some parallels here, of course, with the reception of Heidegger's work in light of his support for the Nazi Party, see *Critical Inquiry*, 1987.

4
EXPRESSIVE ORGANISATION AND EMOTIONAL COMMUNITIES

Expressive identities can be associated with a romantic structure of feeling. This structure of feeling is itself expressed through six underlying principles that help to shape an ethics of aesthetics: experience, identification, location, solidarity, communication and knowledge. In this chapter, I look at the type of organisation of consociates that is often favoured within emotional communities by those who adopt this structure of feeling and the collective identifications associated with it. Following Maffesoli, I have used the term emotional communities to account for this issue of organisation. While this is suitable for discussing the generic issue of the type of identification that is sought, it is too imprecise when trying to account for the particular type of grouping or mode of organisation through which expressive identifications are often achieved and maintained. The term community is far too vague and its association with the organic, traditional and ascriptive ideas of a past way of life is too inaccurate when trying to account for the elective identifications and groupings that we see. The term for this type of organisation I prefer to use, which recognises from the outset its distinctly non-institutional, expressive and elective character is Bund, or communion, first identified sociologically by Schmalenbach in 1922 (1961; 1977; see also Hetherington, 1990; 1992; 1994).

In this chapter I argue that it is the particular conditions that a Bund creates which allow expressive identities to be established. A Bund facilitates the affectual identification with others that gives individuals the elective and expressive identity that they seek. I start by describing the etymological origins of the word 'Bund', followed by a discussion of the use of the Bund concept historically among radical 'neo-tribal' groups such as the Wandervogel and the early kibbutz movement. I describe and analyse Schmalenbach's development of the Bund as a sociological concept and suggest it is worthy of revival. Comparisons can be made also between the concept of the Bund and similar concepts such as communitas (Turner, 1969) and Gemeinde (Weber, 1968), as well as that of a neo-tribe (Maffesoli, 1988b).

The significance of charisma to these Bünde is also important and I evaluate how expressive lifestyles might make use of a Bund as a charismatic form of sociation that provides a means of facilitating the development of expressive individual identities through a shared strongly emotional kind of identification with others. It is this type of organisation in which solidarity and a sense of moral election, something associated with the romantic structure of feeling and its subjectivised occasionalism, are expressed.

In speaking about organisation I am not, therefore, referring solely to formal questions of group structure and its dynamics. Rather, a whole set of issues associated with identity, identification, belonging, and solidarity can be expressed through this idea of organisation. It is the character of organisation, then, that is of particular interest here and not the narrower issue of organisations. In speaking of organisation, we can add another dimension to our understanding of expressive identities. It may well be possible to suggest that there might be a distinct preference for a particular type of organisational form associated with a particular structure of feeling. The Bund does indeed have a very distinct character and type of organisational dynamic to it. It also, however, is a means through which wider questions involved with the issue of association and identification come to be addressed or performed.

The word Bund has a long history yet a rather forgotten place within sociological analysis. Conceived as a sociological concept during the 1920s, it never really caught on. There have been occasional attempts to revive it including my own (see Talmon, 1972; E. Cohen, 1983; Hetherington, 1994) – so far with little success. There are a number of possible reasons for this including: the elusive character of a Bund as an observable empirical form; its intermediary status between other, better known terms; the current fashion in sociology to try and invent things from scratch rather than go back to the past to re-think or re-theorise with earlier and often more precise concepts; and the current unfashionability of questions of organisation within mainstream sociology. We might also add, to focus on organisational form alone is to be too narrow in outlook. I have two main reasons for continuing to advocate the use of this otherwise old and largely forgotten term: first, its conceptual precision works well analytically in describing the types of groups engaged in the quest for expressive and alternative identities; and second, the term, based as it is in feeling and emotion rather than in the more instrumental practices usually associated with organisations, allows us to address this broader question of organisation and its relationship to identity.

Origins of the concept of the Bund

The term 'Bund' is a German word with a long and convoluted history. Over time it has come to be associated with a range of formal and informal types of organisation, all of which in some way imply a sense of looseness in terms of elective membership while at the same time suggesting the strength both of loose organisational forms and of the social bonds they create. 'Bund' comes from the Indo-Germanic verb *bhend*, meaning 'to bind' or 'to tie'. It was first used as a noun to describe something bound or bonded from about the second half of the thirteenth century (Koselleck in Brunner et al.,

1972). After that time the term began, along with words such as *Einugen* (union, as in the modern German *Vereinigung*), to be used as a legal term implying 'that which has been made into one', as in a legal covenant, as distinct from the less personalised notion of contract (Koselleck in Brunner et al., 1972).[1] It also came to mean federation and alliance, often of Germanic principalities or cities, and other forms of legally binding association which historically were often based on oath. The word has continued despite many changes to retain this sense of federation, as with words like Bundesrepublik, Bundesbank and Bundesliga which are all modern German words implying some form of federation (Koselleck in Brunner et al., 1972).

It was from the fifteenth century that the word Bund also began to be used in a different way, distinct from this earlier usage and of more interest to our current concerns here. The initially loose, non-institutional nature of association implied by the word Bund made the word appropriate to millenarian religious movements in the fifteenth and sixteenth centuries, the most significant of which would appear to be the Bundschuh, the 'Tied Boot', that played a prominent role in the peasants' revolts in Germany at this time (see Mullett, 1987: 85). The symbol they used on their banners – a laced peasant's boot – suggested the idea of close union and solidarity, which had religious connotations associated with the ideas of communion and this worldly salvation. In such movements, the connection between the idea of the Bund, as a reference to the legal rights of peasants, and close-knit political and religious association was also made.

Although the Bundschuh was suppressed during the Reformation, the word retained this more religious connotation attached to the idea of a covenant, notably in Luther's ideas about the covenant with God. This religious reading of the word Bund was also to have increasing significance among millenarian movements, notably among the Anabaptists led by Thomas Müntzer, who saw themselves as an elect with an established covenant with God (Koselleck in Brunner et al., 1972: 604). Unlike the English word federation, Bund retains a notion of something holy as in the English word communion, yet it also contains something of an organisational meaning as that found in the word league (as in to be 'in league' with someone). Bund may also approximate to the English word 'band' as in 'a band of outlaws' or a musical band like a brass band.

From the end of the eighteenth century the term Bund began to take on more directly political meanings, notably through calls for a unified Germany, implying in this case a sense of national unity, federation, and self-determination. However, the term was also used to describe informal, sometimes secret societies such as the Freemasons and student fraternities like the 'Deutscher Bund' (1810–1813). While many of these groups can be seen as forming a significant part of what became the political right in Germany, the left also had its use for the term Bund, as in 'Bund der Gerechten' (League of the Just), the precursor of the Communist League. Marx, of course, was associated to some degree with both of these Bund-style organisations (see Nicolaievsky and Maenchen-Helfen, 1976: chapter 7).

The word Bund has also been significant for anarchists, for whom federations, secret societies and more open, leaderless groups of people with a common aim have at one time or another been important (Joll, 1964). A significant figure here is the mystical anarchist, Gustav Landauer, who in the first decade of the twentieth century formed the most notable example of a radical Bund, 'The Socialist Bund'. This organisation offered an alternative way of living that promoted a brand of utopian socialism and a somewhat mystical attempt at the rejuvenation of Spirit or Volk, in this instance without Fascist overtones (Maurer, 1971; Lunn, 1973; Link-Salinger, 1977; Landauer, 1978). Landauer was not only to have influence among anarchists but upon Zionists in the early Jewish youth movements and on kibbutzim.

It is perhaps significant that the theologian Martin Buber, an important influence on the kibbutz movement that was itself to take up the idea of a Bund, should have been influenced by Landauer (Buber, 1958) and that the ideas of close union, with völkisch and mystical associations, should have influenced his thinking as well as that of other Jews associated with Hasidim, early Zionism and the kibbutz movement.[2] In many ways Landauer's Bund was a 'kibbutz' in all but name, something that seems to have been overlooked by those who use the Bund concept to understand the early kibbutz movement (Talmon, 1972; E. Cohen, 1983).

Before going on to consider the sociological significance of the Bund, as originally set out by the sociologist Schmalenbach, one further example of the use of the word Bund has to be given: that found in the early German Youth Movement known as the Wandervogel, which shares much of the romantic structure of feeling found in today's expressive identities and their neo-tribal identifications. The Wandervogel was originally conceived as a means of rejecting what many young people at the time saw as the spiritlessness of Wilhelmism (the German equivalent of Victorianism) in favour of the 'authentic' life of the nomad and the simple pleasures of roaming in the forests among the peasants (Becker, 1946; Lacquer, 1962; Heberle, 1951: 137). The type of social organisation that the early youth movement established was expressed in terms of the idea of a Bund, which was to provide those involved with a sense of common feeling, belonging and the means of regenerating society. Becker gives a good summary of their lifestyle and aspirations:

> In the late nineties and early nineteen hundreds there were no youth hostels, no well travelled routes, no easily transmissible techniques of roaming. The pattern was that of prolonged truancy or vagrancy, accompanied by a little rowdyism . . . Costume was highly individualised and sometimes approached the rags and tatters of the quasi-mythical 'wandering scholar' of medieval times or the nondescript, dirty garb of the 'raggle-taggle Gypsies, O!' (1946: 67)

These young people desired a Bund in the sense of a communion in small groups, which provided an affectual sense of fusion, Bunderlebnis, and an idealised authentic experience of what they saw in a romanticised vision of

Gemeinschaft located in the past. They contrasted the experience of close union in a Bund with what they saw as the spiritless individuating tendencies of modern, bourgeois, gesellschaftlich culture. As Mosse suggests:

> The Bund was no ordinary group, but a specific product of the German Youth Movement. It resolved the urge toward an organic, rather than an alienated man, by positing unity of soul, body and spirit as the prime law. This law bound together individuals who had voluntarily entered the Bund: unity of soul and spirit was to be attained through shared eros. (1971: 99)

The month-long roam into the forests of Bohemia provided this fusion of a set of disparate people into Bund, or what Becker describes as 'conventicles of the elect' (1946: 75):

> [T]hrough identification with the group, as demonstrated by successful assimilation of the unique experience of the expedition, rapidly came to be the way in which the initially random conventicles of dissenters were fused into genuine sects [Bünde] of the like-minded and consciously elect. (1946: 83)

That the Wandervogel had their roots in Romanticism and ended up, although it was not certain at the outset, as one aspect of the conservative revolution in Germany in the first part of the twentieth century is beyond question (see Mosse 1964; 1971). Later still, their original spiritual revolt was politically appropriated by the Nazis – a mass, hierarchical political movement quite different from the much more small-scale Bund – who propagated the idea of Bünde (the plural of Bund) as the germinating cells of a Fascist state (Mosse, 1964: 189). No doubt, these latter uses to which the concept was put were one further reason why the reception of Schmalenbach's seminal sociological work on the Bund in the post Second World War period was minimal (although see Shils and Janowitz, 1948). However, it was the Bund as an idealised form of sociation found in the youth movement that provided one major source of inspiration for Schmalenbach's sociological conceptual formulation and not this later manipulation of the idea of the Bund (see Becker, 1946: 105).

Schmalenbach and the sociology of the Bund

Schmalenbach's work is not particularly well known in the sociological community. Those works which do mention his concept of the Bund generally tend to give only a sketchy outline of its use as a critique of Tönnies's concept of Gemeinschaft (for examples from British sociology, see Abrams and McCulloch, 1976: 165–166; Bell and Newby, 1976: 196–197). Histories of sociology have also generally been cursory in their review, although almost always approving (see Aron, 1964: 18; Shils, 1970: 40–41). Freund is typical:

> [S]chmalenbach tried to complete or correct the distinction established by Tönnies, adding a third category, that of the league [Bund]. The attempt had practically no success. As opposed to community, inspired by tradition, and to society, inspired by rationality, the league was supposed to have a more instinctive and sentimental basis. It would be a place for the expression of

enthusiasms, of ferment, and of unusual doings. And yet, German sociology continued to think – albeit with diverse and sometimes confused variations – in the categories elaborated by Tönnies, the only ones which stayed meaningful. (1978: 183)

Euclideanism again – a way of thinking that is premised on the idea that any notion that introduces some kind of more complex topological arrangement, and third categories have such a tendency of unsettling dualisms, has to be avoided for the sake of conceptual clarity. Schmalenbach's essay was also a critique of Spengler's *Decline of the West* as well as an attempt to apply a phenomenological approach, influenced by Husserl's practice of categorical intuition, to the Simmelian inspired study of forms of sociation. The essay also uses the concept of the Bund in a critique of Weber's theory of the routinisation of charisma and of his famous fourfold typology of social action (1968). The essay on the Bund was originally published as 'Die Soziologische Kategorie des Bunds' (Schmalenbach, 1922: 35–105), with the full English translation following some 55 years later (Schmalenbach, 1977). If the essay is remembered at all, it is usually in the form of an abridged version that was translated into English in the well-known *Theories of Society* collection in the early 1960s (Parsons, et al., 1961: 331–347). Most of the works that do cite Schmalenbach's concept use this as their source. Much of what is said in the full essay, however, is missing in this extract; the result is that only the first of the issues, as a corrective to Tönnies description of Gemeinschaft (Tönnies, 1955), is usually remembered of this essay.

The one body of literature that is an exception to this is that concerned with kibbutzim. Notably, the influential book by Talmon introduced, albeit rather sketchily, the Bund concept in order to show the stages through which a kibbutz passed in its development and routinisation (1972). As Talmon suggested in a footnote, 'for lack of a better term, I use here the term "bund" which was coined by the German Sociologist Schmallenbach [sic] for similar purposes' (Talmon, 1972: 2). More recently, Eric Cohen has attempted to develop a more systematic use of the Bund concept in his research into kibbutzim, in particular, on the means by which the original affectual Bund is transformed into the more stable gemeinschaftlich conditions found in a longer established kibbutz (1983). Significantly, he goes on to add:

> Schmalenbach's much neglected concept can be applied to many of the social and religious movements which, nourished by the discontent of contemporary life, strive to renew and rejuvenate society through a complete abandonment of its established institutions and through a radical or revolutionary transformation of its values and ways of life. (E. Cohen, 1983: 76)

Shils also suggests that, with reservations, he found Schmalenbach's category of the Bund useful in his study of comradeship among German prisoners of war during the Second World War (Shils, 1957: 133; Shils and Janowitz, 1948). He also makes the interesting suggestion that Sorel in his

Reflections on Violence is using the Bund concept, without of course calling it that, as the ideal of the revolutionary cell (1957: 138).

The main sources of empirical inspiration for Schmalenbach's categorical understanding of the Bund, however, were twofold: the Stefan Georg circle, a small group of acolytes who had formed around the charismatic poet Stefan Georg in the early years of the twentieth century (see Leppenies, 1988: 281–282); and, as I suggested above, the early German Youth Movement (see Lüschen and Stone, 1977: 24). In this case, as in both Landauer's socialist Bund and also in kibbutzim, there was an emphasis on elective membership in small groupings that promoted a sense of participation around a set of strongly held values and totemic symbols, and a shared sense of belonging, usually with a charismatic leader as the focus of the group. In each case, the political response was perceived as a utopian rejection of some of the consequences of modernisation, in particular, of the perceived breakdown of organic ties of community and the increasing instrumentalism of everyday life. A Bund can be seen, therefore, as an attempted basis for re-communitisation of social relations within modern, gesellschaftlich conditions but one which applies individual choice as the basis for membership rather than class, gender or ethnic origin.

Most of those sociologists who do remember Schmalenbach's essay make the point that it was originally sociologically conceived by Schmalenbach as a third term which would correct the simplicity of the dualism of Gemeinschaft and Gesellschaft in Tönnies. The difference when comparing a Bund with a Gemeinschaft is precisely that the ascriptive and constraining aspects of Gemeinschaft, based as Tönnies would have it on the natural will, are missing in the Bund. Schmalenbach sees this longing for community, exemplified by Tönnies, as romantic and confused. What this longing seeks, he argues, is not so much the ascriptive conditions of a community based in tradition and custom, but the elective, affective-emotional solidarity of the Bund. The essay goes to some length, therefore, to disentangle the idea of the Bund from that of both Gemeinschaft and Gesellschaft. Schmalenbach's aim is to replace the usual dichotomy with a trichotomy of what he sees as 'fundamental sociological categories' (1977: 102). These are seen as offering a less rigid and more cyclical view of social change than the unilinear one offered by Tönnies (and, indeed, much of sociology ever since).

The main basis for this distinction between Gemeinschaft and Bund, according to Schmalenbach, is that Gemeinschaft is based in the unconscious, in a taken for granted belonging to a group, habitually grounded in what Weber describes as traditional social action (1968: 25). The Bund, on the other hand, is a wholly conscious phenomenon derived from mutual sentiment and feeling – from what Weber describes as affectual social action (1968: 25). However, the three categories are not wholly separate; any approach that wishes to show how society is characterised by either gemeinschaftlich or gesellschaftlich social conditions, which was a part of Tönnies's original intention, must – according to Schmalenbach – take into account the intermediate social category of the Bund. For Schmalenbach, however, Bünde are inherently unstable and fleeting, liable to be turned into either gemeinschaftlich or gesellschaftlich forms of sociation as they break up or are routinised. Schmalenbach uses a number of examples of Bünde to show this, most notably the transformation of religious sects into churches (1977: 100) and the communion of heterosexual love into the community of marriage and family (1977: 103ff.).

The other concerns of Schmalenbach's essay, ones which are less well reported, are exhibited in his use of the Bund concept as a critique of Weber's methodologically individualist typology of social action and, through discussion of the Bund, his production of a less elitist re-evaluation of Weber's ideas about personality implied by his theory of the routinisation of charisma. It is through this critique that Schmalenbach offers an alternative to Weber's model of the individual in modern gesellschaftlich conditions.

In his fourfold typology of social action at the beginning of *Economy and Society*, Weber describes these ideal types as: instrumentally rational; value rational; affectual; and traditional (1968: 24–25). According to Schmalenbach, Weber goes beyond simple dichotomies here but in an incomplete and confused way, which derives from his belief that meaningful social action can only be understood in terms of the intentionality of the act by the individual. Schmalenbach puts this down to Weber's 'epistemological asceticism' (1977: 110). According to Schmalenbach, there remains a false dichotomy in this typology in its distinction between the rational as conscious and the irrational as unconscious. Weber ignores, Schmalenbach argues, the fact that feeling does not derive from unconscious, irrational motivations, but is a conscious phenomenon that is neither simply rational nor irrational but affectual. Schmalenbach thus accuses Weber of subsuming affectual social action within the bounds of traditional social action, which Weber has already described as being based on unconscious motivations such as habit. For Weber, as Schmalenbach puts it:

> Only aspects manifested explicitly in consciousness can be known. This, however, is already derived from a consciousness of feeling, and it abstracts through feeling its understandable meaning in Weber's sense. Consequently, the distinction between the traditional – insofar as it is still understandable – and the affective emotional, between community and communion, is blurred. (1977: 110–111)

Schmalenbach's main aim is to stress the significance of forms of sociation (in a Simmelian sense) into which social action is organised, coupled with a categorical understanding of the motives of individuals engaged in social action. This allows him to treat the individual as both subject and object of analysis in a way that avoids Weber's methodological individualist standpoint, with its stress on the use of Verstehen in relation to trying to understand the individual's conscious motives for action. In so doing Schmalenbach's aim, in particular, is to differentiate between traditional and affective forms of conduct, with the Bund as a form of sociation associated with affective social action. However, he does not dismiss Weber altogether; rather, he sees the basis for his analysis implicit in what Weber has to say about charisma and types of legitimate authority.

Separate from his typology of social action, Weber provides a trichotomy of legitimate authority: legal-rational, traditional and charismatic (1968: 215–216). The importance of this for Schmalenbach is that, unlike Weber's typology of social action, here Weber does provide evidence, in the case of charismatic governance, against his methodological standpoint, of an example of affective social action that reveals it not to be unconscious and irrational at all. Schmalenbach argues this is an example of where affective conduct does have a role to play in the production of rational authority, notably in the manner in which traditional authority is transformed into rational authority via a route through charismatic governance (Schmalenbach, 1977: 118). Schmalenbach establishes, therefore, a trichotomous basis for social action which corresponds to his social forms: 1. Gemeinschaft: traditional social action and governance; 2. Bund: affectual and value-rational social action and charismatic governance; 3. Gesellschaft: instrumentally rational social action and legal-rational governance. With this argument Schmalenbach adds an element of circularity to the idea of the routinisation of charisma, which suggests that a Bund, as an affective-emotional form of sociation, acts reflexively to counter the dominant trend of rationalisation into the Weberian iron cage.

A Bund, and affective social action in general, according to Schmalenbach, offers a means of renewal or reversal of the general trend of rationalisation. While there remains a strong trace of Weber's theory of the routinisation of charisma in Schmalenbach, it is seen historically as a continuous, circular process rather than a unilinear one as in Weber. There are two consequences of this: first, a circular view of history which is developed by Schmalenbach, and second, and more important here, a different view of identity and personality in modern society. In the first case, therefore, it is necessary to say something about Schmalenbach's view of history. He suggests that the transformation of historical epochs is based upon the interplay of the forms of sociation based upon these three social categories. In arguing this, he anticipates many of the current themes in what is now described as a period of postmodernity – a period for which Schmalenbach, in 1922, even had a name: 'The Late Period' (1977: 122–125). However, my main concern here is with what his analysis says about organisation, identity and governance.

The essay by Schmalenbach also suggests a different conception of the individual and of personality to that offered by Weber. As I indicated in Chapter 2, for Weber, like Nietzsche before him, the ideal personality was an individualist personality, an heroic, inner-directed personality, expressed through inner-distance, asceticism and the desire for self-realisation (see Hennies, 1987; Owen, 1991; Schroeder, 1991; Featherstone, 1996). This is the puritan personality that played such a significant role, for Weber, in the emergence of capitalism and, therefore, the modern world, but which is supposedly destroyed by the success of the routinisation of the puritan outlook in the process of rationalisation and capital accumulation (see Bell,

1979; Lasch, 1980; Sennett, 1986; Bauman, 1987). In contradistinction, Schmalenbach, with his focus on the renewal of charisma and affective social action, offers us a different perspective on the effects of gesellschaftlich on the individual. If one were to follow Weber's description of the charismatic community, the Gemeinde – which has many conceptual similarities with the Bund[3] – it is only the person with charisma whose individuality is expressed, while the supporters subsume their individuality to the will of the leader:

> It [Gemeinde] is based on an emotional form of communal relationship (Vergemeinschaftung). The administrative staff of the charismatic leader does not consist of 'officials' . . . It is not chosen on the basis of social privilege nor from the point of view of domestic or personal dependency. It is rather chosen in terms of the charismatic quality of its members . . . The genuine prophet, like the genuine military leader and every true leader in this sense, preaches, creates, or demands new obligations – most typically, by virtue of revelation, oracle, inspiration, or of his own will, which are recognised by the members of the religious, military or party group because they come from such a source. Recognition is a duty. (Weber, 1968: 243–244)

For Schmalenbach, however, and here he is perhaps closer to his teacher Simmel than to Weber, the Bund both promotes and denies individuality:

> The comrades of communion [Bund] have nothing at all to do with one another in the beginning. The communion is originally established when they meet each other . . . The experiences that give rise to communion are individual experiences. While it appears here that the communion is closer to society [Gesellschaft], it approaches community [Gemeinschaft] after it has been established. (Schmalenbach, 1977: 94–95)

In stressing that it is the individual who elects whether or not they want to become part of a Bund, Schmalenbach shows it is intentional acts of joining together with strangers that are the basis of their community of feeling and mutual solidarity. A Bund operates principally through forms of self-governance and control but not at the expense of expressing one's emotions. Weber, on the other hand, reads into the support for charismatic leaders and Gemeinde a set of unconscious motives and irrational behaviour, by subsuming affectual action within his category of traditional action, and thereby tends to overlook or marginalise the elective basis of a Gemeinde. For Schmalenbach, individuation is not a condition of the gesellschaftlich conditions of modernity to be contrasted with the unconsciously accepted dense sociability of a romanticised pre-modern Gemeinschaft; instead, he presupposes, like Simmel, the individual prior to social relations, but an individual who can only realise him or herself within human sociation with others.

Charisma, elective identities and the other

A Bund is a form of sociation, whose conditions facilitate the development of expressive identities and elective identifications with others. These identities are achieved principally through regular, proximate relations with others. These identities are formed and reproduced not through dyadic relationships – which Giddens, for example, implies in his account of how individuals electively narrate, or script, their own biographies (1991) – but through collective identification with others and especially through the emotional solidarity that is generated. Perhaps the most counter-intuitive aspect of the argument I have put forward so far relates to the question of charisma. Charisma implies obedience to the will of a leader (see Weber, 1968: 241ff.; Shils, 1965). While this may have been acceptable to the Bund that made up the Wandervogel or gangs (see Thrasher, 1927), it is less in keeping with the anti-authoritarian, anti-hierarchical stance taken by most of those concerned with establishing expressive identities within the so-called 'new social movements' (although see Roth, 1979).

Perhaps too much of the work on charisma in the past has focused on the charismatic leader and not upon the elective conditions that are the source of the charismatic community. A reliance on leaders among those who adopt an ethically grounded, 'anarchistic' lifestyle will probably be seen as a denial of individual responsibility and likely to lead to egocentric power mongering by the leaders (Bookchin, 1989). There is, therefore, likely to be a strong ideological resistance to the notion of charismatic leadership among new social movement groups and those who want a lifestyle that allows them to express themselves as individuals. Instead, I argue, the goal of collective responsibility and enthusiasm for a set of beliefs is likely to lead to attempts to generalise the condition of charisma through a process of diffusion within the Bund. Terms like 'energy' and 'commitment', describing characteristics that all members are expected to exhibit, are the means by which this generalised charisma is likely to be expressed rather than through adherence to particular leaders (see Mills, 1973; Willis, 1978).

I argue, however, a Bund cannot exist without some form of centrality. As an organisational form it performs a charismatic mode of governance to which individuals submit themselves; this is not the same, however, as saying they submit themselves to the will of individual leaders. Rather it is an expression of the subjectivised occasionalism which those engaged in creating these types of identification are active in promoting. One commits to the group one has joined and its core values rather than to a person. While it is debatable, therefore, whether this has to be embodied in a person, what has to be considered is the means by which this charisma is dispersed to all the members. As a state of grace or calling, charisma has the peculiar status of being perceived as a relational substance (see Shils, 1965: 201). Individuals – 'prophets' – are perceived as having this charismatic substance within them, which takes the form of a calling or a state of grace; it can then leave their body and disperse as a transcendental influence upon others who are in its vicinity. This 'fluid substance' is the presence of the other whose auratic quality is given through the communitas or flow experiences, provided by the sociation of the Bund. I argue that among emotional communities under discussion here, a generalisation of charisma within groups seeking to disperse this 'substance' in the form of 'energy' or 'commitment' to all members of the Bund will probably be favoured over charismatic leaders. Charisma in this more general sense is likely to be perceived as the basis of authentic unmediated interpersonal relationships, expressed through the performativity of the occasion as well as within a Bund rather than through the adoration of a leader. Such empathic relations come to be seen as unmediated and direct, based purely in feeling. Such is the proximity of this experience in love and hate that a Bund may provide a strong positive sense of communitas or, alternatively, bitter recrimination when things do not work out (see Scheler, 1954: 147ff.). The significance of charisma in a Bund is the focus it provides for flow experiences as a source of individual governance.

The disappearance of and nostalgia for communal relations under such conditions has become something of a sociological truism (see Redfield, 1947; Tönnies, 1955). Despite some attempts to find continuing traditional communal relations (Young and Wilmott, 1957; Gans, 1962), the search for community should be considered in most cases (Schmalenbach argued) as being a search for communion (1977). The significance of this communion (Bund) is that it is elective and affectual, and not grounded in tradition and taken for granted routine. Bund-like expressive lifestyles are rejections of the undermining of communal fellowship, but not examples of individual isolation. Gesellschaftlich conditions and the instrumental attitudes they promote towards others are rejected by those who elect to adopt non-kin, close-knit affectual sociations. The intensity of a Bund, while it calls for the complete commitment of individual members, also reflexively promotes their individuality in that it requires continual self-monitoring and self-identification as well as identification with others.

The process of choosing expressive identities, for whatever personal reason, tends to lead some people to organise their lives around interests and enthusiasms that are individually chosen but collectively and affectually realised outside of routine daily activities associated with work and family life. In doing this, however, the enthusiasts are more likely to seek collectivities of like-minded others with whom they can identify. This is especially so in the case of those who seek to create a lifestyle that is ethically committed towards others. Such lifestyles as those associated with 'new social movements' seek to make life meaningful on affectual and value-rational grounds. In both cases, therefore, others – indeed, the category of Other – become of significance on emotional and moral grounds.

This communion can be understood in terms of Buber's notion of 'Thou': an unknowable, but direct relation outside of the realm of relations with things (it) (1958: 25ff.). Buber, of course, is referring to God, not as a thing but as a divine, unmediated state of grace. Such an understanding of the other has been taken up and considered by Levinas, who sees the Other as the unknowable presence of alterity (difference) (1989: 37–59). Levinas says of the Other: '[W]e recognise the other as resembling us, but exterior to us; the relationship with the other is the relationship with a mystery. The Other's entire being is constituted by its exteriority, or rather its alterity, for exteriority is a property of space and leads the subject back to itself through light (1989: 43). In both Buber and Levinas the relationship between self and other is dialogical, involving empathic communication – communion – with an absent Other, through 'I–Thou' relations rather than 'I–it' relations. That this Thou-like communion will often be transformed into an it-like relation associated with a charismatic person or group identification is evidence of the unattainability of the Other. A second sense in which this Otherness is significant is through the related issue of difference, or with Otherness as strangeness and marginality. In seeking to identify with others in a Bund-like sociation, those involved seek the Other not only as a Thou, or social divine (Maffesoli, 1996), but also value difference as a sign of moral election.

Above all, it is through the form of the Bund and the occasionalism that it helps to promote that a sense of moral election is developed among its participants. Often separated from the rest of the world because of their commitment to each other and to shared oppositional goals to those of society at large, those engaged in a Bund are likely to perceive themselves as an elect, with access to some heightened sense of experience. If that sense of experience and the expressive forms it takes are then also associated with moral values about how this is a better way to live and to interact with one another, a sense of moral election may well be achieved. To then go out into the world and – through the occasionalism of the politics of identity, the challenges, protests and forms of resistance in daily life – advocate such a lifestyle is likely further to heighten this sense of elect moral status.

Bund, neo-tribe and communitas

By introducing this third sociological category, Schmalenbach can also say something about ideas once described under the term Gesellschaft that is perhaps only now beginning to be recognised. Just as there is an over-simplification of Gemeinschaft which has its origins in Tönnies romantic view, so too is the world of gesellchaftlich conditions expressed as an alienating world of atomised individuals an overstatement, premised on a fear of the consequences of an anomic or depersonalising condition. While the modern world promotes greater individuation through its weakening of the 'organic' tie of community, it also promotes elective and collective (neo-tribal) conditions of association – Bund – that act to promote individuality as well as provide an intense experience of communion into which that individuality is subsumed (Maffesoli, 1988b; 1996; Bauman, 1991).

This ambivalence as a condition of modern individual experience has best been described by Simmel, notably in his essays on fashion and on mental life in the metropolis (1971a; 1971b) in which the individual uses the alienating experiences of modern life to promote a more cosmopolitan form of individuality. Where Schmalenbach differs on this matter is that in Simmel, his former teacher (see Leppenies, 1988: 281), the old

Gemeinschaft/Gesellschaft dichotomy is retained but Simmel chooses to focus on Gesellschaft, in these essays, in a positive way. Simmel retained the idea that the individual in modern society was ultimately defined by being isolated and alone, whereas for Schmalenbach, under such conditions people reproduce their individuality by forming Bünde. While these Bünde are themselves often nostalgic for the past, promoting the ideology of Gemeinschaft, as indeed more recent expressive lifestyles have done, what they actually achieve is something quite different, given their elective and affectual starting point. Within modernity the experience of individuality is a collective one, promoted by associations of all kinds; it is the significance of a Bund form in such a process that has perhaps, most importantly, been overlooked.

An interesting allusion to the ideas behind the Bund, though not expressed conceptually as such, can be found in Wirth's famous essay 'Urbanism as a Way of Life' (1964) where he talks about what he sees as the detrimental impact that city life has upon traditional, gemeinschaftlich social relationship. The weakening of kinship ties leads, according to Wirth, to the creation of 'fictional kinship groups' based around interests (1964: 82). Indeed, the response to the depersonalising tendencies of the city lead Wirth to suggest the emergence of social groupings that have an uncanny resemblance to Bünde and to contemporary discussions on neo-tribes:

> Reduced to a state of virtual impotence as an individual, the urbanite is bound to exert himself by joining with others of similar interest into groups organised to obtain his ends. This results in the enormous multiplication of voluntary [elective] organisations directed towards as great a variety of objectives as there are human needs and interests. While on the one hand, the traditional ties of human association are weakened, urban existence involves a much greater degree of interdependence between man and man and a more complicated, fragile, and volatile form of mutual interrelations over many phases of which the individual as such can exert scarcely any control. (1964: 81)

Given the extensive empirical studies carried out by members of the Chicago School, no doubt Wirth had in mind not only formal voluntary association but also such things as gangs and subcultures (see Thrasher, 1927).

Similarly, such issues as the massification of society and the neo-tribal response have, as suggested above, been raised in the context of debates about postmodernity by Maffesoli (1988a: 146). Maffesoli speaks of neo-tribes being constituted as Gemeinde or emotional communities into which individual identity is dissolved in collective empathy and identification (1988a: 146). All this is already to be found, however, in Schmalenbach's essay on the Bund.

Maffesoli is not the only person to re-invent the concept of the Bund; there have been others who have tried to conceptualise the same phenomenon: 'communion' for Gurvitch (1941), 'intentional communities' for Moss-Kanter (1976) and, notably, communitas for Victor Turner (1969). The problem has been that all of these concepts appear to have been developed independently of one another. Turner's work, in particular, exemplifies the similarity with Schmalenbach, while offering no knowledge of the earlier concept. Given the significance of Turner's work to the theoretical arguments of this book (see Part II), it is worth drawing out here some of the similarities between the concepts of Bund and communitas.

In his anthropological studies of liminality, pilgrimage and rites of passage (Turner, 1969; 1973; 1974; 1977), Turner introduces the concept of communitas. Liminality is an anthropological concept, associated originally with the work of Van Gennep (1960). Generally the concept is concerned with the study of rites of passage, which, of course have considerable significance in the production of status and identity. A rite of passage can be separated as a process into its three stages: separation, margin and re-aggregation (Van Gennep, 1960: 11). Liminality is associated with the transgressive middle stage: the threshold or limen, the point at which activities and conditions are most uncertain, and the point at which the normative structure of society is temporarily overturned. This liminal state is characterised, according to Turner, by a feeling of communitas, which is described as an affectual and experiential condition of togetherness, comprising a set of 'flow experiences' (1977: 47). These flow experiences are said to involve: the merging of awareness between group and actor; loss of ego; narrowing of consciousness on a limited number of stimuli; ability to control one's actions and gain a subjective sense of control; coherent demands for action; and finally, flow experiences are said to be autotelic, that is, they become their own goals (Turner, 1977: 48). These conditions can be taken as synonymous with the expressive organisation and its form of governance found in a Bund.

Communitas is contrasted with social structure, with Turner making the claim that in periods and places of liminality the normative basis of social order, its social-structure, is allowed to be challenged, as in the case of a festival, by a period of inversions characterised by this intensely affectual communitas or what he calls anti-structure. This, in turn, allows for the renewal of social structures to take place. What is of significance here is that in an earlier study, Turner used the concept of communitas against Tönnies, in the same way that Schmalenbach had done previously:

> The term gemeinschaft, [sic] similar to 'community' as used by Ferdinand Tönnies, combines two major social modalities which I distinguish, structure and communitas . . . Gemeinschaft in that it refers to the bonds between members of tightly knit, multifunctional groups, usually with a local basis, has 'social structure' in this sense. But insofar as it refers to a directly personal egalitarian relationship, gemeinschaft [sic] connotes communitas, as for example, where Tönnies considers friendship to express a kind of gemeinschaft or 'community of feeling' that is tied to neither blood nor locality. (Turner, 1974: 201)

It is quite clear here that Turner's concept of communitas and Schmalenbach's concept of the Bund are attempting to describe the same thing. Where Turner speaks of liminality as a state of transition from structure to structure via a phase of anti-structural liminality, either for individuals or societies, Schmalenbach uses Weber's theory of the routinisation of charisma to explain the unstable nature of Bünde and their transition into more stable gemeinschaftlich or gesellschaftlich states. The principles of transformation and routinisation are ostensibly the same.

Having shown the similarities between these writers I am able to produce my own description of a Bund. This can be set out in the following seven points:

1. A Bund is an elective, unstable, affectual form of sociation. This instability can be associated with its intermediate and often transitory position and character.

2. Bünde are small in scale and generally based on face-to-face inter-action.[4]

3. Bünde are maintained through active, reflexive monitoring of group solidarity by those involved. In other words, they are highly self-referential sociations in which participants define themselves as individuals in relation to the others that make up their Bund. A Bund not only establishes the conditions for identity formation, but sets this process in a form of sociation that requires intense, emotional identification with others based on a strong sense of self-governance.

4. The social bonding involved is intense but because of its elective origin is very weak, requiring considerable effort in self-management (Gurvitch, 1941). The cohesion of the group is maintained through forms of identification often organised around some mode of charismatic identification. This is often expressed through the performance of one's commitment to the group's goals, and through identification with its ethics of aesthetics and tribal symbols.

5. Bünde are self-enclosed and produce a code of practices and totemic symbols which serve as the basis for identification.

6. Bünde involve the blurring of the public and private spheres of life of their members. The sense of belonging provided by this form of organisation and the occasionalism through which one's commitment is often expressed are likely to lead those involved to see themselves as some kind of moral elect.

7. Bünde are both emotional communities and moral communities, involving affectual and value-rational forms of action. One source of their instability may be due to the fact that there is little that is private for the individual; the maintenance of a Bund as a group is paramount and an individual's wishes are secondary to that. As a consequence, however, the continual self-management of the Bund acts reflexively to provide not only a collective identity or lifestyle for its members, but also a greater degree of interpersonal communicative skill which facilitates the development of a new or renewed self-identity.

As a type of organisation, a Bund is well suited to the person who adopts a romantic structure of feeling. It is elective, affectual and expressive in character and those who adopt it seek to find through its emotional intensity not only the freedom to express themselves but also the perceived authenticity of a communal experience with others who share their outlook on life. The Bund is the organisational form of expressive identities, especially although not exclusively those that are based on a search for an alternative way of life. The term Bund, then, escapes many of the formal requirements normally associated with more institutional types of organisation and their dynamics. In doing so it opens up the idea of organisation to wider issues of identity and belonging (see Munro, 1998). It is not, I would argue, for instrumental reasons of political effectiveness that those associated with contemporary identity politics are led into such expressive organisational forms; it has more to do with a desire to share a sense of commitment and belonging with others who are seekers after some kind of expressive alternative to the conditions of modern life that leads to the adoption of such an organisational form. Identity politics can be expressed through the form of the Bund. In addition, the solidarity and sense of commitment to others that such emotional communities foster are likely to facilitate the more overt forms of political action associated with 'new social movements'. For these reasons we can say that the expressive is not antithetical to the organisational and that organisation can, in the form of a Bund, take a distinctly expressive form. It is important, therefore, that we make the Bund a concept for analysing expressive identities.

Conclusion

In this chapter I have examined the claims made previously about the elective, affectual and expressive character of the organisation found in contemporary expressive identity formations. I have suggested that the concept of a Bund, first developed as a sociological concept by Herman Schmalenbach, then later and independently by others, best fits these typical conditions. Identification with others, however, is not just a cognitive exercise in recognition but, more significantly, involves a series of practices through which an identification with the other takes place. The most obvious type of practice within emotional communities which are associated with the search for alternatives is that of protest or social dramas, which often take a visible and symbolic form (Turner, 1974). Less obvious, perhaps, are the practices through which activists' identities are produced in the occasionalism of the public arena as well as in the interstitial spaces of everyday life. There are a number of performative practices, I shall argue, that are of significance in the development of these expressive identities and their quest for meaning, authenticity and belonging: the practices of travel, social drama and forms of protest, and of new or alternative modes of dwelling. I attempt to explain and justify this argument in Part II of this book. In doing so, other factors will become significant: notably the symbolic mobilisation of the 'elsewhere' or spatiality of other 'marginal' spaces (see Foucault, 1986a; Hetherington, 1997a) and their relationship to the performance of identity. What should be apparent from this chapter is that it is the unusual and charismatic form of sociation provided by a Bund that best facilitates such practices.

Notes

1. All etymological references come from the essay describing the etymology of the concept Bund by Koselleck in *Geschichtliche Grundbergriffe: Historisches Lexikon Zur Politische-Sozialen Sprache in Deutschland* Band 1, A-D, under the entry for Bund (Brunner, Conze and Koselleck, 1972). In this chapter I refer to the entry by its author and co-editors: Koselleck in Brunner et al., 1972. I would like to thank Dominique Corazolla for helping me, given my negligible knowledge of German, in understanding this text.

2. It may strike the reader as odd to associate völkisch ideas with radical Jews, given the nationalistic and later Nazi connotations of the idea of the Volk. The reality, however, as Mosse has shown, is that not all völkisch ideas had the racist connotations assumed by the Nazis (Mosse 1971: 77ff.). What is also significant is that the idea of the Bund, strongly associated with the idea of Volk, should have played such an important role not only in the ideas of anarchists such as Landauer, but also in early Zionist movements (1971: 99ff.). It was only later that the Nazis appropriated words like Volk, Bund and Gemeinschaft for their own purposes (1971: 123ff.).

3. Schmalenbach's concept of the Bund bears some similarity to Weber's description of a Gemeinde. Schmalenbach's essay, as I have pointed out, was first published in 1922. Given that Weber died in 1920, he must have made his observations without any knowledge of Schmalenbach's essay. Also, Schmalenbach was just a student at the time of Weber's death. Clearly, given that the essay engages in some detail with Weber's work, it was Weber who was an influence on Schmalenbach when he developed the concept, rather than the other way round. However, the full version of Weber's *Economy and Society*, with its description of a Gemeinde, was not published until after his death and so would not have been fully available to Schmalenbach (Roth, 1968: lx).

4. It would be interesting to see if Bund-like emotional communities can exist via the Internet.

II SOCIAL SPACE AND THE PERFORMANCE OF IDENTITY

INTRODUCTION TO PART II

In Part I I looked at a range of issues associated with identity, expressivism, and identification within that set of identity positions associated with the New Age, alternative lifestyles and new social movements. In Part II I want to look more specifically at the importance of issues of social space within this identity politics. So far I have considered mainly the production of identity within neo-tribal identifications and used this to challenge more individualist conceptions of self-identity (Maffesoli, 1988b; 1996; Giddens, 1990; 1991; Featherstone, 1991b; Beck, 1992; Shields, 1992a). These identities are not particularly new, although they can, of course, take on new forms. The process of identity formation can be seen as responding to a perception of social conditions as overly instrumental and alienating. These expressive identities can also be located within the development of a romantic structure of feeling.

This tradition seeks a re-communitisation of social relations so that they are perceived as more authentic, expressive and fulfilling. This has led to the development of a structure of feeling that seeks to establish identities that are located in perceptions of the past, or of simpler societies, and are informed by the rejected knowledge of modernity. However, while the past and notions of Gemeinschaft and Utopia might be invoked by the protagonists of this position, I argue that it is a distinctly modern approach that seeks to establish individual rather than collective alternatives. The expressive organisation of the Bund is important in this respect. While the collective identifications, some would say neo-tribes, that are produced by this set of expressive identities adopt through their totemism an ideal of community, they do not and cannot produce the imaginary conditions of a perceived authentic community. Instead, they are elective in nature and promote achieved forms of sociation, or a Bund, that in appearance are gemeinschaftlich and Utopian in character, but in reality are something quite different.

The elective basis to neo-tribal identifications means that they create a sociation that is affectual rather than traditional. The identity that is formed is not one that is unified, perfect and lasting, but one that is a monstrous heteroclite, whose syncretism is empowering because its momentary transitional state requires a concerted reflexive process of self-identity in the context of forms of emotional identification with others. It is an identity that is performed and this is the main issue in Part II.

ontext of expressive identities, I shall go on to argue in Part II,
that we need to see this process of identity formation as a
e process that has a distinct spatiality. In certain spaces and
expression, I shall argue, these identities are established through
practices that embody carnivalesque modes of ordering associated
in particular with such practices as social drama – especially in the form of
direct action, travel and communal modes of dwelling. In taking this
position, I draw extensively, albeit critically, on the work of Victor Turner
(1969; 1973; 1974; 1976; 1977; 1982). The main conceptual components of
Turner's position that I have drawn upon are his ideas about the development and effects of communitas within a social order, the significance of
liminal space and the ritual processes of identity performance associated
with it (see also Shields, 1991a; 1992b), and the importance of con-
ceptualisations of dramaturgical performance to identity politics.

In Part I I sought to develop a conceptual framework that allowed me to
understand this issue of identity formation in relation to questions of
identification, a shared structure of feeling and modes of expressive organisation. I suggested that the nexus of identity formation, identification and
identity politics are involved in challenging the instrumentally rational
character of everyday life in contemporary capitalist societies. They do this
from the standpoint of an affectually based revalorisation of everyday life,
lifestyle and interpersonal relations. It has been common within research on
neo-tribes to draw on examples that related to the practices of consumption
(Maffesoli, 1988b; Langman, 1992; Shields, 1992a). While I recognise the
importance of this research, the examples that I have chosen are not
postmodern, consumer lifestyles but what used to be described as counter-
cultural or alternative lifestyles (see Roszak, 1970; Mills, 1973; Martin,
1981). Such new social movement and counter-cultural examples show,
however, how identity formation is not simply a matter of free choice but is
a response to the uncertainties of identity formation that give rise to a
politics of identity.

From within the literature on new social movements, I have suggested that
the work of Melucci (1985, 1989; 1996) most clearly addresses the significance of lifestyle and identity formation on these movements. I discussed
what I saw to be some of the main features of this lifestyle and have argued
that such movements can be characterised as neo-tribal.

I have suggested that this preoccupation with identity and the development of a new personality in the wake of the debates on narcissism (see Bell,
1979; Lasch, 1980; Sennett, 1986) should not lead us into to romanticising
an individualist personality, but instead to recognise the importance of
collective identifications for the development of self-identity. This set of
expressive identities can be associated with the practices of complementary
medicine, spirituality, non-violent political actions, healthy and ethically
motivated eating habits such as vegetarianism or veganism, styles of dress,
alternative modes of dwelling, experimental relationships and sexual practices, travel, and alternative types of employment.

All of these conditions associated with the development of ex
identities provide the basis for attempts to transform the ident
personhood of activists and supporters alike. The spatial context fo
types of grouping suggests that an important place to start is with writ
space within anthropological work on liminality (Van Gennep, 1960; Tʋ　ˌ,
1969; 1974; 1982). Liminal or liminoid practices, such as social dramas and
rituals such as rites of passage generally, take place in spaces that are
symbolically ambivalent. These spaces are similar to what Foucault has
called heterotopia (see Foucault, 1986a); they are spaces, defined in relation
to other spaces in which an alternate social ordering emerges (see Hetherington, 1997a). In the context of identity politics the issue here is the
alternate ordering of identity. I consider the way that space, through the
creation of transgressive situations and embodied displays, shows how
performance in places constituted as marginal has been significant for
transgressive and ludic practices of resistance (see Shields, 1991a; 1992a;
1992b; Hetherington, 1992; 1996; Keith and Pile, 1993; Cresswell, 1996).
Such marginal or liminal space not only provides social centrality for the
groups involved but also sites for the production of identity, through the
enactment of liminoid performances, social dramas and symbolic acts of
protest or resistance. It is important to recognise from the outset, however,
that acts of resistance – what may be described as subjectivised occasions
informed by a romantic structure of feeling – are also ordering acts. Identity
positions constituted in terms of resistance and transgression do not escape a
logic of ordering. All the same, their order, a monstrous or heteroclite one, is
what allows us to call them identities.

Occasions are about the performance of identity and the ordering processes associated with them. My argument is that the empowering, transitional identity of the 'new social movement' or 'counter-cultural' actor is
established through performative repertoires in particular spaces. The constitution of a persona of the Other, which often involves status reversals,
transgressive practices (which may be given a normative justification) and
embodied symbolic forms of resistance to the instrumental rationality of
modern life, is a means through which a new self-identity is ordered and
performed.

5

THE ELSEWHERE OF OTHER MEANING

Spaces of identity

Identity, as well as being about identification and organisation is also about spatiality. In part, this means that identity involves an identification with particular places, whether local or national. It also means that certain spaces act as sites for the performance of identity. I am interested in both of these issues and explore them in Chapters 5, 6 and 7. Here, in order to develop this issue of space and identity in more general terms, let me begin with three quotations:

> Man no longer worships the gods on their heights. Solomon's Temple has slid into a world of metaphor where it harbours swallows' nests and corpse-white lizards. The spirit of religions, coming down to dwell in the dust, has abandoned the sacred places. But there are other places which flourish among mankind, places where men go calmly about their mysterious lives and in which a profound religion is very gradually taking shape. These sites are not yet inhabited by a divinity. It is forming there, a new godhead precipitating in these re-creations of Ephesus like acid-gnawed metal at the bottom of a glass. (Aragon, 1987: 28)

> The characteristic habitat of Chicago's numerous gangs is that broad zone of railroads and factories, of deteriorating neighbourhoods and shifting populations, which border the city's central business district . . . The Gangs dwell among the shadows of the slum. Yet, dreary and repellent as their external environment must seem to the casual observer, their life is to the initiated at once vivid and fascinating. They live in a world distinctly their own – far removed from the humdrum existence of the average citizen. (Thrasher, 1927: 3)

> It [Stonehenge] was the space that allowed people to get a community going [it] created a kind of space in which people could do things that they couldn't do anywhere else . . . You could do what you wanted at Stonehenge and no one would bat an eyelid.[1]

The first of these quotations is from the novel *Paris Peasant* by the surrealist writer Louis Aragon (1987); the second from Frederick Thrasher's classic study of gangs, one of the most famous pieces of ethnographic work to be conducted by a member of the so-called Chicago School of sociologists into what amount to elective and indeed expressive identities (1927); the third comes from an interview I conducted with a New Age traveller in 1991 (see Hetherington, 1993; 1996).[2]

This may seem a strange way to begin a chapter on the spaces of identity, not least because there is a good deal of difference between surrealism and the Chicago School, let alone New Age travellers. However, each of these examples conveys something of the character of the relationship between space and identity that I want to explore here.

Breton, Aragon and their fellow surrealists, as we have seen above in relation to their ideas about everyday life and the city, were fond of wandering amid the 'left-over' parts of the city. In particular, they were interested in places that had been forgotten by the bourgeois culture which had created them in former times – what Lefebvre, following them, has called representational spaces (1991). Sites like brothels, arcades, flea markets and wastelands were, for them, 'elective places' that constituted what they understood as the unconscious of the city and they were keen to explore its ambience (see Breton, 1961; Aragon, 1987; see also Benjamin, 1973; Nadeau 1987: 98; Buck-Morss, 1989). Such magical 'other places' offered them alternative perspectives or ways of seeing the city (see also de Certeau, 1992). As indicated in Chapter 3, this fascination with the hidden spaces of the city has played an important part in the development of the idea of everyday life as containing sites of resistance and creativity (de Certeau, 1984; Lefebvre, 1991; Shields, 1992b; Maffesoli, 1996).

While members of the Chicago School were also interested in the badlands of the city, they were also much more wary of such places associating them with poverty, crime, deviance and unrest (Wirth, 1964; Park, 1967). Thrasher's study, while it illustrated many of these concerns, acknowledged that such 'other places', known in the vernacular as turfs, had an appeal for the marginals of the city – most notably the gang members. More recently Shields has highlighted, in a similar vein, that for some young people shopping malls have a social centrality that provides a focus for the articulation of identity and sense of belonging (1991a; 1992b; see also Hetherington, 1992; 1996).

This concept of social centrality is important in understanding the spaces of identity that characterise a whole array of elective identities, not least those associated with the expressive and alternative lifestyles that are my concern here. While it may not be shopping malls or street corners that have a social centrality for the alternative lifestyles (see Young, 1990; Hetherington, 1992; 1996; Cresswell, 1996), other types of place will have a social centrality that can be analysed in a similar way.

For Shields, social centrality involves the identification of key sites that provide a 'wilful concentration which creates a node in a wider landscape of continual dispersion' (Shields, 1992b: 103). In other words, particular sites take on a symbolic significance around which identities are constituted and performed. Those sites, like Stonehenge for New Age travellers, Greenham Common for the women peace campers, festivals sites, sacred sites, green-field sites marked for road development for anti-road protestors, or even city centre landmarks around which young people may congregate on a Saturday morning to meet their friends, have a social centrality for those who are trying to create some alternative and expressive identification with one another. They are not merely places where like-minded people congregate but symbolic centres around which the values and practices associated with an identity position are performed. While surrealists, Chicago school sociologists as well as recent cultural geography all aid our understanding of the importance of spaces of social centrality to the processes of identity formation, it is the anthropological study of pilgrimage – that liminal process associated with identity rites and its shrines – that provides the most complete picture of this relationship between space and identity.

My argument is that such places have a social centrality such that they act like shrines for those who live outside of the conventions of a society – whether they be Chicago gang members, surrealists or those, like travellers, who have chosen an expressive and alternative identity – because they come to symbolise another set of values and beliefs around which groups can order their identities and the way they want to be identified (see Cohen et al., 1987). Such sites become sites of social centrality for the reproduction of marginal or outsider identities (see Shields, 1990; 1991a; 1992b; Hetherington, 1992; 1996; 1997b; Cresswell, 1996).

In order to analyse this issue of space and its relationship with marginality, I look in this chapter at the processes associated with this issue of social centrality. Taking the practice of pilgrimage to shrines as a model (Turner, 1973), I suggest that the places in question, the ones that are the likely to become a source of social centrality for those who adopt values and beliefs that are perceived as marginal within society, are likely to have some sort of symbolic affinity with the identity in question. Such spaces facilitate opportunities for being different and the constitution of new identities. The sort of places likely to be chosen are marginal ones whose significance has been described by a number of different writers, for example: Lefebvre's concept of representational spaces (1991), Foucault's heterotopia (1986a; 1989a) and Turner's development of the anthropological concept of liminal space (1969; 1974). In more recent cultural geography, marginal space (Shields, 1991a; Cresswell, 1996) and paradoxical space (Rose, 1993) have also been used as terms to try and capture something of the uncertain character of particular sites and the practices through which they are constituted as spaces for all kinds of alternative doings and goings on. I critically analyse the idea of marginal space in detail in Chapter 6; here I want to look more specifically at the processes associated with social centrality and its relationship with the constitution of identity.

What should become immediately apparent is that we are dealing here with what Rose has described as paradoxical space (1993); in this instance, the paradox is that the sites that are socially central to the identifications I have identified in Part I and the structure of feeling that informs them, are likely to be spaces that are seen as in some way marginal within society. As we shall see later, the idea of marginal space is more complex than it may at first appear. Margins are not only things pushed to the edge, they can also be in-between spaces, spaces of traffic, right at the centre of things. At this point, however, I argue that it is around such 'marginality' (and I leave the term marginality in inverted commas throughout this chapter) that new identities, and the collective processes associated with their formation, are expressed (see Hetherington, 1996). As such, 'marginal' sites can be said to take on the character of symbolic centres for marginal out-groups on the margins of society (see also Stallybrass and White, 1986; Shields, 1991a; 1992a; Wilson, 1991; Bondi and Domosh, 1992; Walkowitz, 1992; Cresswell, 1996).

Looking at the relationship between space and identity will aid our understanding of the nature of what has been described as an emerging ludic and transgressive politics, acts of resistance, and the creation of alternative lifestyles through which these Others ritually produce their identities in Other places. In effect, I am arguing that there is an elective affinity between marginal places, as sites of social centrality for those marginal identities that have been assumed (see also Shields, 1991a; 1992b). There is, therefore, a relationship between space and identity which, though not causally neces- sary, is made significant through an attachment to a symbolism of Otherness, difference, and marginality (see Shields, 1991a; 1992b; Hetherington, 1992; 1996; Rose, 1993; Cresswell, 1996).[3]

Symbols come to mean something within a distinct structure of feeling. The creation of alternative ways of life are not on the whole utopian in the sense that they establish new fixed and permanent communities, but more significantly they use marginal places as sites of social centrality to create fleeting but transitional identifications out of which new identities emerge. If not utopian they might be described as 'utopic', involving a spatial play with ideas of Utopia translated into actual spatial practice (see Marin, 1984; Hetherington, 1997a).[4] These may be spaces of alternative communities, encampments, sites of protest, sites of festival; or sites to which one can escape or 'retreat' and to which only those who are part of a 'tribe' are given access; or they may simply be sites chosen for more contingent reasons to make some sort of protest. Whatever the case, such sites will also be spaces for the performance of identity.

The link between establishing an identity and the space is a symbolic one. That symbolism is likely to be a informed in some way by the structure of feeling that lies behind the particular identifications and their modes of expression. In Chapter 3 I identified a particular structure of feeling that I called a romantic structure of feeling. One of its central aspects was the occasion; events that were publicly visible both to others involved and to those outside. Another way of describing this might be in terms of a social drama (see Turner, 1974). The dramaturgical metaphor associated with the performance of identity is an issue I take up in Chapter 7. Here, I want to suggest that spaces that have a social centrality for those who share a structure of feeling and seek to establish an identity around it are likely also to be what we may call spaces of occasion, in which the values and political views of a group might be expressed and around which identities are at the same time performed.

Escape attempts and the elsewhere

An important part of the romantic structure of feeling, as we have seen, is its emphasis on issues of freedom, authenticity and the occasionalism of self-creation. One important sort of occasion which can be said to fit this set of conditions is that of the adventure, another the pilgrimage and a third the more politically expressed social drama. All of these can be seen as examples of escape attempts from the routines of everyday life and their systemic, instrumental domination by institutionalised arrangements (see Cohen and Taylor, 1992). For those who find the conditions of everyday life routine, banal, morally unedifying and oppressive, or somehow perceive them to be inauthentic, the solution is often an escape attempt – an enthused re-centering of life and one's identity around a particular, chosen and, usually, shared interest.

The recently republished work on escape attempts by Cohen and Taylor (1992 [first edition, 1976]), which had originally been written to try and account for the emphasis on freedom from the constraints of everyday routine found in the 1960s counter-culture, borrows the term escape attempt from the authors' earlier research on long-term prisoners and how they negotiate escapes, in an imaginary sense, from the dull routine of a long sentence and provides us with a useful starting point from which to look at this relationship between space and identity. Their work also critically reflects the idea of everyday life as a site of resistance and provides a useful starting point when looking at alternative lifestyles in conflict with the routine expectations of everyday life.

For Cohen and Taylor, escape attempts include: activity enclaves such as hobbies, games, gambling and sex; new landscapes which they associate with holidays, popular cultural interests, and art; and mindscaping which involves the use of hallucinogenic drugs and therapy (1992: chapter 5; see also Rojek, 1993). This is a somewhat arbitrarily chosen list which perhaps reflects the interests of the time and is not a systematic attempt to describe the nature of escape attempts. This is a criticism that the authors now make of their own work (1992: 7). Like Meyrowitz (1985), these writers now tend to assume that electronic media undermine a sense of place, or de-territorialise life, making it all the more difficult to escape from the routines of paramount reality when there is no locatable paramount reality, rather a multiplicity of realities or frames into which everyday life is organised (see Goffman, 1986; Meyrowitz, 1985). While such alternative realities may become routine and mundane or incorporated within a consumerist logic, this does not necessarily stop them being used in the creation of alternative, often marginal or transgressive activities associated with changing one's lifestyle and creating a new identity. In many respects, the type of escape attempt framed by a romantic structure of feeling is one that seeks some sort of holism of everyday life and challenges the instrumentalism that lies behind its fragmentation.

However, the quest for experience and meaning within modern societies, which lies at the core of Cohen and Taylor's account of escape attempts, has often been a collective tribal one, and one which forms a significant part of the romantic structure of feeling. The emotional security of a Bund-like sociation is likely to offer a source of security in the uncertainty of an escape and thus be more likely to be sought as the means through which a life perceived as more authentic is created – more likely than the lonely, stoical inner-directed *Persönlichkeit* Weber would have preferred to see.

Escape attempts, especially those which have a political or religious motive as their basis, often involve a rejection of existing values, notably material ones, but also involve a search for new values, post-material ones, around which collectively to re-centre the identities of the enthusiasts (Inglehart, 1977; 1990). From studies of alternative, politicised identifica-tions, there are two identifiable and related sets of symbolic practices through which such escape attempts are likely to take place: travel and alternative types of dwelling, often of a communal kind (see E. Cohen, 1973; Mills, 1973; Abrams and McCulloch, 1976; Cohen et al., 1987; Pepper, 1991; Rojek, 1995). The first practice, travel, involves a process of removal from everyday life into an exotic realm of new meanings. The second practice, dwelling, seeks to re-centre everyday life upon new values found in the intimacy of dwelling together in the elsewhere of this other meaning.

Liminality, travel, dwelling

The traveller or wanderer is a typical romantic figure associated with the critique of modern, alienated life. The nomad has conventionally been held up as the spirited example of the rejection of the constraints and instrumental rationality of contemporary life, who goes on a quest for authenticity (Graham, 1927; Becker, 1946; Lacquer, 1962; Cohen, et al., 1987: 332).[5] Folklorists attracted by the supposed authenticity of gypsy lifestyles during the eighteenth and nineteenth centuries (Mayall, 1988), numerous young members of the aristocracy who went off on a grand tour to finish their education, are examples of such travellers who have gone in search of their identity in other places (Hibbert, 1987). There were more extreme cases like the 'gentlemen gypsies', such as Bamphylde Moore-Carew, who during the eighteenth century took to adopting a complete gypsy lifestyle (Lambert, 1950: 177). One can also include among such travellers religious pilgrims during many ages, and even go back as far as Homer to find, in the example of Odysseus, the mythical figure of the wanderer searching, on one level, for his home; on another, for wisdom. These examples all have in common this association of travel with truth, in the form of a religious quest (see Eliade, 1969). All such journeys contain the myth of arrival at some truth, a truth that signifies belonging and meaning outside of the routines of daily existence. Those in search of a new identity are in some respects pilgrims in search of the experience of an authentic truth around which to re-centre their lives.

An important place to start in analysing this quest for the elsewhere is with the liminal practices associated with rites of passage and pilgrimage to shrines (see Turner, 1973). From this we can see that 'shrines', in the loosest sense, are the likely source of social centrality or elective centredness (Cohen et al., 1987) for those who adopt beliefs and produce identities that are perceived as marginal within society. As such, they will be taken as symbolic centres for marginal out-groups on the margins of society (see also Stallybrass and White, 1986; Shields, 1991a; 1992b; Wilson, 1991; Lefebvre, 1991).

The issue of liminality, which lies behind much of the anthropological analysis of shrines, has recently become important within cultural geography which has begun to look at the relationship between space and identity (notably Shields, 1991a; see also Featherstone, 1991b; Hetherington, 1996; Cresswell, 1996). Of particular importance in this work is the interest in the symbolic properties of sacred spaces associated with rites of passage, pilgrimage and social dramas, and the social centrality that they have to the constitution of identity (Van Gennep, 1960; Turner, 1969; 1974; 1976; 1977; 1982; for more critical approaches on liminality see R. Werbner, 1989; Handleman, 1990).

Rites of passage are rituals associated with life changes which require the move between different statuses, states, ages or places. They involve a process of symbolic transition that can be separated as a process into the three stages of separation, margin and re-aggregation. In the first stage, in small-scale societies, a person at a particular point in the lifecourse is required to move on to another point – such as from childhood to adulthood, or to pass on to other life stages such as marriage. To do so they are required to go through a set of initiation rites before they can take on their new state. They are separated physically from the rest of their society and stripped of any previous status and identity. Once this has been done they exist in a liminal or marginal phase. Liminality, therefore, is associated with the middle stage of the rite – a stage that describes a threshold or margin, at which activities and conditions are most uncertain. It is during this period of the process that the person assumes an empowered, transitional identity often through various forms of initiation and ritual humiliation or through the assumption of transgressive powers. People during this phase are subjected to ordeals and rites that mark them off as being different, in an unstable identity position that exists between two states (see La Fontaine, 1985). The spaces that they inhabit are also sometimes seen as polluting and marginal (Douglas, 1984). By placing these dangerous liminal initiands in a liminal place, their uncertain and sometimes magical powers are contained and managed. In the final stage of a rite of passage, the person is reintegrated back into society as a new person.

In small-scale societies liminal rituals as rites of passage are an important part of the life of the people. According to Turner, they exist as a means to self-understanding of a particular society and as a means of renewal of that society and a process of integration. The part of this process that has most interested cultural geographers, and indeed cultural studies generally, is that the liminal phase is associated with acts of transgression (see Shields, 1991a; Cresswell, 1996). What this literature often misses is that acts of transgression are also acts of (re)ordering and social integration, rather than an unfettered, counter-hegemonic form of resistance (see Stallybrass and White, 1986; Hetherington, 1997a).

Turner identifies two particular types of liminal ritual in small-scale societies: rituals of status elevation and cyclical rituals (1969: 167). In terms of their relationship with the so-called carnivalesque practices of transgression often associated with identity politics and alternative lifestyles as a significant source of resistance associated with marginal places, it is the latter that are of most importance. Drawing on Bakhtin's analysis of the carnivalesque (1984), Turner shows that such liminal rituals embody the principles of the world turned upside down, where everything becomes its opposite. For Turner, however, unlike Bakhtin, in small-scale societies such rituals embody not only acts of transgression but the means of reintegration and social order. As he suggests:

> Cognitively, nothing underlines regularity so well as absurdity or paradox. Emotionally, nothing satisfies as much as extravagant or temporarily permitted illicit behaviour. Rituals of status reversal accommodate both aspects. By making the low high and high low, they reaffirm the hierarchical principle. (1969: 176).

While liminal rituals such as marriages, christening, funerals and various ceremonies associated with changes of status along with cyclical rituals such as festivals and public events still exist in large-scale complex societies, their significance as an integrated and totalising means of social renewal and integration is weaker and more fragmented than in small-scale societies.

However, the functionalism of Turner's analysis of rites of passage and liminality, debatable in the context of small-scale societies in the way it overemphasises structure at the expense of process, works even less well in the societies of the capitalist West in which social integration and ordering are more diffuse and do not always centre on religious rites. In order to retain some sense of liminality in Western societies which have a more dispersed social structure, and to try and overcome some of the functionalism in his earlier work, Turner also makes the added distinction between what he calls liminal rituals and liminoid rituals (1982). Liminoid rituals resemble liminal ones, but with a number of notable differences. First, liminoid rituals are achieved rather than ascribed; whereas in the liminal rituals of small-scale societies there is little choice involved in rites of passage, in socially differentiated Western societies there is. Second, as a consequence of their achieved status, liminoid rituals are weaker than liminal ones (Turner, 1982: 33).

Liminal rituals involve constraint as well as freedom; liminoid rituals are more ludic in character and do not require the same sort of obligation as liminal rituals. A third difference has to do with the nature of the spaces involved. Liminal spaces are betwixt and between sacred and profane space. They act as a dangerous and polluting margin, dangerous in the symbolic sense of mingling the sacred with the profane, as such liminal spaces have to be clearly demarcated and associated with their own practices. Although profanation may take place, it does so in a symbolically regulated manner. Liminoid spaces exist in societies that do not have clearly demarcated sacred and profane space. Although remnants of sacred and profane space remain, the routine, neutral space of contemporary society is open to contestation, revealing the symbolic nature of space below – a process made particularly visible at marginal spaces, in which the veneer of earlier forms of symbolic representation has worn thin. Liminoid spaces, therefore, are likely to be created out of spaces that still retain some degree of symbolic significance as marginal or transitional spaces. In particular, Turner associates liminoid space with leisure activities and political protests that have a strong carnivalesque element, and sees the spaces in which they take place as being ones associated with the individualism and personal freedom that such practices aim to achieve (1982).

For Turner, one of the most important aspects of liminoid rituals, when freed from the association of liminality with social renewal and regeneration, is their significance as sites for the production of new symbols for new modes of living (1982: 33). In small-scale societies liminal rituals, as well as being rites of passage for individuals, are meaningful collectively as a means of transgressing a society's moral codes such that a process of renewal of identity can occur. Liminality is associated, as we have seen, with what Turner describes as anti-structure and communitas: passing moments of release, usually associated with festivals and ceremonies in which people act up in ways that might otherwise appear strange or threatening, and through which the rules of society that underpin its structure are not only inverted but also re-invented. In liminoid conditions, the emphasis shifts some way towards process as freed from the functionalism of structural constraints. Anti-structure in the occasions, festivals and protests of liminoid 'initiands' do not reintegrate the structure of society, but they do have the effect of producing alternate orderings of identity for those who challenge what they see their society standing for.

There are two other concepts that Turner introduces in his work that have some bearing on these issues of space and identity: communitas (1969) and social drama (1974; 1976; 1982). Communitas, in Turner's analysis and as I indicated in Chapter 3, is associated with anti-structure and is contrasted with social structure. In periods and places of liminality, the means by which social order is maintained is ritually challenged, as in the case of festival, by a period of inversions characterised by the intensely affectual identifications of communitas or shared sense of identity and belonging. The transgressive practices associated with the carnivalesque can be said to embody this experience of communitas. Experiences of ecstasy, solidarity, spontaneity and empowerment are all associated with the communitas of transgression and symbol creation. Turner identifies three types of communitas: existential communitas, normative communitas and ideological communitas (1969: 132). While the first is characterised by its spontaneity, the other two have a more formal basis which involves the organisation of people in the pursuit of particular goals or as utopian models for living. It is these latter two types of communitas, in particular, that can be seen to correspond to the more form-orientated concept of a Bund.

Turner offers us two examples of this: the communitas surrounding St Francis and that found among hippies in late-1960s counter-culture (1969: chapter 4). In both cases the charisma associated with the Bund is also of significance. He also alludes to the routinisation of such a charismatic form of sociation: 'When normative communitas is demonstrably a group's dominant social mode, one can witness the process of transformation of a charismatic and personal moment into an ongoing, relatively repetitive social system.' (1982: 49).

The concept of communitas was originally associated with the rites of passage found in small-scale societies but it can also be found, I would argue, in the form of a Bund in some liminoid social dramas within complex, industrialised societies. The significance of social drama, like the liminal ritual is again a spatial one, associated with the idea of arenas, which Turner suggests are: 'the concrete settings in which paradigms become transformed into metaphors and symbols with reference to which political power is mobilized and in which there is a trial of strength between influential paradigm-bearers. "Social dramas" represent the phased process of their contestation.' (1974: 17). Turner defines a social drama as a 'spontaneous unit of social process' (1982: 68) that consists of four phases: breach, crisis, redress and reintegration or recognition (1982: 69). Again Turner's functionalism is apparent, as is his emphasis on structure rather than process. Turner does not allow for the possibility of process freed from its structural properties; a social drama – what might also be called an 'occasion' in the Schmittian sense (Schmitt, 1986) – for Turner exists in a processual form, like the rite of passage in small-scale societies. In complex societies, the less prescribed liminoid conditions occur in relation not only to rites of passage, but also to social dramas. In liminoid conditions, individuals in choosing whether to involve themselves in social dramas may do so as much for the communitas that it provides as for the goals they may hope to achieve. A Bund, which I consider to be synonymous with normative communitas, can be taken as a precondition of the sociation associated with non-routine, elective social dramas.

Social dramas are often associated with forms of symbolic action that are variously playful, inventive and subversive, or carnivalesque in character, occurring in spaces that are often symbolically uncertain or marginal. As places of uncertainty which have a social centrality, they are endowed with the symbolic properties that allow them to be used as arenas for the generation of new symbols which go into processes of political actions, identifications, and identity formation.

Pilgrimage shares many of the properties of social dramas, also conveying much of the communitas, festival and carnivalesque atmosphere. Pilgrimage in the structured religious sense is also, as Turner describes it, a liminal process. Pilgrimage involves the removal of a person from the routine of their daily life into a communal quest for some 'sacred' site which comes to symbolise renewal or rebirth and a new start, often with new or renewed values. When the pilgrim arrives at their sacred site, having experienced the communitas of the pilgrimage on route, their identity undergoes a process of renewal:

> The peripherality of pilgrimage shrines and the temporal structure of the pilgrimage process, beginning in a Familiar Place, going to a Far Place, and returning, ideally 'changed', to a Familiar place, can be interestingly related to van Gennep's concept of the rite of passage, with its stages of separation, margin or limen, and re-aggregation. . . . a pilgrimage center, from the standpoint of the believing actor, also represents a 'threshold', a place and moment 'in and out of time', and such an actor – as the evidence of many pilgrims of many religions attests – hopes to have their direct experience of the sacred, invisible, or supernatural order, either in the material aspect of miraculous healing or in the immaterial aspect of inward transformation of spirit or personality. (Turner, 1973: 213–214)

Pilgrimages, which tend to follow set routes, generally end at shrines that have significance as sacred places. Perhaps one of the most significant aspects of these pilgrim centres or shrines is that they are often to be found on the margins or peripheries of inhabited areas (Turner, 1973: 211). According to Turner, the peripherality of sacred spaces, symbolically as well as physically on the margins, like shrines, is a significant part of their liminal status.

For the pilgrim, the margin becomes socially central. This reorientation involves an inversion of meanings, from those that are central in the pilgrim's indigenous society. This is largely an issue of ordering. Marginal places come to symbolise other, different sets of beliefs and values and to act as liminal sites for the reordering of the identity of the pilgrim. The pilgrimage to such places uses this marginality in a regeneration of faith (and identity). For those who seek experiences outside of their routine daily existence, the exotic other place, like a shrine, is likely to be of major significance. Just as football fans will make a regular pilgrimage to their team's stadium every other week (see Bale, 1993), so too will those whose core values and beliefs lie symbolically outside the space of their everyday lives, in some more authentic space that is to be found elsewhere.

Edward Shils once argued that every society, no matter how complex, has a centre of values and beliefs (1975). He went on to suggest this centre was not itself spatial in nature, but consisted of values affirmed by elites that took on the sacred quality of authority (1975: 4). Be this as it may, Shils is wrong to suggest that authority and value centrality cannot be spatial in nature. While values and beliefs do indeed transcend both time and space within a society, particular places do, all the same, take on a symbolic role in representing that value centrality. Cathedrals, parliaments, monuments, state buildings and other such places come to represent forms of authority in a society. This is most clearly shown during times of revolt or revolution when these central values are challenged. For example, Wensislas Square in Prague in August 1968, Tiannamen Square in Beijing in 1989 and the Berlin Wall, again in 1989, have been sites of protest directed at the central values of a society's elite symbolised by particular places.

If particular places come to symbolise authority within a society, then it is equally the case that other more 'marginal' places come to symbolise other, different sets of beliefs and values that are in some way resistant to that authority. The shrine, often a site of martyrdom or divine visitation, is such a place which symbolises the inadequacies of existing values. The pilgrimage to such places uses this marginality in a regeneration of faith. For those who seek experiences outside of their routine daily existence, the exotic other place, like a shrine, is likely to be important. In the case of pilgrims, tourists or travellers, the quest for knowledge and identity will quite possibly be symbolised by marginal places on the periphery of everyday life. The weariness with everyday life, a desire for a brief period of recuperation and renewal, and the touristic search for new experiences, makes the tourist – the name given to the modern day pilgrim – a key figure in contemporary society (see MacCannell, 1989; Urry, 1990; Rojek, 1995). The sorts of escape attempts engaged in by those seeking a new morally and emotionally revived lifestyle and the possibilities it offers for the construction of a new identity, can be described as an extreme form of tourism.

Political tourists of the elsewhere

MacCannell's description of tourists as typical modern characters who go in search of experiences in places that are unfamiliar and exotic, in an attempt to escape from the routine of their lives and have their selves liminally renewed in the process, has many similarities with the typifications of the pilgrim (1989). This is no doubt something of an overgeneralisation in that it suggests that all tourists engage in such practices in a similar way. The reality, however, may well be that many tourists take their everyday lives with them in their suitcases when they go on holiday (see Urry, 1990; Rojek, 1995). Indeed, some undoubtedly go on holiday to seek out what is familiar to their home environment in the form of food, drink and entertainment, in places that may simply have better weather or where they can relax away from the familiar sites of their everyday routines. Other tourists, especially those with children, may have no choice but to take that everyday life with them. However, even for some of these tourists, a carnivalesque, liminoid atmosphere of abundant drink, food and sex may also be significant to the experiences that they seek. What makes tourism and the alternative lifestyles I am interested in similar is not only this search for the elsewhere as a source of meaning and identity, but also the expressive mode of much of this experience.

In order to avoid overgeneralising the sort of experiences sought by tourists, Eric Cohen has provided a useful typology that distinguishes between different types of tourist experiences, all of which involve the search elsewhere for new or different types of experience. Some parts of this typology overlap very clearly with alternative lifestyles and their identity politics. His typology consists of: 1. The Recreational Mode; 2. The Diversionary Mode; 3. The Experiential Mode; 4. The Experimental Mode; and 5. The Existential Mode (Cohen, 1979: 183). As a typology it is not perfect. It would appear to presume as its model a lone (male?) traveller. How issues of class, gender, lifestage, sexual orientation, disability and so on might cut across it remains to be explored. All the same, this typology can be used to suggest that tourists' travel experiences differ with regard to their relationship to the centrality of values associated with their own society.

Of course, most of those engaged in some sort of quest for a new identity, symbolised by a move to some Other place which has a meaning different to that of the everyday life they wish to leave behind, would not take to the idea of being called tourists or perhaps even travellers. Equally, they may not travel physically very far at all. They will, however, often identify with other cultures, with native peoples and their culture, and with the life of the nomad free to roam and experience the variety of their location. Travel is first a cultural practice of movement; second, however, it can be a type of identity position that may or may not actually involve the practice of travel itself. To be a traveller one does not necessarily have to get on a plane; equally one can be a high street consumer who buys the identity of the traveller: from Gortex-lined hiking boots and fleecy jackets to Mongolian caps and handwoven Bolivian shawls. The symbolism of movement as much as actual movement found in the idea of travel is important here, and is certainly found among the 'tourists' at one end of Cohen's typology. All the same, the practice of travel is an important part of the identification.

Recreational tourists, according to Cohen, are strongly attached to their own society's culture as the basis for their central system of meaning and values. They act as if at home when they are tourists and are only interested in tourism for the entertainment it provides (Cohen, 1979: 184). Diversionary tourists do not adhere to the centrality of their own culture when travelling, but neither are they looking for an alternative centre. This sort of tourism, according to Cohen, is concerned only with escapism and has no other meaning behind it (1979: 185). It is the experiential tourist who goes in search of experiences in the sense that MacCannell implies. The experiential tourists find meaning for themselves in the life of others (1979: 186). As MacCannell identifies, other lives are perceived as more authentic than the tourist's own (1989: chapter 5). The search for authenticity by the experiential tourist takes on the form of a quest. In this form, the tourists, who will have to return to their routine lives in due course, hope to absorb some of the authenticity of the other and enrich their own lives in the process.

Experimental tourists take this search for authentic experiences a stage further, according to Cohen, by identifying more fully with the centrality of other cultures (1979: 189). These people are likely to reject the central values and beliefs within their own society and, in so doing, try to adopt what they perceive to be the lifestyle of more authentic cultures:

> Examples of such seekers who experiment with alternative lifestyles abound among younger, post-modern sets of travellers: urban American, European or Australian youngsters who taste life in farming communities, the Israeli kibbutzim, the Indian asramas, remote Pacific villages and hippie communes, engage in the experimental mode of tourism. (Cohen, 1979: 189)

This group of tourists begins to approximate to those I have suggested are seekers of an expressive and alternative lifestyle – even though in reality it may mean staying for a while at a muddy commune in mid-Wales in the driving rain, rather than going to some South Pacific island in emulation of Gauguin. Cohen's last category of tourist, the existential tourist, is a more extreme, long-term example of the experimental tourist. Existential tourists choose to identify completely with the elective centre of the other and live in exile from their own society (1979: 190; see also E. Cohen, 1973).

For these last two types of 'tourists', who no doubt would prefer to call themselves travellers, the act of travelling becomes a semi-permanent or permanent adventure which, as Simmel suggested, is an 'exclave of life, the "torn off" whose beginning and end have no connection with the somehow unified stream of existence' (1971c: 196). Travel for adventure, the search for experience or for complete escape involves, as Simmel identified, a fatalism and positive attachment to fleeting and unexpected encounters and events removed from the routine of everyday life (1971b: 192ff.). Adventurers are unconcerned with the passing of time, treating their experiences as if in an eternal present; what concerns them instead are spatialised events and chance encounters over which they have little or no control. The liminality of this state gives this type of traveller a means of breaking with their existing society and identifying with another. In so doing, they become integrated into a new way of life, with a new lifestyle and a new identity.

In rejecting Shils's suggestion that value centrality in society is not spatial, I would argue that the social centrality associated with these experimental and existential modes of travel generally involve identifying with a centre which is a place that serves as a locus of new meaning and authenticity. All of the examples that Cohen gives which I have quoted above involve small-scale communities located in particular places, places in which one supposedly dwells authentically in the presence of an Otherness to their host society. These sites, like the end points of a pilgrimage, are sacred places or 'shrines' that are perceived to embody the Otherness of meaning, rejected knowledge, to the centrality of modern social values and beliefs.

The practice of travel is an act of removal from a person's place of origin. This act of removal is a liminal practice out of which a new status and a new identity are formed (see Turner, 1969; 1973; 1974). These new, or renewed, identities are given symbolic significance by their association with a search for alternative truths symbolised by shrine-like, marginal places. The communion with others occurs in places that are symbolically other.

While travel, modelled on the idea of pilgrimage, is important for those who chose expressive lifestyles, it is the communal presence of others and the process of dwelling with others that adds further significance to this process. There is an extensive literature on communes that could be used to justify this claim (see Mills, 1973; Rigby, 1974; Abrams and McCulloch, 1976; Webster, 1976; Pepper, 1991). Equally, work on kibbutzim also provides further examples of this quest for dwelling within the authenticity with others (see Talmon, 1972; E. Cohen, 1983). To dwell in this sort of way is to seek to live with others an unmediated way in other places, often out in some 'marginal' place. This sense of dwelling is based in a romantic structure of feeling. The elsewhere is more authentic, less tainted by the instrumentalism of modernity; a place where people can, supposedly, be free to live their own lives and discover an identity for themselves. The dweller, in this sense, is often also the traveller who leaves the familiar place for one far away. The figure of the wanderer or rover is, significantly, a person who cuts her or himself adrift from the idea of dwelling in the built world of things in favour of the individual freedom offered by displacement.[6] To dwell, in this sense, is to dwell within the adventure of an uncertain future; to take a chance on a new life elsewhere, informed by the authenticity of the communitas established as part of the pilgrimage or quest and to use particular sites to challenge the lifestyles of the sedentary population.

Through the two related practices of travelling and dwelling, expressive identifications, often Bund-like in nature, will use places located in a symbolic realm outside of perceived central values and beliefs within their indigenous society. This may mean living within small-scale communal societies, but it is more likely to mean creating one's own small-scale 'society' (Bund) on the margins of one's own society. Those electing to adopt a lifestyle whose main features derive from values and beliefs outside of some of the values and beliefs of their own indigenous society, will do so in places that in a symbolic system of placing can be described as marginal. These marginal places give those who adopt such a lifestyle a new source of social centrality around which to re-centre their lives through a ritual process of identity formation, through symbolic practices such as travel and dwelling.

Margins and the structure of feeling

As we have seen, opposition to modern society is often made on the basis of a critique of its instrumental, calculating formal rationality. There is a multiplicity of expressive forms, the identity set, that this opposition can take; 'new social movements', religious movements, alternative lifestyles, and so on. To reiterate, the anti-instrumentalism and expressiveness of these groups operates within everyday life at the level of identity and lifestyle as much as they do in forms of collective protest (Melucci, 1989). These groups seek a revalorisation of their everyday life through value-rational and affectual identifications expressed through a shared structure of feeling. The groupings they produce are not only moral communities but also emotional communities, the lifestyles of which are grounded in ethical and emotional criteria associated with identifications with others. This affectual revalorisation of everyday life concerns the production of new lifestyles and can be described as part of a quest for meaning in sites that have a social centrality, or elective centres (E. Cohen, et al., 1987). This meaning, freedom and authenticity is sought in some symbolic elsewhere, outside of the routines of daily life and values of modern societies.

'Marginal' places, symbolically outside of modern society, are the elsewhere in which these meanings are sought. The symbolic meanings attached to these spaces, often associated with rejected or non-modern, non-Western knowledge, allow for the metonymical transferral of meaning from place to neo-tribal identity. Because of the anti-instrumental rationality of these groups, the places chosen are likely to have some sacred, ambivalent, forgotten or mysterious meaning attached to them. Such places will have a social centrality for the people involved.

The process of removing oneself from the familiar spaces in which one lives and travelling to be somewhere else, on either a temporary or permanent basis, is one in which both the process of movement and the process of being somewhere else are important to the constitution of new identities and the communitas of identification with others. These affectually based identifications have two main areas of significance: 1. a re-establishment of a moral proximity with the other, and 2. a search for an 'authentic' affectual sociality that offers a non-instrumental, direct mode of experience in relation to both the self and others.

These two interrelated practices locate affectual-ethical lifestyle protagonists in a search or quest for authentic experiences and identity – much to Habermas's chagrin (1981) – outside of the cultural spheres of modernity and modes of communicative rationality. These experiences are ones which develop in association with the rejected knowledge to which those with this type of lifestyle are attracted and by the emotional identification with others found within a Bund. I suggest, following Cohen, Ben-Yehuda and Aviad (1987), that this sort of escape attempt involves the rejection of the central values of society and a quest for new, elective centres on the margins of modern life. These elective centres, I suggest, are more than just metaphorical spaces; more often, they are actual sites that have a social centrality for a specific Bund (see Shields, 1992a).

The practices of travel and dwelling, involved respectively in the search for experience, and a new sense of belonging and recovery of dispersed beliefs and values, can be described as practices that are involved in the re-sacralisation of space. One can see in the practices of both travel and dwelling a desire to overcome the banality of everyday life in favour of one lived more 'authentically'. The lifestyle practices of travel and dwelling involve both a communal and spatial re-centering. The re-sacralisation, however, is as much a process of resistance and transgression as it is a work of the imagination. The two, however, should not be seen as incompatible.

Travel as pilgrimage to particular shrines and dwelling in such places involves the seeking out of forgotten or 'marginal' places. As we have seen, religious shrines and pilgrim centres are often found on the margins (Turner, 1973). What is significant about travel and dwelling is that both practices involve different ways of seeing, especially seeing through the prism of rejected knowledge (Webb, 1974). It is places that are seen as marginal, forgotten or somehow hidden, on the edges of modern society – the spaces that fascinated both the surrealists and the Chicago sociologists – that are likely to be the sites of social centrality for those who adopt the sort of identities I have described in Part I. They are either placed in such a way that they act as places of exclusion or have multiple and contested meanings attached to them, or they simply do not figure within the system of placing and are therefore forgotten or overlooked.

Travel and dwelling, I argue, along with more overtly political social dramas are the main types of performance to be found among those who elect to adopt alternative lifestyles. It is these performances that facilitate an escape attempt into what are perceived as more authentic experiences out of which identities are constituted.

Conclusion

The social centrality of key 'marginal' sites provides a symbolic resource in establishing and maintaining alternative and expressive identities. Sites that have social centrality for those engaged in transgressive and alternativist activities are likely to be seen as in some way marginal. The 'marginality' of such places provides a source of new meaning, outside the main forms of knowledge within society. These places are the elsewhere of Other meaning or 'elective centres' (E. Cohen, et al., 1987) which have a social centrality around which the practices and performances that facilitate the production of new identities are ordered.

Travel involves the process of removal and a new start; social dramas involve a liminoid reversal of the norms of a society that those adopting an alternative lifestyle wish to reject; and dwelling provides a sense of belonging in a new type of ethically and affectually committed lifestyle with others. Travel is a symbolic practice in which the person, seeking new and more authentic experiences, leaves their host society and embarks on a quest for a new way of life and new meanings. Travel, as a practice, symbolises pilgrimage to some new exotic other place, freedom, starting again, a break with the past and all that is seen as wrong or inauthentic. The practice of travel is also a quest for new truths symbolized in Other, more exotic places. The social drama involves the development of alternative identities, and takes place in a manner that publicly inverts social norms and values. The constraints of former lifestyles are thrown off in preparation for new ones. To dwell is to belong, drawing on the past but aiming, by example, to change things in the future – to create alternatives to conventional modes of living, and to create new lifestyles and become someone else.

We might argue, therefore, that identities are transformed in 'marginal' places. The enactment of a visibly different identity, that has its origins in the affectual sociality of the Bund, becomes a source of both conflict and empowerment. These places become sites of cultural or political resistance, in which processes of identity formation and neo-tribal identifications are reproduced. It remains for me to discuss what might be meant by marginal place. Simply invoking the term 'marginal place' in itself is not enough.

Notes

1. Interview with Traveller Key Informant No. 1. (TKI 1) 26 March 1991. London. Two Tapes. Male, late twenties, long-term traveller and festival attender.

2. Fieldwork, in the form of participant observation, interviews with key informants and documentary research was carried out for this study between 1990 and 1993. A more detailed account can be found in my PhD thesis, 'The Geography of the Other: Lifestyle, Performance and Identity' (1993), Department of Sociology, Lancaster University. This was funded by a research studentship provided by the Economic and Social Research Council (see also Hetherington, 1999).

3. By symbolism, I refer to symbols in the manner in which Turner defines as 'a thing regarded by general consent as naturally typifying or representing or recalling something by possession of analogous qualities or by association in fact or thought.' (1967: 19). It is the association in thought or socially constructed basis of symbols that is important here. Such symbols may not be generally acknowledged within a society, but they are likely to have particular significance to those whose shared identifications and identities derive particular meaning from them.

4. The issue of utopics and what they mean in relation to Utopia is one that I explore in more detail in Chapter 6.

5. Nomadism is also a theme in the wandering philosophy of Deleuze and Guattari, who celebrate the nomad, in the form of nomad thought, for its vitalism and creativity (1988).

6. This is perhaps part of the reason why the Nazis hated, persecuted and exterminated travelling or wandering peoples, notably Jews and gypsies.

6

MARGINAL SPACES AND THE TOPOLOGY OF UTOPIA

Marginality, utopics and identity

Expressive identities and their associated alternative lifestyles and identity politics have always been seen as either utopian or idealistic. Utopia is, however, about more than just ideas about a new type of (perfect) society. It is above all about spatial practice (see Hetherington, 1997a). The geography of what I have described as the expressive identities of identity politics, their structure of feeling and the cultural and political practices in which they are involved, provides an example of a spatial practice that Louis Marin has called utopics (1984; 1992).

Utopics are a type of spatial play whereby a utopian outlook on society and the moral order that it wishes to project, are translated into practice through the attachment of ideas about the good society onto particular places. The particular places in question are those that have a social centrality for the group involved. In the case of the type of groups with which I have been concerned here, this involves the constitution of identities through the occasion of performance around sites which have a social centrality and that social centrality is expressed specifically through a utopics of the margin.

How margins can be seen as socially central was an issue I began to address in the previous chapter in my discussion of liminality, pilgrimage and the identity practices associated with it. Here I want to look more specifically at what is meant by this utopics of the margin, what it entails and its relationship to identity politics. Utopics are not associated only with identity politics. Any group that wishes to make some change to society and seeks to bring about that change will engage in some form of spatially located action. If the spaces themselves become invested with the values of the groups involved, if they come to have a social centrality, then that process can be described as a utopic one (see Hetherington, 1997a). Marin's own analysis of the spatial play associated with utopics can best be seen in his reading of Disneyland (1984) and America (1992). In this chapter, however, I want to look more specifically at the utopics of the margin and the way it informs the identity spaces of expressive identities and the way this, in turn, is informed by the romantic structure of feeling associated with identity politics.

As we have seen in Chapter 5, identity politics has always had an element of making space for oneself, of creating a turf and finding one's place – often on the margins of society (see Thrasher, 1927; Becker, 1946; Shields, 1991a). Finding one's place has sometimes meant going elsewhere into a supposedly free space, a space perceived as more authentic (see E. Cohen, 1973; 1979) or more one's own, where issues of inclusion and exclusion can be determined by establishing categories of belonging and group identifica-tion. At other times, it has meant staying put and trying to change one's situation there, either in the spaces of one's everyday life or by challenging authority at its spaces of social centrality. In either case, certain sites come to be seen differently – they take on a value that is different to the rest of society. In other words, they take on a social centrality that comes to be invested with values that express an alternative to the existing society.

For those who reject the norms and beliefs of society, such places facilitate the ordering of a new identity or identities. In this geography of the elsewhere, margins become centres, centres become margins, and the meaning of centres and margins becomes blurred. Those who see themselves as marginal or different are likely to see such places as socially central to their alternative values and beliefs. The question that remains for this chapter is to work to understand what is meant by a marginal space and how its topology might fit within the constitution of expressive identities.

Cultural geography has been preoccupied with margins for a number of years now. The cultural turn that has influenced the whole of social science from the mid-1980s through the 1990s has also influenced geographical analysis profoundly. That cultural turn in geography and in sociology interested in issues of space followed on from an earlier move to making space central to questions of social theory (see Ley, 1976; Relph, 1976; 1989; Tuan, 1977; Sack, 1980; Thrift, 1983; Giddens, 1984; Massey, 1984; Gregory and Urry, 1985). These two interests in theory and culture really came together at the end of the 1980s and into the 1990s, especially in relation to the question of postmodernism (see Meyrowitz, 1985; Soja, 1989; Harvey, 1989; Shields, 1991a; Zukin, 1992). Throughout, the emphasis in this field has been to see space as socially constructed and to open up the possibility of rejecting one closed view of space, replacing it instead with a multitude of competing spatial representations which make up the imaginary, symbolically constructed, spatial worlds of people and societies. The notion of the 'gaze' in the tourist experience (Urry, 1990), of 'figural signification' (Lash, 1988), 'scopic regimes' (Jay, 1992), or of 'Scapes' (Zukin, 1992), all imply in some way that place should be understood by means of the social construction of different visual perceptions of space by which places are given symbolic meaning (see Berger, 1972). As a result, places are often seen not as something essential to a site but the construct of social spatialisations: imaginary representations of space that give particular spaces their mythical meaning and significance (Shields, 1991a).

In looking at the possibility that places have relational significance, it is useful to recognise the significance of what Schutz once described as multiple realities associated with perception (1967). Schutz was concerned in particular with the subjective construction of reality and its intersubjective basis for understanding in the natural attitude. While his work was mostly concerned with the mundane and routine everyday life of 'performance' in paramount reality (1967: 211), he also left open the possibility for what he described as 'phantasm': intentions to act which remain latent, as in day dreaming, which serve the purpose of creating alternative realities (see also Bachelard, 1969).

We might argue that place, while generally associated in everyday life as something familiar and part of the natural attitude, may also be produced as place at the level of phantasm or, in other words, in the utopic dreams of sections of society for a better world and an identity constituted around that vision of the future. We are dealing here again with strategies and tactics (de Certeau, 1984). The creation of alternative ways of life, sought by those who have become involved in identity politics, are not on the whole utopian in the sense that they establish new fixed and permanent communities; more significantly they are heterotopic in that they use marginal 'other' places as sites of social centrality to create fleeting but transitional identifications out of which new identities emerge (Foucault, 1986a; Lefebvre, 1991).

The importance of margins, alongside these other concerns with social construction and multiple spatial ways of seeing, is also apparent within this 'new' cultural geography; as, indeed, is the social centrality of marginal spaces to marginal groups. Shields's analysis of margins within the social spatialisations of Britain and Canada (1991a), and his work on the social centrality of shopping malls (1989; 1992b), has been influential in establishing the place of the margin – often seen as a liminal place – within cultural geography. In addition, feminist geographers such as Massey (1994) and Rose (1993), and feminist historians such as Walkowitz (1992) and Wilson (1991), have also raised the issue of women's marginal position within the space of the city and society more generally and seen in the idea of the margin (albeit one seen as a more complex or folded 'paradoxical' space in some cases, notably by Rose) a space of women's resistance to patriarchal social relations. Marginal spaces as spaces of difference, spaces for identity politics in particular, have come to be associated with marginal space across a wide ranging literature (see in particular Keith and Pile, 1993; Bell and Valentine, 1995; Pile and Thrift, 1995; Ryan and Fitzpatrick, 1996; Cresswell, 1996; O'Connor and Wynne, 1996a). In particular, this work has tended to draw attention to the particular location of identity politics. The city and its marginal spaces has been a major focus for much of this work, looking at the social spaces, clubs, and networks in which identity politics is to be found. The women's peace camp at Greenham Common during the 1980s has been another favoured site for analysis (see Stallybrass and White, 1986; Young, 1990; Cresswell, 1996). One might also include my own work on New Age travellers and the importance of a site like Stonehenge to their identity politics as contributing to this work (Hetherington, 1991; 1992;

1993; 1996; 1997b; see also Lowe and Shaw, 1993; Earle et al., 1994; Halfacree, 1996; Cresswell, 1996).

While all of this research emphasises the importance of marginal spaces for the constitution of marginal identities, what a margin actually might be remains, however, rather under-theorised in most of this work (the notable exception, perhaps, is Rose, 1993). Invariably margins are taken to be counter-hegemonic spaces at the edges, from which the centre – itself seen as a unified and hegemonic space – is in some way challenged through practices of resistance and transgression. A simple Euclidean view of the geometry of social space underlies this position. Social space is divided up into neat geometric shapes with discernible, culturally established lines between those spaces. While some of these practices might be understood as being about trying to blur those lines, there is little attempt, except in Rose's concept of paradoxical space, to introduce a non-Euclidean topology to the analysis of margins that allows us to see the more complex relationship they have to questions of centrality (1993; on complex topology see also Mol and Law, 1994; Doel, 1996; Hetherington, 1997c).

As anthropological work on liminality would suggest, however, margins do not exist only at the metaphorical edges of society but also as spaces between. Neither are there always clearly defined, unified spaces. The line between two things is also a margin; a site of traffic, like a boundary space, is also a margin. One might also think of marginal spaces as 'hidden' or submerged, like a water mark, within the sites of daily life – a point that Jacob made many years ago in her analysis of the changing character of street life in the city (1961). Margins are, therefore, more complex spaces than may at first appear. If we are to speak of them at all, I argue, we should do so in terms of a complex, folded and crumpled topology rather than the simpler Euclidean one (see Deleuze, 1986; Deleuze and Parnet, 1987; Deleuze and Guattari, 1988). The identity positions of those who adopt an expressive alternative to society are multiple and heteroclite. If we are to say that such identity positions can be mapped onto space, then we should treat that space in kind. Centrality comes together in a space which is socially central but that does not mean it comes together in one space. The pilgrimage to a particular site passes through a number of other sites whose continuity makes up the pilgrimage. Equally, margins are not just single sites that are spaces connected together by a type of marginality that, in turn, can be taken as central. The space of identity politics might best be seen as folded spaces. If we are to see expressive identities as heteroclite and topologically complex and argue that these can be mapped onto space, then we should treat the spaces accordingly in the same manner.

Margins can be perceived as sites of deferral as well as of difference; they do not have thick dark lines around them that make them visible to all. They are, rather, often constituted in practice and in the representations of that practice rather than in the ontology of things. All the same, their deferred character makes them useful in the organisation or ordering of dispersed, composite, fragmented identities. That this is done in spaces which are themselves uncertain in their 'geometry' is, therefore, significant.

The social centrality of these uncertain sites provides a symbolic resource in establishing and maintaining an alternative lifestyle. Sites that have social centrality for those engaged in transgressive and alternativist activities are likely to be seen as marginal. The uncertainty of such places provides a source of new meaning, outside the main forms of knowledge within society. These places are the elsewhere of other meaning or 'elective centres' (E. Cohen et al., 1987) around which the practices and performances that facilitate the production of new identities can occur. The liminoid character of the identities, the rituals associated with group identification, its rites of passage and status reversals all help to establish new identities out of new identifications with the other of one's tribe/Bund. The search for authentic, sacralised, non-instrumental experiences is met by the normative communitas produced under these conditions.

If we are to follow the suggestion of Doel and treat social space as a crumpled geography rather than a Euclidean one (1996), this means that it is not only the relationship between centres and margins that becomes more complex, but also the relationship between those marginal spaces and the identity politics that have been associated with them. If the relationship between centres and margins is a folded one, so too is the relationship between resistance or transgression and the social order it seeks to challenge. Identities, as I suggested in Part I, like the identity politics associated with these expressive identities, are also topologically complex. The term often used is hybrid; we might also say heteroclite or monstrous or anomalous, confused, multiple, dispersed, and fragmented. It is through the relationship between these complex margins and complex identity positions that a semblance of unity, an ordering that we describe as an identity position, is established.

I shall argue further in Chapter 7 that this is established through forms of performance. It is performances of monstrous identities in monstrous spaces that impart a sense of giving order to identities and what they come to stand for. While the whole issue of identity as performance is one that I look at in detail then in the next chapter, I have already begun to explore this issue in Chapter 5 through discussion of the practices of travel, dwelling and social drama. Travel involves the process of removal and the search for a new start in a new place, an elsewhere that has important symbolic connotations. Social dramas are liminoid reversals of the norms of a society which those adopting an alternative lifestyle wish to reject. Dwelling provides a sense of belonging in a new type of ethically and affectually committed lifestyle with others.

We have seen that travel can become a symbolic practice in which the person, seeking new and more authentic experiences, leaves their host society and embarks on a quest for a new way of life and new meanings. Travel, as such a practice, symbolises pilgrimage to some new exotic Other place, freedom, starting again, a break with the past and all that is seen as wrong with or inauthentic in society. The practice of travel is also a quest for new truths symbolised in Other, more exotic places. Out of the liminoid practices comes a desire to live together in a new way. To dwell is to belong, drawing on the past and on memory, but aiming, by example, to change things in the future; to create alternatives to conventional modes of living, and to create new lifestyles and become someone else. Before developing the point about performance, however, I want to establish what I see to be the relationship between the spaces chosen as sites of social centrality, their complex 'marginality' and the identities in question. A lot of this has to do with a structure of feeling but it also has to do with utopics.

To think about Utopia as practice rather than literary writing and imagined future worlds, we can best begin with Marin's seminal deconstruction of the term Utopia and all that it implies for practice. The word Utopia, first used by Thomas More in his book *Utopia* (1985), is a pun which plays on two Latin terms: eu-topia or good place and ou-topia meaning no place. More brought these together to convey the idea of a perfect society represented by an imaginary place – a satirical idea to challenge many of the fantastic writings of travellers to the East which emerged during the Renaissance (see Campbell, 1988). For Marin, pulling the word apart and holding it in tension sets up an unbridgeable space of deferral that reveals the practice that goes into the spatial play associated with both ou-topia and eu-topia (1984; 1992). Utopics, the spatial practice associated with making Utopias, involves attempts to cross this gap to create out of a no-place, a place whose existence appears insignificant, a eu-topia that can serve as a model for a future society (see Hetherington, 1997a). Like some of his contemporaries, such as Derrida, Foucault and Lefebvre, Marin is interested in the difference established in this deconstructive reading and the space it establishes, which he calls the neutral (1984). While Marin's work is perhaps closest to Derrida's deconstructive method (1976), we can also see similarities with Foucault's analysis of forms of representation through similitude and the heterotopia that it establishes (1983; 1986a; 1989b) and with Lefebvre's analysis of representational spaces (1991).[1]

While there are theoretical differences associated with these concepts, what they all have in common is their non-Euclidean topological character. All of these terms might be used as substitutes for the simpler and more problematic 'marginal space'. Elsewhere I have tended to prefer to follow Foucault in the use of his term heterotopia, defining heterotopic spaces as sites of alternate ordering (1996; 1997a). I continue to use that term here and discuss what it means below. However, my main interest here is not with heterotopic sites as such but with the utopics invested in them and the opportunities that they allow for the performance, in conditions of un-certainty and incongruity, of expressive identities.

Margins and alternate orders

Rather than see margin spaces as clearly defined counter-hegemonic sites and marginal identities as defined by practices of resistance and transgression *per se*, established through a Euclidean geometrical relationship with centres, I want to suggest that it is better to see both as being about responses to uncertainty and complexity and the new types of social ordering they generate. While utopian stories have always been about a free society, they have also been associated with ideals of social order. The good place, represented by the nowhere, is one in which freedom, social harmony and order invariably go hand in hand (see Manuel and Manuel, 1979; Kumar, 1987; 1991). Part of my interest in the utopics that underlies this question of how freedom and order might go together, has been to see it as one of the defining characteristics of modern societies (Hetherington, 1997a). The idea of modernity is established around the utopic play across the gap between freedom and control, seeing that gap in spaces associated with the modern polity and economy as heterotopic in character (Hetherington, 1997a). Here, my interest is narrower, not at the level of modernity, but related to the constitution of expressive identities and their identity politics within modern societies. All the same, this is still a utopic practice and one that often occurs in uncertain or incongruous spaces in which opportunities for alternate modes of social ordering such as of identity, might best be achieved.

In the gatherings, festival sites, squats, encampments, protest sites, occupations, cafes, communes, and so on that make up the topography of expressive identities, we see a utopic at work – a utopic of the margin as a space of freedom, resistance, alternative moral order and authenticity (see McKay, 1996; Cresswell, 1996; Hetherington, 1996; 1997a). This utopic is something that expresses what happens at such sites as a model alternative to modern societies or some important part of that society. The space itself, as is often seen by observers, will tend to be one which within that society is seen as somewhat marginal. Cheap, run-down parts of a city that one can make one's own, bits of disused or common land (in England, at least, associated with a radical tradition of protest over land rights for commoners extending back several centuries), sites that have a long association with radical or alternative political practices, sites of wilderness 'unspoilt' by civilisation, sacred pagan sites associated with earth mysteries, sites of medieval fairs, sites of political 'martyrdom', sites that symbolise everything a group might oppose, such as a nuclear reactor, vivisection laboratory, sex shop and so on – these are the likely sites chosen for the occasionalism of protest and/or identity performance.

The women at Greenham Common chose the roadside verge next to a USAF base used to site Cruise missiles to make their protests against nuclear weapons, the threat of war and the patriarchy underlying it all (see Liddington, 1989; Young, 1990; Roseneil, 1995; Cresswell, 1996). New Age travellers chose Stonehenge, an ancient megalith and a site associated with mystery and paganism dating back millennia, for their annual summer solstice free festival between 1975 and 1984 (see Chippindale, 1983; Michell, 1982; Chippindale et al., 1990; Hetherington, 1996). Anti-road protesters in Britain have chosen to set up camps in tree houses and underground tunnels on the actual sites of proposed bypasses or road extensions on greenfield sites, such as those around Winchester and Newbury in the chalk downlands of southern England (see Docherty, 1996; McKay, 1996). Such groups are not only found in Britain. 'New Age Pilgrims' in Australia, for whom Ayers Rock has a social centrality, are another example not dissimilar to the New Age travellers in Britain (see Marcus, 1988). In the context of claims over Aboriginal land rights in Australia, this 'authentic', sacred space has become a contested marginal place in the centre of the margin of Australia, the outback (St. John, 1997). Travelling into the outback in search of new meanings associated with this mysterious site involves a pilgrim-like communitas: 'Those who move out towards the centre, adopt new, more authentically Australian garments (rough clothes – the felt hat, the boots, the tough trousers or ripped shorts, often ex-army gear); a new language of mateship and equality with a distinctive vocabulary and accent, and new attitudes to those whom they encounter' (Marcus, 1988: 262). Mateship – perhaps this is another way of talking about a Bund. These are sites that are either already represented as marginal or become marginal because of their contested character. People make pilgrimages to these sites, social dramas occur there and in some cases they become places where people choose to dwell. They are spaces in which identities are not only performed through cultural and very often overtly political performances, they are also sites at which those identities – and the values and beliefs that lie behind them – are made visible to the rest of the world. They are spaces that, while they are not in any way perfect little island Utopias (despite the best efforts of many involved in setting up alternative, self-sufficient communities), are invested with a utopic, an attempt at turning no-places into good-places, in which the margin becomes central to the development of alternatives that can be seen as a challenge to the ways of society.

The utopic is a spatial practice in which ideas about a better society – defined as 'better' within a structure of feeling – are made visible through the spatial practice associated with the identity performances that occur there. These may be places on the edge of things, forgotten sites where one can go and live an alternative life away from the society one no longer wants to be a part of, but they can also be spaces right at the centre of things, spaces in which the State or big business may express their own utopic and may choose to surround them with barbed wire, and police with dogs and tear gas. They may also be insignificant, everyday sites that are only made visible by what unusual goings on may be seen to occur there. In other words, they may be margins at the edge, margins at the centre, or transparent margins that are normally hidden from view. These are all ways in which we might define a margin. They are spaces that come to be marginal because of the difference and uncertainty that comes to surround them. That difference and uncertainty may be well established, over decades or centuries, or it may be newly inaugurated by a particular event that has just happened. There is no ontology of the margin. Marginality is constituted in practice and through how those practices come to be represented rather than given in the order of things.

As margin is generally conceived in a Euclidean sense, it is a problematic term and it would be useful to find an alternative. I have already discussed Lefebvre's concept of representational space in Chapter 2 (Lefebvre, 1991); Foucault has also provided us with one of the most interesting analyses of such spaces through his concept of heterotopia (1986a). It is on Foucault's term that I want to concentrate here. Representational spaces, as Lefebvre describes them, may well be useful in helping us to analyse the spatiality of resistance; however, for Foucault, while heterotopia may well be about acts of resistance and transgression, they are also about issues of ordering and control — something that is largely lacking in Lefebvre's analysis. As Foucault recognised, freedom and order cannot be completely separated out: they are folded into one another (1982; 1986a).

Meaning literally 'other places', heterotopia are sites established through incongruous spatial relations that challenge the spaces of representation and their mode of representation within society. I have argued in detail else-where that heterotopia be defined as sites of alternate order constituted through their incongruous character and its relationship to other less incon-gruous sites (Hetherington, 1997a). Heterotopia has been used in a variety of different contexts in recent years with varying degrees of clarity (see Teyssot, 1980; Connor, 1989; Soja, 1990; 1996; Delaney, 1992; Chambers, 1994; Lyon, 1994; Bennett, 1995; Genocchio, 1995; Hetherington, 1996; 1997a). The idea for the term originally comes from the study of anatomy where it has a specific medical usage. In particular, it is used to refer to parts of the body that are where they should not be: out of place organs, missing pieces, extra fingers or toes, or, like tumours, alien to the body as a whole.[2] For Foucault, such places of otherness can be seen in two forms: non-discursive literary sites, associated with incongruous grammar and dis-cursive statements; and actual sites of contrast whose existence sets up unsettling juxtapositions of incommensurate 'objects' that challenge the way we represent and especially the way our representations are ordered (1986a; 1989b). Heterotopia are constituted through the way they unsettle estab-lished modes of representing and ordering rather than because of any intrinsic otherness within a site itself.

The key, for Foucault, in understanding such sites has to do with the issue of representation. Heterotopia are established through the juxtaposition of things not usually found together and the confusion that the resulting representations creates. Heterotopia signify through similitude, through a series of deferrals that are established between a signifier and a signified rather than with direct reference to a referent (Foucault, 1983; 1989b). Representation through similitude represents without any depth or relation to a referent, it involves a semiotic glide across the surface, a surface constituted by mobile signifiers and signifieds. Heterotopia, for Foucault, are sites that bring together heterogeneous collections of unusual things (or words), without allowing them to settle into a definite unity of meaning through direct resemblance to some anterior reality. Their meaning is derived from a process of similitude which produces, in an almost magical way, monstrous anomalies that unsettle the flow of discourse rather than produce a static order (1989a: xvii).

Such a spatialised process can be seen to facilitate acts of resistance and transgression in that they generate spaces where there is no clearly defined order of how things should occur; they are like battle sites, full of smoke and confusion. They do not remain in a condition of disorder, however, but allow new modes of ordering to emerge. Similitude, very like the more familiar term bricolage, is about an assembly of the incongruous, but, as Levi-Strauss pointed out, such incongruity is usually given some ordering into an homology (1966). For Foucault, therefore, heterotopia also act as spaces for the means of alternative ordering. That ordering is established through the way that such sites come to be seen in contrast to others. As Foucault suggests:

> Either their [heterotopia's] role is to create a space of illusion that exposes every real space, all the sites inside of which human life is partitioned, as still more illusory . . . Or else, on the contrary, their role is to create a space that is other, another real space, as perfect, as meticulous, as well arranged as ours is messy, ill constructed, and jumbled. (1986a: 27)

Heterotopia are not easily located within a system of representation but neither do they exist in the realist sense of existence. Heterotopia do not exist in the order of things, rather they are constituted through the very ordering of things that they help create. Heterotopia are sites in which all things displaced, marginal, rejected or ambivalent are represented and this representation becomes the basis of an alternate mode of ordering that has the effect of offering a contrast to the dominant representations of social order.

There is nothing intrinsic about a particular space that might lead us to call it a heterotopia, rather heterotopic relations are produced in the relationship between sites that come to stand for different forms of social ordering and representation. A sense of Otherness comes to hang over a site once it begins to be used in such a way. How it comes to be used may vary: it may have to do with tradition, a site having always having had a degree of uncertainty or mystery associated with it; it may have to do with its aesthetic appeal or lack of it; it may have to do with the use to which it is put by a particular group to which others may be opposed. What a space represents has to do with social and cultural practices and the representations those practices generate (see Lefebvre, 1991; Shields, 1992b). It is these practices that I would follow Marin in describing as utopic.

Utopics and identity

The utopics of the margin, and the ordering effects they establish, are made up within the practices and performances found within heterotopic spaces.

While Marin starts from a deconstructive reading of More's *Utopia* focusing on the play of difference between the ou/eu-topia that More introduced within this signifier, his key concept is 'the neutral', the gap that develops out of this tension or deferral of meaning within the term Utopia. For Marin, utopian discourse emerged at a time of social conjunction between feudalism and capitalism, from the end of the fifteenth century in Europe. This utopian discourse is, for Marin, a discourse that derives its significance from the practices of a spatial play over this no-place/good-place ambivalence. It is, for Marin, through utopics that the significance of this deferred 'gap' is revealed. The desire for another world, a Utopia of the good life, the eu-topia, is to argue against its lack in the present. Utopia is about challenging the order of society through a new imaginary picture of future conditions of possibility. But this other place only exists as a ou-topia, an imaginary no-place, that is not to be found anywhere except in a form of social critique. Utopics are the spatial practices that emerge from the vacillation between the no and the good in a neutral realm of pure différance. The neutral is what lies between these two poles of More's pun. It is neither 'the good' nor 'the no' place. The neutral for Marin is both an 'Other place' in that it represents an alternative to society and the 'Other of Place' in that it is not attached to any specific locality or site (1984: 13). He sees this neutral space as an impossible space, a realm of différance as Derrida would, no doubt, have expressed it (1976). It involves an endless deferral of meaning that derives from the unresolvable tension contained within this linking together of the terms eu/outopia. What should hopefully be apparent is that Marin's 'neutral' has much in common with Foucault's 'heterotopia', such that the two terms might be seen as interchangeable. In both cases we are dealing with the issue of order and its conditions of possibility (see Foucault, 1989a: xxii). Such spatial configurations lie outside the known conditions of possibility within a society. Furthermore, they might be said to challenge the very possibility of a condition of order.

For Marin, the character of Utopia reveals social conjunction as an example of the neutral:

> As [Utopia's] organizing principle [social conjunction] is the centre of the structure and the rule for its coherence. It allows for the elements inside the whole system to be substituted. This term designates the process at the very same time it comes into being between the contraries. It ontologizes this duration in the synchrony of an opposition it henceforth masters and orders. The neutral will constitute the *principle* of the conjunction of contraries, it will join them in their very opposition, tying them together and dominating them, it is the very contrariety of contraries. It allows each of them to be contraries and at the same time escapes from the relation that founds them. (1984: 15)

The conditions of possibility for order come to be altered within the utopic practices associated with this neutral or heterotopic space. The agency associated with such an uncertain space is one that is unknown or under-determined. It attains something of the character of a blank figure (see

Serres, 1991). That blankness, that underdetermined state – something that we can associate with both space and the identity associated with it – has the power to shift the terrain of the conditions of possibility for social order, if not for ever then at least for a moment. The realm of the neutral stands outside as something separate but also as a transition. The neutral stands apart, it constitutes sites of difference within a process, a neutralisation, and from this emerges a new social ordering; a new form of sameness, what in this case might be called identity. Blank elements are always figures of both change and order (see Hetherington and Lee, 1998). The process of utopics is what lies behind the spatial practices associated with, in this case, alternative, expressive identities. The practices of identity politics, their desire for both social change and collective identifications as the basis of their expressive identities, creates a neutral or heterotopic space that establishes a mode of ordering out of the incongruous conditions in which these identities are performed. Unlike the idea of liminal space, these terms are freed from the functionalism and focus on structure found within Turner's analysis of liminality. They are much more to do with the uncertainties of process and the way it performs order than with social reproduction in which the model for order is already established. I would argue that spatial relations involve play between utopic practice and hetero-topic or neutral space. This is also a contested space, a space with many actors who all wish to project their ideas about society, their utopics, through that space.

Utopics are associated, therefore, with the translation of ideas about a good society into spatial practice, and can be described as a cultural performance of moral orderings through spatial practice. Utopics are an important aspect of the way of life of many of those engaged in the creation of expressive identities. Like the 'ethics of aesthetics' formed within a structure of feeling, they also contribute to the occasionalism of identity politics in which identities are performed.

The cultural and political performance of identity takes place in a hiatus, in this gap that Marin calls the neutral that emerges from the conditions of undecidability that lie behind representations of space. This is the space in which representations of the good society and its moral order are articulated and contested. Utopias do not exist in themselves as the end product of those practices, even though that may well be the desired goal of many of those involved. What exist are the translations of ideas about the good life and about social and moral order into social reality, and that reality takes on a distinctly spatial character as it comes to be represented in particular heterotopic spaces (see Hetherington, 1997a). As we have seen, certain sites have had, in Shields's terms, a social centrality, a focal identity as if they were shrines (Shields, 1992a; see also Hetherington, 1996). It is around these sites of social centrality, and through the processes and spaces leading up to them, that this utopics is expressed. It is through this utopics that the values of a group are expressed in spatial terms.

Utopics and the structure of feeling

The expressive utopic is one that often looks to the past for its authenticity but selectively, often focusing on, and identifying with, the marginal and oppressed – the peasant, the vagrant, the circus, gypsies, native Americans – and their ways of life. It is shaped by a distinctly romantic outlook and aesthetic which places above all else a sense of the marginal at the centre of this notion of the authentic. The character of the utopic, the spatial practice that comes to take on the values of the identifications of the groups who are seeking to establish some kind of alternative, is one that is constituted within a structure of feeling. A number of the key features of that structure of feeling are likely to be associated with the utopic and the sites through which they come to be expressed, in particular: freedom, authenticity, rejected knowledge and the occasion for the performance of identity.

There will, of course, be a good deal of variety across the array of different groups with their different tribal identifications and identities, and this difference will be reflected in the utopics of the particular groups and their favoured sites of social centrality. The first distinction might be an urban/rural one. There are few, however, who would argue that the urban can be more closely associated with authenticity than the rural. Those who may favour an urban setting might be the less politicised but still opposi-tional youth subcultures that overlap at the fringes of other forms of identity politics. It is also the case that there are many sites associated with iden-tity politics to be found in towns and cities: clubs, bookshops, refuges, vegetarian cafes and restaurants, wholefood shops and co-operatives as well as certain parts of university and college campuses. The social centrality of these sites may well spring from contingent economic factors. Some areas of the city will have lower rents than others, attracting people to live and set up either political or business ventures; student accommodation areas around universities are often a common site for such activities. The utopic here is one very much submerged within everyday life. While the idea of a turf is one better suited to gangs and youth cultures, something of having control over one's own space, having the freedom visibly to live an alternative lifestyle given by the relative tolerance to be found in a local community (often of students and young people), the opportunities for networks of activists and supporters to flourish, as well as the low rents available, are all reasons why such spaces might have a social centrality.

At a more overtly political level, squatting has for many years provided an opportunity for alternative urban communities to flourish. In cities like Amsterdam and Berlin, in particular, large scale squatting of whole districts and the establishment of anarchist communities has been a common feature and one that has often led to conflict with state authorities and police. In urban areas, therefore, it is particularly the ideas of freedom and visibility that influence the location of identity politics. If the idea of authenticity is involved at all, then it is most likely that this will be associated with the types of community or communal living arrangements rather than with particular spaces.

Ideas of authenticity and rejected knowledge are more likely to be associated with the establishment of alternatives and identity politics in rural areas. As such, there is likely to be a strong environmentalist slant to these ideas of authenticity. There are some rural communities, Earth First! style environmentalist groups, and some New Age travellers in Britain, North America and Australia who adopt a deep green attitude of living lightly on the land, and see nature as a being (Gaia) from whom we are drawn and for whom we must care. The bus, Tipi or makeshift 'bender' is perhaps the favoured dwelling of such people. For others, notably in Britain where increasingly strong laws against trespass are enforced, the old Digger idea dating from the Civil War of common land for the people is more apparent and has at times influenced the idea of a land squat. In this sense, as with those who advocate rights of access and common land, the countryside is seen as belonging to everyone. Many people who see the rural as more authentic may also identify with nature religions and earth mysteries.

Through these forms of rejected knowledge the rural comes to be seen as a sacred and mysterious place, focused in ancient sacred sites and best understood through forms of rejected pagan spiritual knowledge (Michell, 1982; 1986; Devereaux, 1990). Earth mysteries generally refers to the study of ancient sites from a standpoint which is, at the outset, critical of modern science (see Michell, 1982; 1986; Devereaux, 1990). Earth mysteries practitioners adopt a more holistic approach which refers back to ancient folk ways of understanding and trying to interpret the landscape: dowsing, ley line hunting, and recovering folklore and custom associated with particular sites. The earth mysteries tradition challenges the modes of understanding offered by modern science and seeks to find in the landscape forgotten practices of knowing and understanding both the natural and the social. In its analysis of ancient landmarks and pathways, the tradition treats ancient societies as technically accomplished and as having acquired knowledge about nature that has been lost to us or rejected and marginalised by modern science.

In countries like the USA, Canada and Australia where there are still large areas of 'wilderness', the social centrality of rural sites is often associated with protecting that wilderness against agri-business, logging and mineral extraction. In a country like Britain, where there is little land that is not either inhabited or farmed, this may translate into protecting areas of natural beauty or with a varied habitat, or it may simply mean dwelling in remote upland areas in Cornwall, Wales and Scotland, as far away from urban life as it is possible to get on a small island.

The contrast between urban and rural is also, therefore, often significant. While it is true that a utopics of rural authenticity plays a significant part in shaping the identity of many like New Age travellers and commune dwellers (see Pepper, 1991), this is not a picturesque authenticity but an authenticity grounded in an identification with small-scale communal solidarity, often expressed through the idea of tribes or through an identification with nomadism, which is seen to be more authentic than the sociality of modern industrial societies. The countryside is not, therefore, seen as a rural Arcadia expressed through images of pastoral peace. Rather it is a place of mystery in which the sacred is reinvested into the landscape through a syncretist paganism and holism. The theme of travel as a quest for meaning, community and self-discovery takes place in that landscape (see Eliade, 1969; Turner, 1973).

While many who seek to establish alternative and expressive identities may share with tourists as well as with those who live in the countryside what Urry has described as a romantic gaze (1995), which emphasises the authentic as a source of moral order and which is the basis of an idea of home, their senses of what constitutes authenticity are quite different. For the alternativists the authenticity of the rural lies not in the picturesque and the pastoral – as it does for most country dwellers and tourists – but in an authenticity of nature as something mysterious and spiritual, and that of society as something expressive and communitarian that exists in harmony with this view of nature.

Identity politics is a distinctly spatial politics. It is one where ideas of freedom, nomadism, tribalism, and harmony with nature and with other people are expressed through a utopics in which this outlook on society is translated into spatial practice. That spatial practice may often come into conflict with the spatial practice of others: locals, farmers, landowners, local authorities, police, and guardians of the countryside like The National Trust and English Heritage. This contest may produce the countryside as a contested space. That contest – while it may be manifested in issues of trespass, rights of access, land use, rights of assembly, respect for property, and so on – is principally a contest of representation. The politics that many of these alternative and environmental groups engage in with their opponents is a politics of representation where one utopic comes up against another. Many engaged in identity politics have come into existence and developed in the space constituted by this politics of representation, they exist in a hiatus between the no and the good, in an ambivalent space in which contested representations of rural authenticity exist.

Marginality and performance

Marginality, therefore, is not something that exists within a site, it is constituted in the representation of that site in practice. Invariably within the literature on identity politics, this issue of spatial representation has come to be associated with acts that are seen as either forms of overt political resistance or acts of transgression (see Stallybrass and White, 1986; Shields, 1991b; Young, 1990; Cresswell, 1996). Clearly, the two cannot really be separated. While the latter may be less direct in its form of opposition, more playful and carnivalesque in character, this too can come to be seen by both protagonists and opponents as a form of political resistance. The relationship between resistance and transgression is not at issue. What is at issue is the idea that these acts are always forms of opposition to social order. Identities, however, are forms of ordering. Those orderings may not be stable or fixed but they are still ways of making sense of who one sees oneself to be and how one relates to others, both within a shared identification and with those outside.

The utopics associated with heterotopic space are not only about resisting, transgressing and making visible an alternative, they are also about ordering identities within conditions of uncertainty. Heterotopia, as I define them, are spaces of alternate ordering. This does not mean we have to assume a functionalism that suggests that acts of transgression and resistance will always end up reproducing the social order as Turner assumes it will in his analysis of liminal rites. Heterotopia address the conditions of possibility for orders both old and new, real and imaginary. That is why we can associate them particularly with the idea of utopia and the spatial practices through which it is expressed. It does, however, mean we should recognise the process associated with acts of resistance or transgression, which does not mean we fall into the other trap of assuming these acts to be ones defined by a pure voluntarism, freed from any structuring conditions. Utopics are about spatial practices, associated with uncertain, heterotopic sites, that come to have a social centrality for a particular group of people. They are about trying to put into practice ideas about a better society which at the same time allows for the development of a new, expressive identity. This is clearly both a political as well as a cultural act. It is not an act that can be separated from acts of resistance or transgression; neither, however, can it be separated from the issue of ordering. I specifically use the word ordering rather than order because as a verb it implies action and process rather than a static state (see also Law, 1994).

Conclusion

In this chapter I have suggested that the ideas of social centrality and marginal space should be seen together. Certain marginal, or heterotopic sites, come to take on a social centrality within the spatial politics of the expressive alternative groups and identifications associated with the New Age, new social movements, youth subcultures and so on. The development of such sites is expressed through a utopic, a spatial practice that seeks to make use of the marginality of certain sites to articulate ideas about alternative futures for society. Identities are performed in these spaces, symbolised through practices such as pilgrimage, dwelling and more political forms of social drama. These performances, I shall go on to add in Chapter 7, are the subjectivised occasions for the constitution of identity as well as the expression of a utopic. As such, issues of identity and politics are inseparable in this domain.

It is to the issue of performance that I now want to turn. Throughout this book, I have sought to show the different ways in which we should consider the idea of identity, focusing on the alternative and expressive identities once associated with the term counter-culture. In Part I this involved discussion of what the term identity means, its relationship to issues of identification and tribalism, a shared structure of feeling and the Bund-like emotional communities found among many such alternative groupings. In Part II, I have so far looked in more detail at the spatiality and spatial politics surrounding these issues of identity. In the final chapter I want to add one further, yet equally important aspect of this process of identity formation – its performative character. I shall argue, in particular, by making use of Schechner's concept of restored behaviour (1985), that the occasion-alism of performances such as pilgrimage, dwelling and social drama, can be seen as a way of recognising the way that identity and politics are intertwined as identity politics. To go to the margins and live a different life is a political act, just as acting up or protesting in a visible way is a means of establishing and articulating a distinct identity.

Notes

1. I have discussed the concepts of utopics and heterotopia in detail in my book *The Badlands of Modernity* (1997a). Chapter 2 of that book also involves a detailed discussion of the ideas of marginality and liminal space found in much of the contemporary cultural geography that I also refer to here.

2. *Oxford English Dictionary*, Vol. VII (Second Edition) (1989). Prepared by J. Simpson and E. Weiner, p. 191. Oxford: Clarendon Press.

7

SPACES FOR THE OCCASION: EMBODIMENT AND THE PERFORMANCE OF IDENTITY

Identity, performance and the body

In Chapter 6, I looked at marginal places and the utopics that are attached to them by groups who construct margins as their spaces. I have argued that such spaces have a social centrality associated with an outlook that is informed by a romantic structure of feeling. It is around these ideas of social centrality and utopics, therefore, that issues and practices of space can be seen to be important for the development of identity and its associated politics and lifestyles. I have looked at how spaces come to symbolise alternative ways of life and how the spatial practices associated with those symbols become a resource for challenging a range of issues and practices within society. It should be clear that these margins, better described as heterotopia (Foucault, 1986a; 1989a), because of their complex topological character have, therefore, an important role in the process of identity formation among alternative and expressive groupings of neo-tribalists. So far, then, I have looked at how certain types of spaces become adopted in terms of their social centrality and have indicated something of the character of the spaces that are likely to be chosen. In this chapter I want to bring together these issues of space and identity and see what happens during particular occasions that are often associated with particular sites. I do this by analysing the spatiality of identity in terms of performance and the ways in which identity is expressed through ongoing performative repertoires. An important dimension of this question of performance is the significance that the body assumes within the occasionalism of identity creation. I look at questions of embodiment in terms of ideas about carnivalesque.

In this chapter, therefore, I discuss the practices through which alternative and expressive identities are enacted and embodied, and the importance that such a performance perspective gives us on the issue of identity. I analyse, in particular, the practices associated with identity politics in terms of performances that are situated in spaces that actually matter to the performance. Heterotopic spaces act as a symbolic *mise-en-scène* for the production of identity through the affectual, tribal and embodied identification with others as well as through contests with opponents. I intend to explain these issues by drawing on a number of key ideas from theatre studies which have shown the significance that the theatrical space has in facilitating and framing transgressive performances, social dramas and rites of passage associated with the production and ordering of dispersed and fragmented identities. The importance of the theatrical work, starting with the seminal ideas of Artaud on the theatre of cruelty (1977) and following with the work of Richard Schechner (1985), it offers a broader understanding of the relevance of social space to the ongoing production of identities through performances that are often politically charged and extend beyond a single and distinct performance on a 'stage'.

In the course of this analysis, I shall show how heterotopic space and the activities that it frames can be seen as a political manifestation associated with performances that are affectual, transgressive, excessive and associated with what has become known as the carnivalesque (Bakhtin, 1984; see also Leach, 1961; Huizinga, 1970; Martin, 1981; Stallybrass and White, 1986; and Fiske, 1989, Featherstone, 1991b). These issues – heterotopia, the carnivalesque, performance, and the body – are all manifestations of the occasionalism of identity politics and its romantic structure of feeling. Through events associated with particular spaces, political protests, alternative ways of living and the processes of identity formation, come to be intertwined, situated and embodied.

While I have taken the concept of the occasion from Schmitt (1986; 1988), these perspectives will not be brought together through the dubious use that he makes of this term in his elitist and decisionist political stance but by looking at the work of the theatre director and theorist, Schechner, who draws upon both Turner and Artaud in his analysis of restored behaviour (1985). I use his work to summarise what I take to be the character of identity performance, drawing on this notion of restored behaviour, which not only shows how such performances are recognisable to others who share a particular identification, but how they produce distinct identity positions through their performances in a 'theatrical space'. The uncertainty surrounding such performances and the uncertainty of the spaces in which they occur have a symbolic importance in performing new or alternative orderings of identity positions. In particular, such performances articulate a monstrous 'heteroclite' identity which comes to be defined by its hybrid, uncertain and multiple forms. The character of the performances involved has already been indicated in Chapter 5, where I singled out travel, dwelling and social dramas as being the types of performative practice most associated with expressive identities and their romantic structure of feeling. Here these performances, often associated with forms of resistance or transgression, or with what Bakhtin and others have described as the carnivalesque (1984), can be seen as forms of restored behaviour.

Much has been made of Bakhtin's study of the carnivalesque in recent cultural studies, notably in relation to themes concerning the playful, ironic and transgressive nature of contemporary 'postmodern' cultural change. (see Fiske, 1989: 67–102; Featherstone, 1991b: 79–83; Stallybrass and White, 1986 and Shields, 1989; 1991a; Cresswell, 1996). Despite Bahktin's over-celebratory association of the ideas of freedom from and transgression of the social order found in the practices of carnival, and his lack of attention to its mode of ordering (see Stallybrass and White, 1986), his study still brings something to our understanding of the performance of alternative and expressive identities. Not least are the importance of the body and its display within those performances; the relationship between the space and the performance; and the highly theatrical character of the types of protest associated with traditional carnival. It is not the momentary overthrow of authority that we should see as the most important aspect of carnivalesque cultural forms but rather the free flow of symbols and identity positions, uses of the body, and the repertoire of acts and their development into an ordering of identities.

Above all, it is through the idea of performance that we can see the old separation which characterises the study of new social movements, polarised into those interested in the politics and its effectiveness and those interested in the identity and its denotative significance, can be avoided. I say avoided rather than resolved. My intention throughout this book has been to try and avoid resolving tensions in the main bodies of literature that I have drawn upon. Performance gives us an alternative perspective – one among many, as this book has tried to indicate throughout the various chapters – that sees both identity and political action as manifestations of the occasionalism of action. Repertoires of action and identity formation are inseparable parts of the expressive performance that goes into the making of forms of identity politics.

The occasionalism of identity politics

The context for the idea of occasionalism is one that does not begin with the 1960s counter-culture but with the 'counter-culture' of the bourgeoisie in Europe during the seventeenth and eighteenth centuries. For Schmitt, analysis of the ways in which the bourgeoisie laid claim to political authority through an elevation of the moral over the political, and the elect character it assumed for itself in doing so, led to his discussion of political romanticism and his concept of subjectivised occasionalism (1986; see also Koselleck, 1988). This set of ideas can be applied to both the bourgeoisie during that time and the contemporary identity politics of today. In the public spaces of the Enlightenment, the bourgeoisie created a performative mode that allowed it to express its identity through political action. The groups involved today may be different from then, and the forms that both the identities and the politics take certainly are; however, there are still a number of similarities that suggest that the idea of subjectivised occasionalism is an appropriate term to use when talking about contemporary forms of expressivism.

The bourgeoisie, excluded from political office in the absolutist regimes of seventeenth-century European societies, asserted its identity through the development of a public sphere located in the coffee-houses, salons and masonic lodges in the town as opposed to the court (see also Sennett, 1986; Koselleck, 1988; Habermas, 1989; Hetherington, 1997a). Through these public spaces, members of the bourgeoisie began to see themselves as a moral elect above the political intrigue and manipulation which was to be found within court society. They believed that only they were fit to govern, and sought to change society on the basis of a view that their position was one of moral election above intrigue and courtly interests. Through this sense of elect self-perception, this class developed a view of their identity as one that was untainted, morally correct, and the basis for trust in one another. They assumed their identity was a sovereign identity. For Schmitt, like Weber (1985), that sense of sovereignty came from the sense of individual freedom which this class had been able to develop in the private sphere of the household, and over the mercantile and industrial economies of these nascent capitalist societies. In that private sphere, a sense of self, something which had to be reflexively cultivated as morally elect, was constituted. This cultivation of self, something that had been limited to the patriarchal private sphere (and it should be clear that this idea of sovereign identity was extended only to men and not to women), could only be developed in the public sphere of civil society and not in that of the State – from the power of which this class was often excluded.

While we might take issue with this public/private split and the development of the idea of the modern individual (see Hetherington, 1997a), it is also clear that the public sphere of the last thirty years of the twentieth century has witnessed the emergence of groups, known by convention as counter-cultures and new social movements, which have sought to effect changes upon society of a political kind through their own sense of moral election. These 'new social movements' too – feminists, environmentalists, pacifists – have often been excluded from having influence either through parliamentary democracy or a legal system which has not recognised their claims; similarly the media has often ignored their message. As a result they have often had to resort to other and more direct means outside of legally sanctioned political participation to get their message across. They have often done so with the sense of themselves as a moral elect. As an elect group, and we have seen how expressive organisational forms like the Bund facilitate this sense of election, they have sought not only to address narrow institutional issues but have linked those issues with questions of identity and expression. For these groups, the personal has indeed been as political as the political acts they have become associated with through various forms of protest.

Their desire to change society has emerged around ideas of changing how one sees one's self through issues of identity. Engaging in such politics often begins, as I highlighted in Part I, with the development of a morally elect position, articulated through a structure of feeling, facilitated by emotional communities (Bund), and expressed in utopic forms of changing society through limited and highly symbolic action. This subjectivised occasionalism and its organisation around a romantic idea of the development of a moral self is, therefore, one that is as characteristic of the identity politics of the late-twentieth century as it was of the late eighteenth.

To engage in protests against society – whether against forms of discrimination and victimisation, environmental degradation, exploitation of animals; defence of the rights of minorities; opposition to nuclear missiles or reactors; proactive attempts to establish alternative communities or ways of life which are seen by many as deviant – is also to engage in an occasionalism in which the development of one's identity is articulated through that protest. The highly symbolic character of many 'new social movement' protests, their emphasis on making government and business practices visible, symbolic confrontation with symbolic targets, emphasis on non-violent forms of protest, adoption of anti-hierarchical forms of organisation, desire for media coverage through which to convey their message to the masses so that they too may become educated, and so on, all highlight the ways in which those involved see themselves as the progressive members of their society: its moral elect, able to speak on society's behalf.

We have seen that some view these new social movements as generators of new knowledge (Melucci, 1989; Eyerman and Jamison, 1991), yet, as I have argued, the emphasis on the expressive and the affectual as well as value-rational forms of action against the instrumental rationality that characterises many of the conditions of modern societies is one that often leads into a romantic critique of modernity that draws on forgotten or rejected forms of knowledge to challenge the current values of society. These groupings see themselves, therefore, not as an elite in the political sense, but as a moral elect who challenge the instrumental, means–ends approaches of contemporary capitalist societies with their value-rational and expressive outlook on everyday life.

One particular example in which this occasionalism can be illustrated is through the emphasis that is often placed on the idea of direct action, especially non-violent direct action (NVDA). Often associated with pacifist forms of political protest and during the twentieth century with the teachings of Ghandi, NVDA involves direct, yet non-violent, confrontations with authority in order to try and stop something from happening, to highlight a practice that is seen as wrong, or to challenge that authority at a moral level through symbolic forms of protest. There are a multitude of different examples that show NVDA to be the preferred form of protest associated with the identity politics of the new social movements: the campus sit-ins of the 1960s; the mass protests in Europe against nuclear weapons and the escalation of the arms race in the early 1980s; the peace camps outside the nuclear missile bases in Britain at Greenham, Faslane and Molesworth; hunt saboteurs disrupting fox hunting; and camps set up to protest against logging, mineral extraction and road building. In all of these cases, as no doubt with others, being involved, making one's opposition visible, risking arrest or assault, attempting to get media coverage for one's non-violent actions, all involve those who are active setting themselves up as a moral elect who can do so by their unwillingness to lose sight of their moral principles while engaging in protest.

Therefore, such protests are not only occasions where particular governmental or business practices can be challenged through both actual disruption and symbolic challenge, but also occasions for strengthening one's sense of moral rightness and one's identity around that position. Success is not measured solely by whether a particular activity such as logging or road building is halted, but by the sense of achievement a person might get in terms of coverage, in terms of building and strengthening networks of protestors, and especially in terms of affirming who one identifies with as well as expressing one's identity in the process. A protest may or may not succeed in instrumental political terms, but it is not measured solely in that way by activists and their supporters; it is also measured in moral and symbolic terms as well – and here the criteria for success will not necessarily be instrumental measures of success. Alternative criteria include a sense of group belonging, communitas and solidarity, personal achievement through being involved, converting sceptics to a cause, and highlighting the alternative values expressed by a group, of which the direct action is just one part, to a wider public. In the occasion, therefore, political action and the performance of identity are inextricably intertwined. The symbolism and the performance are what holds the two together. The political actions as well as the alternative ways of living with which they tend to be associated, which often may in themselves become acts of protest if and when the State seeks to clamp down on them, are occasions in which identities are performed. The issue, therefore, is how we might analyse the character and significance of that performance in relation to the question of identity formation.

Order, disorder and the carnivalesque

We have seen from many of the recent analyses of these types of protest within cultural geography that the issues of resistance and transgression are often seen as paramount to the study of identity politics (see Stallybrass and White, 1986; Young, 1990; Shields, 1991a; Rose, 1993; Bell and Valentine, 1995; Cresswell, 1996; O'Connor and Wynne, 1996a). In making this particular claim, this work often draws upon the anthropological concept of liminality. Another related analysis, one that Turner himself uses in his outline of liminality, is Bakhtin's seminal discussion of Rabelais's account of the medieval carnival and the so-called carnivalesque in his novel *Gargantua and Pantagruel* (see Bakhtin, 1984). It is the transgressive practices and the disorder said to be entailed in these that have come to be associated with identity politics. In particular, the festival character and the open challenge it makes to the varied conventions of social order and authority, has been seen to have relevance to the type of protests associated with many forms of contemporary identity politics and its occasionalist mode of ordering.

Bakhtin's work on the carnivalesque looks at medieval popular culture and the influence it had on Rabelais. Bakhtin considers the way that carnival behaviour – in particular discussing the role of laughter, the mocking of civil and ecclesiastical authority, and the importance it places on the grotesque, secreting, sensual and desiring 'unfinished' body – inverts the cultural norms of the society, mocking social order through the carnival forms: what he calls the carnivalesque (1984). This carnivalesque culture, often associated with the market and the fair, involves a highly theatrical spectacle in which people assume monstrous or exaggerated personae, notably through the wearing of masks, 'excessive' costume and through wasteful acts of consumption, associated with food, drink and in some cases other kinds of drugs. Through these carnival-like performances people behave in an excessive way in which the order of social conventions is turned on its head. Through this type of performance, carnival is said to provide a release from the routines of daily life and the constraints it places on individuals. Through being different in a carnivalesque way, through its tactics of disorder and transgression, a new identity position can be adopted – one that assumes the status of an alternative to the identity positions constituted within the routines of daily life.

The issue within this carnivalesque that has most interested recent cultural studies has been the emphasis that Bakhtin places on its theatrical acts of transgression against the moral and social order, and normative forms of behaviour and the identities associated with it. This transgression takes place, as Stallybrass and White have also suggested, through a process of symbolically inverting the meanings associated with the established binary codes that make up a culture (1986). In particular they stress the importance in carnival of the inversion of the classical/grotesque duality, where normally all that is classical dominates over the other category of the grotesque (1986: 18, see also Steig, 1970; Thompson, 1972; Greenblatt, 1982). The grotesque is celebrated at the expense of the classical in carnivalesque performance. In so doing, this grotesque as a cultural form can take on the character of a tactic of resistance in which boundaries between the orderly and disorderly become blurred or confused. Through acts of transgressive wastefulness, eroticism, drug-induced states, foul language and the rejection of taboos, especially those associated with bodily wastes, the boundaries of social order are crossed and a challenge to the idea of order is made. While the boundaries of social space are redrawn by the carnival form and are important to this process, it is the boundary of the body – that of the inside/outside – which is most visibly transgressed. The grotesque body becomes a site or place of heterogeneity, waste and excess; it becomes what might be called a monstrous body that celebrates the orifices, the lower bodily strata rather than the head and all that is 'classical'. With this body, the symbolism of the high and the low are reversed; dirt, gluttony and waste are celebrated and through that the visibility of the boundaries of the body becomes blurred. The body comes to express matter out of place, it becomes a site for the celebration of the out of place and of dirt (see Douglas, 1984). This grotesque body, as Stallybrass and White suggest, becomes a space of 'mythopoetic transgression' (1986: 24).

It is important to note also that the performance of such a body through the grotesque forms of carnival is well suited to the utopic of the margin, and to spaces whose incongruous character makes them a suitable *mise-en-scène* for the transgressive acts associated with the carnivalesque. There is an association, therefore, between such performances and the spaces of ambivalence within which they occur. The carnivalesque as a performative mode has traditionally had its type of spaces: fairs, festivals, markets in addition to that of carnival. To these spaces we might add the space of the occasionalism of identity politics.

For Bakhtin the most important site in medieval carnival was the marketplace. For others, like Turner, the shrine is a model site (1973; 1974). In either case, in the carnivalesque we see an association made between a heterotopic space and the transgressive acts associated with the performance of some monstrous and oppositional kind of identity. The identity that is produced can be described as an eclectic, heteroclite 'monstrosity'. The mixing of genres and inversions of the high/low hierarchy of the body within the carnivalesque have led me to suggest that this identity, established in heterotopic places, can be termed a heteroclite identity.

In the time of Rabelais and until the eighteenth century, the marketplace was a theatrical space of encounters with both the familiar and the strange (see Agnew, 1986). It was this ambivalence that allowed the marketplace to be seen as a marginal space in which the ambivalent and transgressive practices of the carnivalesque were allowed to take place. Stallybrass and White are right, however, to criticise Bakhtin for his overemphasis on the transgressive freedoms associated with carnival festivities; such practices were tolerated by the civil and ecclesiastical authorities during this period (1986: 10). As a heterotopia, the market, especially in relation to its association with the fair, gathers and organises nearness and remoteness into a unity (see Shields, 1992b). We should avoid the Euclideanism that sees spaces of order and disorder as separate and distinct. Their topology, rather, is more akin to a Möbius strip, a folded space in which order and disorder can be transformed into each other. The very idea of identity – even in unfinished, hybrid and monstrous forms – still involves an idea of ordering, even if that ordering is not finished. It is as much involved in issues of ordering as it is in forms of transgression and resistance. Such a criticism cannot be levelled only at Bakhtin's celebration of the freedoms of the carnivalesque, but also at its use in much of the recent cultural geography (notably Shields, 1991a; 1992b; Cresswell, 1996).

Shields, for example, has developed the theme of the carnivalesque associated with markets in relation to new spaces of consumption and pleasure (1989; 1990; 1991a; 1992a). The beach as a marginal space, along with the seaside resort, is one such space that has been seen as a space of the carnivalesque (Shields, 1990; 1991a). Another space is the shopping mall, a market space whose exuberant and excessive emphasis on the pleasures of consumption encourages a carnivalesque atmosphere (Shields, 1989; Shields, 1992b). However, these marginal places are places in which marginality becomes a source of ordering just as much as it does a source of transgression. A person can safely take part in transgressive and carnivalesque activities at the beach because it remains acceptable to do so. The heterotopic nature of these places is incorporated within the conditions of order associated with the practices of consumerism. It is debatable whether shopping malls have a carnivalesque atmosphere. Although the use of mirrors, water and themed interior design does provide an element of exoticism, the 'transgressive' activities are limited to shoplifting, wanton impulse buying, and young people using commercial spaces as public spaces in which to meet and loiter. The threat and fear associated with out of place transgression seems rather limited. It is places that do not fit into the dominant representation of space, and continue to effuse an aura of marginality and otherness, that are the sort of spaces which retain the appeal of the carnival and are likely to be the sorts of heterotopia that will attract politically motivated symbolic acts of transgression.

While such examples may be seen as overstating the importance of acts of transgression, the real significance of this work and indeed Bakhtin's own analysis lies in the emphasis it places on such forms of resistance, not as rational and discursive but as ludic and affectual, involving a high degree of communitas that allows for the development of identities (see Maffesoli, 1988a; 1996; Featherstone, 1991b; and Shields, 1992a). Acts of transgression are fundamentally spatial in nature. They are not a rupture of society and the overthrow of social order but involve an interplay between challenging society and ordering new social practices. These practices are attracted to a certain space by the social centrality given to it by a particular group and the symbolism they attach to it. The utopic that comes to be expressed within a space, the alternative values that are expressed in its symbolic importance, link with this issue of transgression as a mode of ordering. It is at the level of symbol and representation, formulated in terms of rejected knowledge and a utopics of the marginal, that such spaces have appeal to those who are trying to create new politics and new identities. Such places, that I have described as heterotopic, can be used in playful and transgressive practices associated with the carnivalesque in the creation of transgressive performances or occasions. Such places, whose heterotopic significance lends them a sense of uncertainty, are suitable for the process of self-creation. They act as the *mise-en-scène* for the enactment of a symbolic politics and protest, and identifications with others – all of which are significant in the occasionalism of identity performances.

Through the practices of travel, dwelling and social drama we can witness the carnivalesque at work. But those practices, those acts of resistance do not bring about the dissolution of society. Rather, they produce alternate modes of social ordering, expressions of a utopic that becomes a means through which identity is acted out. Its protagonists seek to change both society and themselves through the occasionalism of this process. The outcomes they desire may or may not be the ones they achieve, but such confrontational acts will bring about a change of some kind. That change may be a positive one in terms, say, of a change in government policy around a particular issue: stopping the building of a particular road across ancient green fields, for example. It may, however, be a negative change as in the case of free festivals and raves in Britain during the 1980s and 1990s bringing about stronger government legislation against trespass and the right to protest or to party (see Halfacree, 1996). The intended and unintended consequences of either positive or negative outcomes will influence further actions; they will also influence the identities constituted within these occasions. Within the spaces of the carnivalesque, identities are both made and unmade. This ordering of identities, in the context of contemporary expressivism, relies in particular on the festivals, protests and symbolic action of a group who come to see themselves as a moral elect. They express this through alternative ideas about lifestyle, about dress and about the body, just as much as through values and ideas. Subjectivised occasionalism relies on a spatial politics of performance. Identity and politics are, therefore, inextricably intertwined within this performativity.

Enactments of identity: performance, space and restored behaviour

> Everything that acts is cruelty. Theatre must rebuild itself on a concept of this drastic action pushed to the limit. (Artaud, 1977: 65)

Types of sociation, symbolic action, the carnivalesque, social dramas, occasionalism, heterotopic spaces, the creation of identity, and identification with others have one thing in common: theatricality. All of these issues associated with identity are in some way linked with ideas of performance. The character of the performance, while it may share many things with the everyday performances that we all engage in, also has a distinctive and often more visible character, defined in particular by its difference to the everyday and the routine. The idea that there is a theatricality to everyday life is, of course, not a new idea. The theatricality of daily life when considered by sociologists has invariably been associated with the work of Goffman (1971a). This provides much that is of use in the understanding of presentations of self as performances and the spaces in which they occur, within a dramatic idiom in which, through roles, individuals create their own biographies. The presentation of self in particular, associated with impression management, the regionalisation of behaviour, and role discrepancy are all areas of Goffman's work that have something to offer when discussing unusual performances (1971a). The main limitation of Goffman's work for the position developed here, however, is that in its concern with interactions, face work and the setting in which they take place, the dramaturgical references are often used metaphorically in order to suggest that, although people do assume personae and roles and take part in performances, there is a real and inaccessible self existing outside such practices – the real identity of the 'I'. In order to use the theatrical idea as more than a metaphor, and see the self as a social construct reflexively created through performances and the creation of personae, I draw instead on the work of writers involved in theatre studies (Brook, 1968; Grotowski, 1975; Schechner, 1985). The person who has influenced all of these directors, as indeed he influenced other writers on space like Foucault, Deleuze, Guattari and Lefebvre, is the surrealist Antonin Artaud.

In two manifestos and a number of articles on what he called the 'theatre of cruelty' written in the 1930s (1977), Artaud was to have a profound and lasting impact on twentieth-century theatre, notably through his influence on Brecht, the Theatre of the Absurd, and on the experimental theatre of Grotowski and his followers during the 1960s. This theatre was itself to share many of the characteristics of the protests and direct actions of the 'counter-culture' of the same time, making it especially significant here.

A central position of Artaud's was the desire to fuse art with life. It is the contention of theorists of postmodernism that this has now been achieved through consumption and the development of a spectacular consumer culture or an 'aestheticization of daily life' (Featherstone, 1991b: chapter 5; Benamou and Caramello, 1977). Consumer culture and its tendency to produce an aestheticisation of daily life, the 'effacement of the boundary between art and everyday life' (see Featherstone, 1991b: 65), can be seen as the basis for the challenge to older established identifications such as class as well as providing an opportunity to style one's life through the use of fashion (Hebdige, 1979; Wilson, 1985; Willis, 1991), music and style (Hall and Jefferson, 1976; Hebdige, 1979), and politics (Melucci, 1989).

The main claim that Artaud made in his manifestos on the theatre of cruelty was that theatre had become separated from everyday life. Bourgeois theatre, he believed, had become too intellectual and cerebral and had lost its original connection with feeling, emotion, the experience of the unconscious and, above all, with the experiences of the body. In other words we might say that his ideal theatre was a theatre organised through the multiple and complex expressions of desire. His own desire was not, however, only to create a new type of theatre but also to achieve a fusion between theatre and everyday life. He wanted theatre and life to become one, for the emotions of daily life to be reintroduced into theatre, making it a total experience and a shock on the senses of the 'audience'. As a means of expressing desire, Artaud wanted theatre to become a direct and unmediated situation – an occasion we might also call it – which required feeling rather than intellectual analysis. In effect, Artaud wanted theatre to be a liminal experience, as can be seen from his enthusiasm for the rituals expressed in Balinese theatre (1977: 36–49).

Such a theatre was also seen by Artaud as the basis of the production of new symbolism (1977: 72); it also required a space that did away with the separation of stage from auditorium and was to take place spontaneously in such a way that the peculiarities of the spatial setting be allowed to enliven the action. By application, such a theatre should become a theatre in which body can fully express itself: an idea Artaud expresses through his concept of cruelty. With this, Artaud meant a hungering after life in its most passionate and immediate form as a blind unmediated form of desire (see also Deleuze and Guattari, 1988).

In such a theatre, based on the idea of the event, the total and innovatory use of space, often to create an ambience of mystery, and the emphasis on the body effectively expresses in an extreme form the idea of a social drama. This is a theatre involving carnivalesque, liminoid rituals, and processes of enactment which are involved in the creation of new symbolic modes of expression. There is no possibility that such an experience could be sustained for long, but its elemental forms can be seen as the basis for the processes by which people create new identities and identifications with one another, unsettling and making use of their chosen spatial setting as they do so. It is under such liminally transgressive conditions that symbol production, the performance process, and their spatial framing become important.

Analysis can be made of the process of identification involved here; it can be seen as one in which spatially framed performances involve the adoption of a persona and a form of sociation that removes the fears of uncertainty associated with routine performativity and everyday life. The persona, as a mask, does not only hide, but also allows the individuals to free themselves from the expectations of self-identity while expressing who they want to be through the accoutrements of their lifestyle: use of style, values and disposition of the body, practices (Mauss, 1985; Featherstone, 1991a; Frank, 1991, B. Turner, 1991). The idea of a theatre expressed through an idealisation of a desiring body rather than a disembodied intellect has much in common with ideas associated with the carnivalesque and the transformations of identity.

The embodied identity found within the 'theatre of cruelty' is a carnivalesque one, as we have already seen; it can be described as an eclectic 'monstrosity'. Note for instance the importance of the mixing of genres and inversions of the high/low hierarchy of the body within the carnivalesque, notably the carnivalesque associated with the protest, festival or rave. Of course the language of youth subcultures associated with bricolage and signifying practices is an appropriate way of understanding some aspects of this process (see Willis, 1978; Hebdige, 1979), but this is not just a body that has an identity attached to it through subcultural style. It is a body that has values and beliefs as well. This is a body that flows out through extension into the places where its performance is called upon. In either case, it is a body fit for the *occasion*, a means of expressing either one's opposition to society or one's identification with an alternative. This meaning is not one that can be seen merely as a use of signs, as some form of magical resistance to class position or a simple embodiment of a social critique as Hebdige and other subcultural theorists would have us believe (1979), it is an ordering process that addresses the issues of identity and embodiment through hybridity and incommensurability as the basis for alternate orderings.

The process of identity transformation that is involved here is one that requires the use of the body in ways that are in some way liminally out of place, 'excessive' or challenging. Through an extended carnivalesque embodiment, these identities come to be associated with new modes of ordering their social world – a process that is represented by the use or deployment of the body. This ordering conveys social messages about the position of this person within a terrain of contestation: notably that between rejected centrality and affirmed marginality. Such an expression of embodiment plays with the themes of carnival, grotesque, freedom, dispossession, the culture of travel and dwelling in a new or alternative space. This identity, an embodied identity through which it comes to express itself, can be described as an identity which seeks to be marginal, different, other, unrepresentable and in flux. It valorises marginality and uncertainty. The contemporary free festival is the epitome of the carnivalesque: a subversive, threatening, grotesque occasion with its untamed communitas, disorder, drug taking, hedonism, anti-authoritarianism, and bizarre costume; all of which are articulated through visible, bodily expressions of release from imposed social constraints (see Hetherington, 1999). However, it can be found in other kinds of occasion as well. The symbolism of the body flows beyond its own boundaries and is incorporated into the symbolism of the space in which it is performed. The issue is, then, to understand the character of that performance. To this end I turn to the work of the director and theorist of performance Richard Schechner.

The theatricality of the occasion

Schechner's work on the acting process in the theatre is of significance here, not least because of the ways he draws upon and adopts Turner's ideas on liminality in relation to the theatre (1985) as well as following in the experimental theatre tradition, which can trace its roots back to the ideas of Artaud. The main claim that Schechner makes is that a performance is characterised by what he calls restored behaviour (1985: 35). By this he means action that is remembered and can be rehearsed so that it may be incorporated into future performances. This simple idea has far-reaching consequences. This view of action comprises ideas about performances which see them as independent of the actors who perform. Particular 'strips' of restored behaviour, performative repertoires that can be learned, may be arranged and rearranged to make up a performance. In this respect, there is never an original action, no performance is ever for the first time. Like role playing, which involves restored behaviour, a performance can never be completely spontaneous and will always involve, as Goffman also suggests, recognisable elements (1971a). The creative aspect involves not the bits of performance themselves but the ways that they are arranged and the expressive, embodied ways in which this is often done. Learning strips of behaviour means that the totality of the performance is unbounded and can be unscripted while at the same time having a visibly performative character to it.

The question of identity along with the practices associated with identity politics can be seen in terms of restored behaviour. What persona one adopts, the embodiment expressed through this persona, what identity one wishes to have and how one identifies with others; these will all depend on the type of restored behaviour, the strips of action which are chosen and the way they come to be arranged. In a more sociological sense, restored behaviour will comprise part of the stock of knowledge that individuals have but its use will not necessarily follow the conventions of everyday life. Rather, it will follow the conventions of the occasion. Just as routine social activity involves performance by skilled agents, so too do liminal, playful and transgressive activities involved in the maintenance of new identities and identifications through recognisable performative repertoires and their strips of behaviour.

The symbolic and reflexive nature of restored behaviour makes it meaningful within a particular performance (Schechner, 1985: 36). Even the most unusual or experimental performance will be contextually meaningful and routine. Restored behaviour is not something learned once; as in the theatre, it involves a continuous process of rehearsal, adaptation and experiment. Restored behaviour is made meaningful by an ongoing process of rehearsal; the past is used to make the actions that are intended meaningful. The question of a real self does not enter into such a process as one is always performing 'as if' scenarios with one's identity, assuming the role of the other, whether in the imagination or in action. Identity, while it can within certain limits be chosen, is not something one attains but something one performs and reflexively monitors by arranging strips of restored behaviour into a distinctive performance. In doing so, strips of recognisable behaviour are chosen through a continuous process of experiment and rehearsal, involving forms of sociation – assumed personae – which emerge in relation to their spatial setting.

The heterotopic/liminoid settings for contemporary identifications and the protests associated with identity politics are part of such a process of ongoing rehearsal and performance, under changing social conditions, requiring a high degree of experimentation, as well as challenging the former arrangement into established performances, of strips of restored behaviour. Experimental theatre, under the influence of Artaud, challenged the former preconceptions of the theatrical performance and the role of the actor's body within that performance. So too do the performances associated with identity politics and their expressive search for alternatives. These involve experimental personae and the use of strange settings in the nature of the performance to create the right ambience in which a new identity can be produced.

It is because there is no boundary to such a conceptualisation of performance that we can say that the politics associated with expressivism, the politics of the so-called 'new social movements', is inseparable from the process of making an identity. One lives such a performance whether one is on a demonstration protesting some kind of state action or whether one is making a cup of coffee from organic beans grown, marketed and sold in a non-exploitative way. Both are strips of restored behaviour – one public, the other more private – which together and with other strips of behaviour, make up the totality of the identity performance. No one 'strip' is more important that another, rather it is the arrangement of all strips of behaviour that is important.

Conclusion

The space of identity is a space of performance and embodied transformation. Around the act of making one's body visible to a world that takes it for granted we see the character of the occasionalism of contemporary identity politics and the lifestyles that it helps to create. The sense of election which can be associated with this kind of politics comes not only from the ethical stance that is taken – against the practices which characterise contemporary societies and what gets done to different groups of people, animals, the environment and so on – above all it comes from the idea of putting one's body on the line. The emotional and expressive character of these types of identities and their politics draws upon the body both as a resource for performance and as a symbol for change.

The spaces of identity politics and the identity positions are linked metonymically through utopic ideas of marginality and its uncertain state. This too is expressed in an embodied way. We cannot speak of expressive identities without recognising that we are also talking about an embodied identity that expresses itself through a performing body. Questions of style, of well-being, of vulnerability, of empowerment, of disease, are all questions raised through the occasionalism of identity performances. Above all, it is through the unresolved or unfinished body (see Falk, 1994) that we see expression of identity at work. Through the language of the carnivalesque and its historical links with forms of protest and resistance we can come to speak of this type of embodiment, and its performative repertoires and their spaces.

We have to recognise, however, that such an embodiment is not just about disorderly, leaky, boundary transgressing bodies, it is also about issues of ordering. Order and disorder are inseparably intertwined. We should avoid another kind of Euclideanism that sees one kind of orderly embodiment being challenged, from a separate counter-hegemonic space, by the forces of disorder. The body is a complex topological arrangement. Its performance also calls upon types of restored behaviour that operate through multiple arrangements of disorder, order and transformation.

An embodiment that is expressed through the grotesque and the carnivalesque is often taken by those involved to be a more authentic body, one that resists the repressive constraints of industrial, scientific, medical and political processes of social ordering. It challenges directly their conditions of possibility but it does so by creating some of its own. As such, identification can work just as well at the level of the body as it can at the level of solidarity or that of shared ideas. The ways in which the body comes to be used and the symbolism attached to such a kind of embodiment can be seen as just as important a source of moral election as adherence to a set of beliefs.

It is through the idea of the occasion that we can see all of these features of the practices of identity politics coalesce. Today's expressive identities must be seen in relation to the question of a situated performance of identity. I have argued that these identifications are both elective in their choice of Other, and affectual in their relation between self and others. The relationship between time, space and identification is one of the significance of presence and proximity. I have argued, by way of establishing the existence of heterotopic places that have social centrality, that it is the unusual setting, or unusual use of a setting, that is favoured by these neo-tribes. The heterogeneous status of such places allows for the communitas, generation of new symbols, and experimentation with restored behaviour which is required in the production of identity.

AFTERWORD
TELLING HORIZONTAL STORIES

The metaphor of the horizon is one I have used before to conclude a book (Hetherington, 1997a: 139–143). It means more here, however, than things are unfinished; rather, I have tried to think about horizons as a strategy for writing. As I indicated in the Introduction, I intended through this book to adopt the Deleuzian strategy to theorising expressive identities in a manner that could be summarised as: saying and and and without an equals sign. To have a conclusion, therefore, might seem to contradict this. Conclusions usually appear after the equals sign. To say, then, that this book does not add up might be to invite unwanted sarcasm. But, of course, adding is a cumulative process, an ongoing process into infinity that does not necessarily need an equals sign. My connotative approach is of this kind of adding. In particular, I have added concept to concept in order to see how they resonate together, how they fit and the story which that might allow us to tell. My argument has, therefore, followed a linear and cumulative narrative; what I have resisted is the move to turn that story, that multiplicity into something else. I have resisted, above all, the denotative move and being locked into a singularity where all the little numbers come together in one big one.

Here, therefore, I offer an afterword rather than a conclusion. Although it is an afterword, it might be better read as a preface. I make no apology to Hegel in saying this (see Spivak, 1976: x). The preface is written last but read first. Not so an afterword. It is often written (second to) last and read last. The issue is not one of a symmetry of folding writing/reading. It can, however, be used to bring awareness to what has come before and might, therefore, be better if it were read first. The afterthought is a reflection on the whole. But here there is no whole; I offer no conclusion to this book. Any point in this book might be the starting point or the finishing point. Where I have chosen to end might, under other conditions of writing, have been the point at which to start.

My own starting point was with the term 'new social movement'. All that I have described here might have gone under the name of new social movements. Using these words may have allowed me to avoid the tumult of different terms I have used in place of these three words (often abbreviated to NSM). My starting point, however, was also not to begin with the term new social movement. I have tried very hard in this book, not always totally successfully, to avoid using the term new social movement. To have laboured with it would have produced a quite different book. I would have had to address above all the questions of time and social change. New social movement implies new agents of change that have emerged now. My approach has been spatial rather than temporal. I have used the much more vague term 'expressive identities' in place of new social movements. That vagueness has been important; it has provided me with a way in, to look at an assemblage, a constellation, a multiplicity – whatever we might call it – rather than a singular entity. To the constellation of terms counter-culture, alternative lifestyle, identity politics, new social movements, I have added neo-tribes, Bund, subjectivised occasionalism, structure of feeling, liminality, heterotopia, heteroclite identity, social centrality, restored behaviour – the list could continue. I have suggested these other terms so that we can go on adding and go on thinking about the complexity that makes up the creation and maintenance of an identity, rather than bring this all together in a singular term which then allows us to avoid asking questions as to what is really happening.

This conceptual stuttering suggests that all of the concepts are useful and all are in some way connected to the others, but that none of them alone is enough to explain things in their totality or to allow us fully to move beyond the particular. Using all of the terms I have used here, allows us to theorise 'new social movements' as an heterogeneous, multiple and diverse assemblage of practice. These concepts help us make sense but they do not lead on to greater things. They are local yet interconnected standpoints which allow us partial, multiple, yet connected perspectives on what we choose to study. I have argued for the importance of connecting issues of identity to political actions and structures of feeling in the study of expressive identities, and have tried to suggest ways in which such phenomena might be considered in their own right rather than as an illustration of wider political and social processes. I have tried to stick with connotation rather than denotation. The only denotative move I have made has been to suggest that expressive identities can be analysed as situated, diverse, heterogeneous and multiple activities that go on within everyday life and which cannot be assimilated to any global, historical understanding as to the shape which society is taking.

While some of the concepts I have adopted imply some form of structure, the emphasis on the creative, expressive and emotional character of identity politics means that this is never a rigid structure but one that operates more like a genre within film – something that while it may seem to lead to a canon is always mutating, being added to and having to deal with inconsistencies and incompatibilities from within. Such an approach is, for me, a more suggestive way of addressing the importance and significance of 'new social movements' than trying to pin them onto some social conjuncture that they are then expected to exploit as agents of history.

It is not, however, just a question of replacing temporal with spatial metaphors. The character of the spatial metaphor is important too. I have used here the metaphor of topology to try and organise this book. The implications are ones of complexity, folding, rhizomic connections – in a word, horizons. I have wanted to try and challenge some of the Euclidean assumptions about the world. To date, much of the writing on 'new social movements' has focused on questions of marginality, resistance, transgression and identity. This book is no exception. However, I have tried to challenge the idea that there has to be a certain fixity to ideas about order and resistance, centres and margins, and so on – which has stemmed from Euclidean assumptions about the world. The world can also be described as comprised of flows rather than bounded regions, folds rather than smooth surfaces, crumpled and heterogeneous spaces rather than ones that are contained and geometrically defined (see Law, 1999). As long ago as 1961 Edmund Leach suggested that mathematical ideas about topology might be important for anthropology (1961). One of the main questions I have tried to ask in this book is: 'How do we think about identity in non-Euclidean ways that allow for conditions of topological complexity to be expressed?'

Social theory has always been in love with Euclid in that a fixed geometric space allows for the perspective of fixed subject positions – and indeed fixed ideas about identity. The 'god trick' of social theory, as Donna Haraway has called it (1991), is not an option when looking at spaces which are topologically complex. A topological approach is one that tries to find ways of expressing the subtle and complex character of the processes under study rather than home in on the great ruptures and transformations.

BIBLIOGRAPHY

Abercrombie, N., Hill, S. and Turner, B. (1986) *Sovereign Individuals of Capitalism*. London: Allen and Unwin.

Abrams, M. (1971) *English Romantic Poets*. Oxford: Oxford University Press.

Abrams, P. and McCulloch, D. (with Abrams, S. and Gore, P.) (1976) *Communes, Sociology and Society*. Cambridge: Cambridge University Press.

Adkins, L. (1995) *Gendered Work*. Milton Keynes: Open University Press.

Adorno, T. (1991) *The Culture Industry*. London: Routledge.

Adorno, T. and Horkheimer, M. (1979) *The Dialectic of Enlightenment*. London: Verso.

Agnew, J-C. (1986) *Worlds Apart: the Market and the Theatre in Anglo-American Thought, 1550–1750*. Cambridge: Cambridge University Press.

Althusser, L. (1971) *Lenin and Philosophy and Other Essays*. London: New Left Books.

Amirou, R. (1989) 'Sociability/"Sociality"', *Current Sociology*, 35 (2): 115–120.

Anderson, B. (1983) *Imagined Communities: Reflections on the Origin and Spread of Nationalism*. London: Verso.

Aragon, L. (1987) *Paris Peasant*. London: Picador.

Aron, R. (1964) *German Sociology*. Glencoe, NY: Free Press.

Artaud, A. (1977) *The Theatre and its Double*. London: John Calder.

Bachelard, G. (1969) *The Poetics of Space*. Boston: Beacon Press.

Bacon, F. (1974) *The Advancement of Learning*. Oxford: Clarendon Press.

Bagguley, P. (1992) 'Social Change, the Middle Class and the Emergence of "New Social Movements": a Critical Analysis', *The Sociological Review*, 40 (1): 26–48.

Bagguley, P. (1997) 'Beyond Political Sociology? Developments in the Sociology of Social Movements', *The Sociological Review*, 45 (1): 147–161.

Bakhtin, M. (1984) *Rabelais and his World*. Bloomington: Indiana University Press.

Bale, J. (1993) *Sport, Space and the City*. London: Routledge.

Barthes, R. (1968) *Elements of Semiology*. New York: Hill and Wang.

Barthes, R. (1973) *Mythologies*. London: Paladin.

Bataille, G. (1985) *Visions of Excess*. Minneapolis: University of Minnesota Press.

Bataille, G. (1991) *The Accursed Share: an Essay on General Economy, Volume 1: Consumption*. New York: Zone Books.

Bataille, G. (1994) 'The Moral Meaning of Sociology', pp. 103–112 in M. Richardson (ed.) *The Absence of Myth*. London: Verso.

Bauman, Z. (1982) *Memories of Class*. London: Routledge and Kegan Paul.

Bauman, Z. (1987) *Legislators and Interpreters: On Modernity, Postmodernity and Intellectuals*. Cambridge: Polity Press.

Bauman, Z. (1989) *Modernity and the Holocaust*. Oxford: Basil Blackwell.

Bauman, Z. (1990) 'Effacing the Face: On the Social Management of Moral Proximity', *Theory, Culture and Society*, 7 (1): 5–38.

Bauman, Z. (1991) *Modernity and Ambivalence*. Cambridge: Polity Press.

Bauman, Z. (1992) *Intimations of Postmodernity*. London: Routledge.

Bauman, Z. (1995) *Life in Fragments*. Oxford: Blackwell.

Bauman, Z. (1996) 'From Pilgrim to Tourist – or a Short History of Identity', pp. 18–36 in S. Hall and P. du Gay (eds) *Questions of Cultural Identity*. London: Sage.

Beck, U. (1992) *Risk Society*. London: Sage.

Beck, U. (1995) *Ecological Politics in an Age of Risk*. Oxford: Polity.

Beck, U. (1996) *The Reinvention of Politics*. Oxford: Polity.

Beck, U., Giddens, A. and Lash, S. (1994) *Reflexive Modernisation*. Oxford: Polity.

Becker, H. (1946) *German Youth: Bond or Free?* London: Kegan, Paul, Trench, Trubner.

Bell, C. and Newby, H. (1976) 'Community, Communion, Class and Community Action: the Social Sources of the New Urban Politics', pp. 189–207 in D. Herbert and R. Johnston (eds), *Social Areas in Cities, Volume Two*. London: John Wiley and Sons.

Bell, D. (1979) *The Cultural Contradictions of Capitalism* (Second Edition). London: Heinemann.

Bell, D. and G. Valentine (1995) 'The Sexed Self: Strategies of Perfomance, Sites of Resistance', pp. 143–157 in S. Pile and N. Thrift (eds), *Mapping the Subject*. London: Routledge.

Benamou, M. and Caramello, C. (eds) (1977) *Performance in Postmodern Culture*. Madison, WI: University of Wisconsin–Milwaukee/Coda Press.

Benjamin, W. (1973) *Charles Baudelaire: a Lyric Poet in the Era of High Capitalism*. London: New Left Books.

Benjamin, W. (1979) 'Surrealism', pp. 225–239 in *One Way Street and Other Writings*. London: New Left Books.

Bennett, T. (1995) *The Birth of the Museum*. London: Routledge.

Berger, J. (1972) *Ways of Seeing*. Harmondsworth: Penguin/BBC.

Berman, M. (1971) *The Politics of Authenticity*. London: Allen and Unwin.

Berman, M. (1982) *All That is Solid Melts into Air*. London: Verso.

Bhabha, H. (1994) *The Location of Culture*. London: Routledge.

Billington, J. (1980) *Fire in the Minds of Men*. London: Temple Smith.

Bondi, L. (1993) 'Locating Identity Politics', pp. 84–101 in M. Keith and S. Pile (eds), *Place and the Politics of Identity*. London: Routledge.

Bondi, L. and Domosh, M. (1992) 'Other Figures in Other Places: On Feminism, Postmodernism and Geography', *Environment and Planning D: Society and Space*, 10: 199–213.

Bookchin, M. (1989) 'New Social Movements: the Anarchic Approach', pp. 259–274 in D. Goodway (ed.), *For Anarchism: History, Theory and Practice*. London: Routledge and Kegan Paul.

Bourdieu, P. (1984) *Distinction: a Social Critique of the Judgement of Taste*. London: Routledge and Kegan Paul.

Bradshaw, S. (1978) *Cafe Society*. London: Wiedenfeld and Nicholson.

Breton, A. (1961) *Nadja*. New York: Grove Press.

Brook, P. (1968) *The Empty Space*. London: Penguin.

Brubacker, R. (1984) *The Limits of Rationality: an Essay on the Social and Moral Thought of Max Weber*. London: George Allen and Unwin.

Brubacker, R. (1996) *Nationalism Reframed*. Cambridge: Cambridge University Press.

Brunner, O., Conze, W. and Koselleck, R. (eds) (1972) *Geschichtliche Grundbergriffe: Historisches Lexikon Zur Politische-Sozialen Sprache in Deutschland*. Stuttgart: Ernst Klett.

Bryson, N. (1983) *Vision and Painting*. Basingstoke: Macmillan.

Buber, M. (1958) *I and Thou* (Second Revised Edition). Edinburgh: T and T Clark.

Buck-Morss, S. (1989) *Dialectics of Seeing: Walter Benjamin and the Arcades Project*. Cambridge, MA: MIT Press.

Calhoun, C. (1995) 'New Social Movements of the Early Nineteenth Century', pp. 173–215 in M. Traugott (ed.) *Repertoires and Cycles of Collective Action*. Durham, NC and London: Duke University Press.

Campbell, C. (1987) *The Romantic Ethic and the Spirit of Modern Consumerism*. Oxford: Basil Blackwell.

Campbell, M. (1988) *The Witness and the Other World*. Ithaca, NY: Cornell University Press.

Carroll, J. (1977) *Puritan, Paranoid, Remissive: a Sociology of Modern Culture*. London: Routledge and Kegan Paul.

de Certeau, M. (1984) *The Practices of Everyday Life*. Berkeley: University of California Press.

de Certeau, M. (1992) 'Walking in the City', pp. 151–160 in S. During (ed.) *The Cultural Studies Reader*. London: Routledge.

Chambers, I. (1994) 'Leaky Habits and Broken Grammar', pp. 245–249 in G. Robertson, M. Mash, L. Tickner, J. Bird, B. Curtis, T. Putnam (eds), *Travellers Tales*. London: Routledge.

Chippindale, C. (1983) *Stonehenge Complete*. London: Thames and Hudson.

Chippindale, C., Devereux, P., Jones, R. and Sebastian, T. (eds) (1990) *Who Owns Stonehenge?*. London: Batsford.

Chtcheglov, I. (1981) 'Formulary for a New Urbanism', pp. 1–4 in K. Knabb (ed.), *Situationist International Anthology*. Berkeley, CA: Bureau of Public Secrets.

Clarke, J., Hall, S., Jefferson, T. and Roberts, B. (1976) 'Subcultures, Cultures and Class', pp. 9–74 in S. Hall and T. Jefferson (eds), *Resistance Through Rituals: Youth Subcultures in Post-War Britain*. London: Hutchinson/Centre for Contemporary Cultural Studies.

Clifford, J. and Marcus, G. (1986) (eds) *Writing Culture*. Berkeley, CA: University of California Press.

Cohen, E. (1973) 'Nomads from Affluence: Notes on the Phenomenon of Drifter Tourism', *International Journal of Comparative Sociology*, 14 (1–2): 89–103.

Cohen, E. (1979) 'A Phenomenology of Tourist Experiences', *Sociology*, 13 (2): 179–201.

Cohen, E. (1983) 'The Structural Transformation of the Kibbutz', pp. 75–114 in E. Krausz (ed.), *The Sociology of the Kibbutz: Studies of Israeli Society, Volume 2*. London/New Brunswick: Transaction Books.

Cohen, E., Ben-Yehuda, N. and Aviad, J. (1987) 'Recentering the World: the Quest for "Elective" Centers in a Secularized Universe', *The Sociological Review*, 35 (2): 320–346.

Cohen, P. (1972) 'Sub-cultural Conflict and Working Class Community', *Working Papers in Cultural Studies*, No. 2. Birmingham: CCCS

Cohen, S. (1980) 'Preface', *Folk Devils and Moral Panics* (Second Edition). London: Granada.

Cohen, S. and Taylor, L. (1992) *Escape Attempts: the Theory and Practice of Resistance to Everyday Life*. (Second Edition). London: Routledge.

Connor, S. (1989) *Postmodernist Culture*. Oxford: Blackwell.

Cresswell, T. (1996) *In Place/Out of Place*. Minneapolis: University of Minnesota Press.

Debord, G. (1981a) 'Report on the Construction of Situations and on the International Situationist Tendency's Conditions of Organization and Action', pp. 17–25 in K. Knabb (ed.), *Situationist International Anthology*. Berkeley, CA: Bureau of Public Secrets.

Debord, G. (1981b) 'Introduction to a Critique of Urban Geography', pp. 5–7 in K. Knabb (ed.) *Situationist International Anthology*. Berkeley, CA: Bureau of Public Secrets.

Debord, G. (1983) *Society of the Spectacle*. Detroit: Black and Red.

Delaney, J. (1992) 'Ritual Space in the Canadian Museum of Civilization: Consuming Canadian Identity', pp. 136–148 in R. Shields (ed.), *Lifestyle Shopping*. London: Routledge.

Deleuze, G. (1986) *Foucault*. Baltimore: Athlone Press.

Deleuze G. and Guattari, F. (1988) *A Thousand Plateaus*. London: The Athlone Press.

Deleuze G. and Guattari, F. (1994) *What is Philosophy?* London: Verso.

Deleuze, G. and Parnet, C. (1987) *Dialogues*. Baltimore; London: The Athlone Press.

Derrida, J. (1976) *Of Grammatology*. Baltimore: Johns Hopkins University Press.

Devereaux, P. (1990) 'Stonehenge as an Earth Mystery', pp. 35–61 in C. Chippindale, P. Devereux, R. Jones and T. Sebastian (eds), *Who Owns Stonehenge?*. London: Batsford.

Docherty, B. (1996) 'Paving the Way: The Rise of Direct Action Against Road-Building and the Changing Character of British Environmentalism', *Keele Research Paper*, No. 21. Keele University: Department of Politics.

Doel, M. 1996, 'A Hundred Thousand Lines of Flight – a Machinic Introduction to the Nomad Thought and Scrumpled Geography of Gilles Deleuze and Felix Guattari', *Environment and Planning D: Society and Space*, 14 (4): 421–439.

Douglas, M. (1984) *Purity and Danger: An Analysis of the Origins of Pollution and Taboo*. London: Ark/Routledge.

Durkheim, E. (1964) *The Division of Labour in Society*. New York: Free Press.

Durkheim, E. (1971) *The Elementary Forms of the Religious Life*. London: George Allen and Unwin.

Earle, F., Dearling, A., Whittle, H., Glasse, R., and Gubby (1994) *A Time to Travel? An Introduction to Britain's Newer Travellers*. Lyme Regis: Enabler Publications.

Eder, K. (1985) 'The New Social Movements: Moral Crusades, Political Pressure Groups or Social Movements?', *Social Research*, 52 (4): 869–900.

Eder, K. (1993) *The New Politics of Class: Social Movements and Cultural Dynamics in Advanced Societies*. London: Sage.

Eliade, M. (1969) *The Quest: History and Meaning in Religion*. Chicago: University of Chicago Press.

Elias, N. (1978) *The Civilizing Process*, (2 vols). Oxford: Blackwell.

Evans, D. (1997) 'Michel Maffesoli's Sociology of Modernity and Postmodernity: an Introduction and Critical Assessment', *The Sociological Review*, 45 (2): 220–243.

Eyerman, R. and Jamison, A. (1991) *Social Movements: a Cognitive Approach*. Cambridge: Polity Press.

Falk, P. (1994) *The Consuming Body*. London: Sage.

Featherstone, M. (1991a) 'The Body in Consumer Culture', pp. 170–196 in M. Featherstone, M. Hepworth and B. Turner (eds), *The Body: Social Process and Cultural Theory*. London: Sage.

Featherstone, M. (1991b) *Consumer Culture and Postmodernism*. London: Sage.

Featherstone, M. (1996) *Undoing Culture*. London: Sage.

Featherstone, M., Hepworth, M. and Turner, B. (eds) (1991) *The Body: Social Process and Cultural Theory*. London: Sage.

Fiske, J. (1989) *Understanding Popular Culture*. Boston: Unwin/Hyman.

Foucault, M. (1977) *Discipline and Punish: the Birth of the Prison*. Harmondsworth: Penguin.

Foucault, M. (1980) 'A Question of Geography' (interview with the editors of the journal *Hérodote*), pp. 63–77 in C. Gordon (ed.), *Power/Knowledge: Selected Interviews and Other Writings 1972–1977*. London: Harvester Press.

Foucault, M. (1982) 'The Subject and Power', pp. 208–226, Afterword in H. Dreyfus and P. Rabinow *Michel Foucault: Beyond Structuralism and Hermeneutics*. Brighton: The Harvester Press.

Foucault, M. (1983) *This is Not a Pipe*. J. Harkness (ed.). Berkeley: University of California Press.

Foucault, M. (1986a) 'Of Other Spaces', *Diacritics*, 16 (1): 22–27.

Foucault, M. (1986b) 'Space, Knowledge, and Power', pp. 239–256 in P. Rabinow (ed.), *The Foucault Reader*. Harmondsworth: Penguin.

Foucault, M. (1989a) *The Order of Things: an Archaeology of the Human Sciences*. London: Tavistock/Routledge.

Foucault, M. (1989b) *The Birth of the Clinic: an Archaeology of Medical Perception*. London: Routledge.

Foucault, M. (1991) ' "But Structuralism was not a French Invention" ' (interview with D. Trombadori), pp. 83–113 in *Remarks on Marx*. New York: Semiotext(e).

Frank, A. (1991) 'For a Sociology of the Body: an Analytical Review', pp. 36–102 in M. Featherstone, M. Hepworth and B. Turner (eds), *The Body: Social Process and Cultural Theory*. London: Sage.

Freund, J. (1978) 'German Sociology in the Time of Max Weber', pp. 149–186 in T. Bottomore and R. Nisbet (eds), *History of Sociological Analysis*. London: Heinemann.

Gabel, J. (1967) *False Consciousness: an Essay on Reification*. K. Thompson (ed.). Oxford: Basil Blackwell.

Gans, H. (1962) *The Urban Villagers*. New York: Free Press.

Genocchio, B. (1995) 'Discourse, Discontinuity, Difference: The Question of "Other" Spaces', pp. 35–46 in S. Watson and K. Gibson (eds), *Postmodern Cities and Spaces*. Oxford: Basil Blackwell.

Giddens, A. (1984) *The Constitution of Society: Outline of the Theory of Structuration*. Cambridge: Polity Press.

Giddens, A. (1990) *Consequences of Modernity*. Cambridge: Polity Press.

Giddens, A. (1991) *Modernity and Self Identity*. Cambridge: Polity Press.

Giddens, A. (1992) *The Transformation of Intimacy*. Cambridge: Polity Press.

Gilroy, P. (1993) *The Black Atlantic*. Cambridge, MA: Harvard University Press.

Girard, R. (1979) *Violence and the Sacred*. Baltimore: Johns Hopkins University Press.

Goffman, E. (1971a) *The Presentation of Self in Everyday life*. Harmondsworth: Penguin.

Goffman, E. (1971b) *Relations in Public: Microstudies of the Public Order*. Harmondsworth: Penguin.

Goffman, E. (1986) *Frame Analysis: an Essay on the Organization of Experience*. Boston, MA: Northeastern University Press.

Goldman, H. (1988) *Max Weber and Thomas Mann*. Berkeley: University of California Press.

Gouldner, A. (1973) *For Sociology*. London: Allen Lane.

Graham, S. (1927) *The Gentle Art of Tramping*. London: Ernest Benn.

Grana, C. (1964) *Bourgeois and Bohemians*. New York: Basic Books.

Greenblatt, S. (1982) 'Filthy Rites', *Daedalus*, 111 (3): 1–16.

Gregory, D. and Urry, J. (eds) (1985) *Social Relations and Spatial Structures*. Basingstoke: Macmillan.

Grotowski, J. (1975) *Towards a Poor Theatre*. E. Barba (ed.). London: Methuen.

Gurvitch, G. (1941) 'Mass, Community and Communion', *Journal of Philosophy*, 38: 485–496.

Habermas, J. (1981) 'New Social Movements', *Telos*, 49: 33–37.

Habermas, J. (1984) *Theory of Communicative Action: Reason and the Rationalization of Society, Volume 1*. London: Heinemann Educational Books.

Habermas, J. (1987) *The Philosophical Discourse of Modernity: Twelve Lectures*. Cambridge: Polity Press.

Habermas, J. (1989) *The Structural Transformation of the Public Sphere: an Inquiry into a Category of Bourgeois Society*. Cambridge, MA: MIT Press.

Halfacree, K. (1996) 'Out of Place in the Country: Travellers and the Rural Idyll', *Antipode*, 28 (1): 42–72.

Hall, S. (1990) 'Cultural Identity and Diaspora', pp. 222–237 in J. Rutherford (ed.), *Identity*. London: Lawrence and Wishart.

Hall, S. (1992) 'The Question of Cultural Identity', pp. 274–316 in S. Hall, D. Held and T. McGrew (eds), *Modernity and Its Futures*. Cambridge: Polity Press/The Open University.

Hall, S. (1996) 'Who needs Identity?', pp. 1–17 in S. Hall and P. du Gay (eds), *Questions of Cultural Identity*. London: Sage.

Hall, S. and du Gay, P. (eds) (1996) *Questions of Cultural Identity*. London: Sage.

Hall, S. and Jefferson, T. (eds) (1976) *Resistance Through Rituals: Youth Subcultures in Post-War Britain*. London: Hutchinson/Centre for Contemporary Cultural Studies.

Handelman, D. (1990) *Models and Mirrors*. Cambridge: Cambridge University Press.

Haraway, D. (1991) 'Situated Knowledges: The Science Question in Feminism and the Privilege of Partial Perspective', pp. 183–201 in *Simians, Cyborgs and Women*. London: Free Association Books.

Haraway, D. (1996) 'Modest Witness: Feminist Diffractions in Science Studies', pp. 428–441 in P. Galison and D.J. Stamp (eds), *Disunity of the Sciences*. Stanford: Stanford University Press.

Harding, S. (1986) *The Science Question in Feminism*. Milton Keynes: Open University Press.

Harvey, D. (1989) *The Condition of Postmodernity: an Enquiry into the Origins of Cultural Change*. Oxford: Basil Blackwell.

Hebdige, D. (1976) 'The Meaning of Mod', pp. 87–98 in S. Hall and T. Jefferson (eds), *Resistance Through Rituals: Youth Subcultures in Post-War Britain*. London: Hutchinson/ Centre for Contemporary Cultural Studies.

Hebdige, D. (1979) *Subculture: The Meaning of Style*. London: Routledge.

Hebdige, D. (1988) *Hiding in the Light*. London: Routledge.

Heberle, R. (1951) *Social Movements: an Introduction to Political Sociology*. New York: Appleton Century Crafts.

Heelas, P. (1996) *The New Age Movement*. Oxford: Blackwell.

Heelas, P., Lash, S. and Morris, P. (eds) (1996) *Detraditionalisation*. Oxford: Blackwell.

Held, D. (1980) *Introduction to Critical Theory: Horkheimer to Habermas*. London: Hutchinson.

Hennies, W. (1987) 'Personality and Life Orders: Max Weber's Theme', pp. 52–74 in S. Whimster and S. Lash (eds), *Max Weber, Rationality and Modernity*. London: Allen and Unwin.

Hetherington, K. (1990) 'On the Homecoming of the Stranger: New Social Movements or New Sociations?', *Lancaster Regionalism Group Working Paper No 39*. Lancaster: Department of Sociology.

Hetherington, K. (1991) 'The Geography of the Other: Stonehenge, Greenham and the Politics of Trust', *Working Paper No. 42*. Lancaster: Lancaster Regionalism Group.

Hetherington, K. (1992) 'Stonehenge and Its Festival: Spaces of Consumption', pp. 83–98 in R. Shields (ed.), *Lifestyle Shopping*. London: Routledge.

Hetherington, K. (1993) 'The Geography of the Other: Lifestyle, Perfomance and Identity', Unpublished PhD Thesis, Lancaster University: Department of Sociology.

Hetherington, K. (1994) 'The Contemporary Significance of Schmalenbach's Concept of the Bund', *The Sociological Review*, 42 (1): 1–25.

Hetherington, K. (1996) 'Identity Formation, Space and Social Centrality', *Theory, Culture and Society*, 13 (4): 33–52.

Hetherington, K. (1997a) *The Badlands of Modernity*. London: Routledge.

Hetherington, K. (1997b) 'Vanloads of Uproarious Humanity: New Age Travellers and the Utopics of the Countryside', pp. 328–342 in T. Skelton and G. Valentine (eds), *Cool Places: Geographies of Youth Cultures*. London: Routledge.

Hetherington, K. (1997c) 'Museum Topology and the Will to Connect', *Journal of Material Culture*, 2 (2): 199–218.

Hetherington, K. (1999) *New Age Travellers*. London: Cassell – Forthcoming.

Hetherington, K. and Lee, N. (1998) 'Social Order and the Blank Figure', Forthcoming.

Hetherington, K. and Munro, R. (eds) (1997) *Ideas of Difference: Social Spaces and the Labour of Division*. Oxford: Blackwell.

Hibbert, C. (1987) *The Grand Tour*. London: Thames Television International/Methuen.

Hinton, J. (1989) *Protests and Visions*. London: Hutchinson/Radius.

Hirsh, A. (1982) *The French Left: A History and Overview*. Montreal: Black Rose.

HM Government (1985). *Public Order Bill*. London: HMSO.

Hochschild, A. (1983) *The Managed Heart*. Berkeley: University of California Press.

Home, S. (1988) *The Assault on Culture: Utopian Currents From Lettrisme to Class War*. London: Aporia Press/Unpopular Books.

Honour, H. (1979) *Romanticism*. London: Allen Lane.

Huizinga, J. (1970) *Homo Ludens: a Study of the Play Element in Culture*. London: Granada/ Paladin.

Inglehart, R. (1977) *The Silent Revolution: Changing Values and Political Styles among Western Publics*. Princeton, NJ: Princeton University Press.

Inglehart, R. (1990) 'Values, Ideology, and Cognitive Mobilization in New Social Movements', pp. 43–66 in R. Dalton and M. Kuechler (eds), *Challenging the Political Order: New Social Movements in Western Democracies*. Cambridge: Polity Press.

Jacob, J. (1961) *The Death and Life of the Great American Cities*. Harmondsworth: Penguin.

Jacob, M. (1991) *Living the Enlightenment*. Oxford: Oxford University Press.

Jameson, F. (1984) 'Postmodernism, or the Cultural Logic of Late Capitalism', *New Left Review*, 146: 53–92.

Jameson, F. (1991) *Postmodernism or, The Cultural Logic of Late Capitalism*. London: Verso.

Jay, M. (1973) *The Dialectical Imagination: a History of the Frankfurt School and the Institute for Social Research*. London: Heinemann Educational.

Jay, M. (1984) *Adorno*. London: Fontana.

Jay, M. (1992) 'Scopic Regimes of Modernity', pp. 178–195 in S. Lash and J. Friedman (eds), *Modernity and Identity*. Oxford: Basil Blackwell.

Jencks, C. (1986) *What is Postmodernism?*. London: Academy Editions.

Jenkins, C. and Klandermans, B. (eds) (1995) *The Politics of Social Protest*. London: UCL Press.

Jenkins, R. (1996) *Social Identity*. London: Routledge.

Joll, J. (1964) *The Anarchists*. London: Eyre and Spottiswoode.

Keith, M. and Pile, S. (eds) (1993) *Place and the Politics of Identity*. London: Routledge

Knabb, K. (ed.) (1981) *Situationist International Anthology*. Berkeley, CA: Bureau of Public Secrets.

Koselleck, R. (1988) *Critique and Crisis: Enlightenment and the Pathogenesis of Modern Society*. Oxford: Berg.

Kumar, K. (1987) *Utopia and Anti-Utopia in Modern Times*. Oxford: Basil Blackwell.

Kumar, K. (1991) *Utopianism*. Milton Keynes: Open University Press.

Lacquer, W. (1962) *Young Germany: a History of the German Youth Movement*. London: Routledge and Kegan Paul.

La Fontaine, J. (1985) *Initiation: Ritual Drama and Secret Knowledge Across the World*. Harmondsworth: Penguin.

Lambert, R. (1950) *The Fortunate Traveller: a Short History of Touring and Travel for Pleasure*. London: Andrew Melrose.

Landauer, G. (1978) *For Socialism*. St Louis: Telos.

Langman, L. (1992) 'Neon Cages: Shopping for Subjectivity', pp. 40–82 in R. Shields (ed.), *Lifestyle Shopping: The Subject of Consumption*. London: Routledge.

Lasch, C. (1980) *The Culture of Narcissism*. London: Abacus.

Lasch, C. (1984) *The Minimal Self*. London: Picador.

Lash, S. (1988) 'Discourse or Figure? Postmodernism as a 'Regime of Signification', *Theory, Culture and Society*, 5 (2–3): 311–336.

Lash, S. (1993) 'Reflexive Modernization: the Aesthetic Dimension', *Theory, Culture and Society*, 10 (1): 1–23.

Lash, S. and Friedman, J. (eds) (1992) *Modernity and Identity*. Oxford: Basil Blackwell.

Lash, S. and Urry, J. (1987) *The End of Organized Capitalism*. Cambridge: Polity Press.

Lash, S. and Urry, J. (1994) *Economies of Signs and Space*. London: Sage.

Latour, B. (1993) *We Have Never Been Modern*. London: Harvester Wheatsheaf.

Law, J. (1994) *Organizing Modernity*. Oxford: Blackwell.

Law, J. (1999) *Aircraft Stories: Technoscience and the Decentering of the Object*, Forthcoming.

Law, J. and Hetherington, K. (1998) 'Allegory and Interference: Representation in Sociology', Forthcoming.

Leach, E. (1961) 'Time and False Noses', pp. 132–136 in *Rethinking Anthropology*. London: The Athlone Press. (London School of Economics Monographs on Social Anthropology 22.)

Le Bon, G. (1967) *The Crowd: a Study of the Popular Mind*. London: Ernest Benn.

Lee, N. (1997) 'Values: Pyraminds and Blank Dominoes', Paper presented at the *Advanced Seminars in Childhood and Social Theory*, Keele University, March 1997.

Lefebvre, H. (1971) *Everyday Life in the Modern World*. London: Allen Lane/Penguin.

Lefebvre, H. (1991) *The Production of Space*. Oxford: Blackwell.

Leppenies, W. (1988) *Between Literature and Science: the Rise of Sociology*. Cambridge: Cambridge University Press.

Levinas, E. (1989) *The Levinas Reader*. Oxford: Blackwell.

Levi-Strauss, C. (1966) *The Savage Mind*. London: Weidenfeld and Nicholson.

Ley, D. (1976) 'Social Geography and the Taken-For-Granted World', *Institute of British Geographers, Transactions*, New Series, 2 (4): 498–512.

Liddington, J. (1989) *The Long Road to Greenham: Feminism and Anti-Militarism in Britain Since 1820*. London: Virago.

Liebersohn, H. (1988) *Fate and Utopia in German Sociology, 1870–1923*. Cambridge, MA: MIT Press.

Link-Salinger, R. (1977) *Gustav Landauer: Philosopher of Utopia*. Indianapolis: Hackell Publishing.

Lowe, R. and Shaw, W. (1993) *Travellers: Voices of the New Age Nomads*. London: Fourth Estate.

Lunn, E. (1973) *Prophet of Community: The Romantic Socialism of Gustav Landauer*. Berkeley: University of California Press.

Lüschen, G. and Stone, G. (1977) 'Introduction', pp. 1–45 in G. Lüschen and G. Stone (eds), *Herman Schmalenbach: On Society and Experience*. Chicago: University of Chicago Press.

Lyon, D. (1994) *Postmodernity*. Milton Keynes: Open University Press.

Lyotard, J.-F. (1984) *The Postmodern Condition: a Report on Knowledge*. Manchester: Manchester University Press.

MacCannell, D. (1989) *The Tourist: a New Theory of the Leisure Class*. New York: Schocken Books.

McKay, G. (1996) *Senseless Acts of Beauty*. London: Verso.

McRobbie, A. (1991) *Feminism and Youth Culture*. London: Macmillan.

Maffesoli, M. (1988a) 'Jeux de Masques: Postmodern Tribalism', *Design Issues*, 4 (1–2): 141–151.

Maffesoli, M. (1988b) *Les Temps des Tribus*. Paris: Meridiens Klincksieck.

Maffesoli, M. (1991) 'The Ethic of Aesthetics', *Theory, Culture and Society*, 8 (1): 7–20.

Maffesoli, M. (1996) *The Time of the Tribes*. London: Sage.

Mannheim, K. (1938) *Ideology and Utopia*. London: Kegan Paul, Trench, Trubner.

Manuel, F.E. and Manuel, F.P. (1979) *Utopian Thought in the Western World*. Oxford: Basil Blackwell.

Marcus, G. (1992) 'Past, Present and Emergent Identities: Requirements for Ethnographies of Late Twentieth Century Modernity Worldwide', pp. 309–330 in S. Lash and J. Friedman (eds), *Modernity and Identity*. Oxford: Blackwell.

Marcus, J. (1988) 'The Journey Out to the Centre. The Cultural Appropriation of Ayers Rock', pp. 254–274 in A. Rutherford (ed.), *Aboriginal Culture Today*. Kunapipi: Dangeroo Press.

Marin, L. (1984) *Utopics: Spatial Play*. London: Macmillan.

Marin, L. (1992) 'Frontiers of Utopia: Past and Present', *Critical Inquiry*, 19 (3): 397–420.

Martin, B. (1981) *Sociology of Contemporary Cultural Change*. Oxford: Basil Blackwell.

Marx, K. (1938) *Capital, Volume 1*. London: Allen and Unwin.

Massey, D. (1984) *Spatial Divisions of Labour: Social Structures of the Geography of Production*. London: Macmillan.

Massey, D. (1994) *Space, Place and Gender*. Cambridge: Polity Press.

Maurer, C. (1971) *Call to Revolution: the Mystical Anarchism of Gustav Landauer*. Detroit: Wayne State University Press.

Mauss, M. (1985) 'A Category of the Human Mind: the Notion of Person; the Notion of Self', pp. 1–25 in M. Carrithers, S. Collins, and S. Lukes (eds), *The Category of the Person: Anthropology, Philosophy, History*. Cambridge: Cambridge University Press.

Mayall, D. (1988) *Gypsy-Travellers in Nineteenth Century Society*. Cambridge: Cambridge University Press.

Mellor, P. and Shilling, C. (1997) *Re-Forming the Body*. London: Sage.

Melucci, A. (1985) 'The Symbolic Challenge of Contemporary Movements', *Social Research*, 52 (4): 789–816.

Melucci, A. (1989) *Nomads of the Present*. London: Hutchinson Radius.

Melucci, A. (1996) *Challenging Codes*. Cambridge: Cambridge University Press.

Mercer, K. (1990) 'Welcome to the Jungle: Identity and Diversity in Postmodern Politics', pp. 43–71 in J. Rutherford (ed.), *Identity: Community, Culture, Difference*. London: Lawrence and Wishart.

Meyrowitz, J. (1985) *No Sense of Place: the Impact of Electronic Media on Social Behaviour*. New York: Oxford University Press.

Michell, J. (1982) *Megalithomania: Artists, Antiquarians and Archaeologists at the Old Stone Monuments*. London: Thames and Hudson.

Michell, J. (1986) *Stonehenge: Its History, Meaning, Festival, Unlawful Management, Police Riot '85 and Future Prospects*. London: Radical Traditionalist Papers.

Mills, R. (1973) *Young Outsiders*. London: RKP.

Mitterauer, M. (1992) *A History of Youth*. Oxford: Blackwell.

Mol, A. and Law, J. (1994) 'Regions, Networks and Fluids: Anaemia and Social Topology', *Social Studies of Science*, 24: 641–671.

More, T. (1985) *Utopia*. London: J.M. Dent.

Moss-Kanter, R. (1976) 'The Romance of Community: Intentional Communities as Intensive Group Experiences', pp. 146–185 in M. Rosenbaum and A. Snadowsky (eds), *The Intensive Group Experience*. New York: Free Press/Macmillan.

Mosse, G. (1964) *The Crisis of German Ideology: Intellectual Origins of the Third Reich*. London: Weidenfeld and Nicholson.

Mosse, G. (1971) *Germans and Jews: the Right, the Left and the Search for a 'Third Force' in Pre-Nazi Germany*. London: Orbach and Chambers.

Mullett, M. (1987) *Popular Culture and Popular Protest in Late Medieval and Early Modern Europe*. London: Croom Helm.

Munro, R. (1998) 'Belonging on the Move': Market Rhetoric and the Future as Obligatory Passage', *The Sociological Review*, 46 (2): 208–243.

Nadeau, M. (1987) *The History of Surrealism*. London: Plantin Publishers.

Nicolaievsky, B. and Maenchen-Helfen, O. (1976) *Karl Marx: Man and Fighter*. Harmondsworth: Penguin.

O'Connor, J. and Wynne, D. (eds) (1996a) *From the Margins to the Centre*. Aldershot: Arena.

O'Connor, J. and Wynne, D. (1996b) 'Left Loafing: City Cultures and Postmodern Lifestyles', pp. 49–89 in J. O'Connor, and D. Wynne (eds), *From the Margins to the Centre*. Aldershot: Arena.

Owen, D. (1991) 'Autonomy and "Inner Distance": A Trace of Nietzsche in Weber', *History of the Human Sciences*, 4 (1): 80–91.

Pakulski, J. (1991) *Social Movements: the Politics of Moral Protest*. Melbourne: Longman Cheshire.

Park, R. (1967) 'The City: Suggestions for the Investigation of Human Behaviour in an Urban Environment', pp. 1–46 in R.E. Park, E.W. Burgess and R.D. McKenzie (eds), *The City*. Chicago: University of Chicago Press.

Parkin, F. (1968) *Middle Class Radicalism: the Social Bases of the British Campaign for Nuclear Disarmament*. Manchester: Manchester University Press.

Parsons, T., Shils, E., Naegele, K. and Pitts, J. (eds) (1961) *Theories of Society: Foundations of Modern Sociological Theory*. New York: Free Press.

Peckham, M. (1962) *Beyond the Tragic Vision*. Cambridge: Cambridge University Press.

Pepper, D. (1991) *Communes and the Green Vision: Counterculture, Lifestyle and the New Age*. London: Green Print/Merlin Press.

Pile, S. and Thrift, N. (eds) (1995) *Mapping the Subject*. London: Routledge.

Plant, S. (1992) *The Most Radical Gesture: the Situationist International in a Postmodern Age*. London: Routledge.

Purkis, J. (1996) 'The City as a Site of Ethical Consumption and Resistance', pp. 203–224 in J. O'Connor, and D. Wynne (eds), *From the Margins to the Centre*. Aldershot: Arena.

Rajchman, J. (ed.) (1995) *The Identity in Question*. London: Routledge.

Redfield, R. (1947) 'The Folk Society', *American Journal of Sociology*, 52 (4): 293–308.

Relph, E. (1976) *Place and Placelessness*. London: Pion.

Relph, E. (1989) 'Geographical Experiences and Being-in-the-World: the Phenomenological Origins of Geography', pp. 15–31 in D. Seaman, and R. Murgerauer (eds), *Dwelling, Place and the Environment*. New York: Columbia University Press.

Riesman, D. (with Glazer, N. and Denney, R.) (1950) *The Lonely Crowd: a Study of the Changing American Character*. New York: Doubleday Books.

Rigby, A. (1974) *Alternative Realities: a Study of Communes and their Members*. London: Routledge and Kegan Paul.

Rojek, C. (1993) *Ways of Escape*. London: Macmillan

Rojek, C. (1995) *Decentred Leisure*. London: Sage.

Rose, G. (1993) *Feminism and Geography*. Oxford: Polity.

Roseneil, S. (1995) *Disarming Patriarchy*. Buckingham: Open University Press.

Roszak, T. (1970) *The Making of a Counter Culture*. London: Faber and Faber.

Roth, G. (1968) 'Introduction', pp. xxvii–cviii in M. Weber, *Economy and Society: an Outline of Interpretive Sociology, Volume 1*. G. Roth and C. Wittich (eds). New York: Bedminster Press.

Roth, G. (1979) 'Charisma and the Counterculture', pp. 119–143 in G. Roth and W. Schluchter, *Max Weber's Vision of History: Ethics and Methods*. Berkeley: University of California Press.

Rotman, B. (1993) *Signifying Nothing: The Semiotics of Zero*. Stanford: Stanford University Press.

Rucht, D. (1990) 'The Strategies and Action Repertoires of New Movements', pp. 156–175 in R. Dalton and M. Kuechler (eds), *Challenging the Political Order: New Social and Political Movements in Western Democracies*. Cambridge: Polity Press.

Rutherford, J. (ed.) (1990) *Identity: Community, Culture, Difference*. London: Lawrence and Wishart.

Ryan, J. and Fitzpatrick, H. (1996) 'The Space that Difference Makes: Negotiation and Urban Identities Through Consumption Practices', pp. 169–201 in J. O'Connor and D. Wynne (eds), *From the Margins to the Centre*. Aldershot: Arena.

Sack, R. (1980) *Conceptions of Space in Social Thought: a Geographic Perspective*. Basingstoke: Macmillan.

Said, E. (1979) *Orientalism: Western Concepts of the Orient*. London: Penguin.

St. John, G. (1997) 'Going Feral: Authentica on the Edge of Australian Culture', *The Australian Journal of Anthropology*, 8 (2): 167–189.

Sarup, M. (1996) *Identity, Culture and the Postmodern World*. Edinburgh: Edinburgh University Press.

Scaff, L. (1989) *Fleeing the Iron Cage: Culture, Politics and Modernity in the Thought of Max Weber*. Berkeley: University of California Press.

Schechner, R. (1985) *Between Theatre and Anthropology*. Philadelphia: University of Pennsylvania Press.

Scheler, M. (1954) *The Nature of Sympathy*. London: Routledge and Kegan Paul.

Schmalenbach, H. (1922) 'Die Soziologishe Kategorie des Bundes', *Die Dioskuren*, Vol. 1. München: 35–105.

Schmalenbach, H. (1961) 'The Sociological Category of Communion', pp. 331–347 in T. Parsons, E. Shils, K. Naegele and J. Pitts (eds), *Theories of Society: Foundations of Modern Sociological Theory*. New York: Free Press.

Schmalenbach, H. (1977) 'Communion – A Sociological Category', pp. 64–125 in G. Lüschen and G. Stone (eds), *Herman Schmalenbach: on Society and Experience*. Chicago: University of Chicago Press.

Schmitt, C. (1986) *Political Theology*. Cambridge, MA: MIT Press.

Schmitt, C. (1988) *Political Romanticism*. Cambridge, MA: MIT Press.

Schroeder, R. (1991) ' "Personality" and "Inner Distance": The Conception of the Individual in Max Weber's Sociology', *History of the Human Sciences*, 4 (1): 61–78.

Schutz, A. (1967) 'On Mutiple Realities', pp. 207–259 in M. Natanson (ed.), *Collected Papers, Volume 1*. The Hague: Martinus Nijhoff.

Scott, A. (1990) *Ideology and the New Social Movements*. London: Unwin Hyman.

Sennett, R. (1977) 'Destructive Gemeinschaft', pp. 171–197 in N. Birnbaum (ed.), *Beyond the Crisis*. Oxford: Oxford University Press.

Sennett, R. (1986) *The Fall of Public Man*. London: Faber and Faber.

Serres, M. (1991) *Rome: The Book of Foundations*. Stanford: Stanford University Press.

Serres, M. (1995) *The Natural Contract*. Ann Arbor, MI: University of Michigan Press.

Serres, M. and Latour, B. (1995) *Conversations on Science, Culture and Time*. Ann Arbor: University of Michigan Press.

Sharma, U. (1992) *Complementary Medicine Today*. London: Routledge.

Shields, R. (1989) 'Social Spatialization and the Built Environment: the West Edmonton Mall', *Environment and Planning D: Society and Space*, 7 (2): 147–164.

Shields, R. (1990) 'The "System of Pleasure": Liminality and the Carnivalesque at Brighton', *Theory, Culture and Society*, 7 (1): 39–72.

Shields, R. (1991a) *Places on the Margin: Alternative Geographies of Modernity*. London: Routledge.

Shields, R. (1991b) 'Introduction to "The Ethics of Aesthetics" ', *Theory, Culture and Society*, 8 (1): 1–5.

Shields, R. (ed.) (1992a) *Lifestyle Shopping: the Subject of Consumption*. London: Routledge.

Shields, R. (1992b) 'Individuals, Consumption Cultures and the Fate of Community', pp. 99–113 in R. Shields (ed.), *Lifestyle Shopping: the Subject of Consumption*. London: Routledge.

Shields, R. (1996) 'Foreword: Masses or Tribes', pp. ix–xii in M. Maffesoli, *The Time of the Tribes*. London: Sage.

Shilling, C. (1993) *The Body and Social Theory*. London: Sage.

Shilling, C. (1997) 'Emotion, Embodiment and the Sensations of Society', *The Sociological Review*, 45 (2): 195–219.

Shils, E. (1957) 'Primordial, Personal, Sacred and Civil Ties', *British Journal of Sociology*, 8: 130–145.

Shils, E. (1965) 'Charisma, Order, and Status', *American Sociological Review*, 30 (2): 199–213.

Shils, E. (1970) *Selected Essays*. Chicago: University of Chicago Press.

Shils, E. (1975) 'Center and Periphery', in: *Center and Periphery: Essays in Macrosociology*. Chicago: University of Chicago Press.

Shils, E. and Janowitz, M. (1948) 'Cohesion and Disintegration in the Wehrmacht in World War Two', *Public Opinion Quarterly*, 12 (2): 280–315.

Simmel, G. (1971a) 'The Adventurer', pp. 187–198 in D. Levine (ed.), *On Individuality and Social Forms*. Chicago: University of Chicago Press.

Simmel, G. (1971b) 'The Metropolis and Mental Life', pp. 324–339 in D. Levine (ed.), *On Individuality and Social Forms*. Chicago: University of Chicago Press.

Simmel, G. (1971c) 'Fashion', pp. 294–323 in D. Levine (ed.), *On Individuality and Social Forms*. Chicago: University of Chicago Press.

Smelser, N. (1963) *Theories of Collective Behaviour*. London: Routledge and Kegan Paul.

Soja, E. (1989) *Postmodern Geographies: the Reassertion of Space in Critical Social Theory*. London: Verso.

Soja, E. (1990) 'Heterotopologies: A Remembrance of Other Spaces in Citadel-LA,' *Strategies*, 3: 6–39.

Soja, E. (1996) *Thirdspace*. Oxford: Blackwell.

Spivak, G. (1976) 'Translator's preface', pp. ix–xxxviii in J. Derrida, *Of Grammatology*. Baltimore: Johns Hopkins University Press.

Spivak, G. (1988) 'Can the Subaltern Speak?', pp. 272–313 in C. Nelson and L. Grossberg (eds), *Marxism and the Interpretation of Culture*. Urbana: University of Illinois Press.

Stallybrass, P. and White, A. (1986) *The Politics and Poetics of Transgression*. London: Methuen.

Star, S.L. (ed.) (1995) *The Cultures of Computing*. Oxford: Blackwell.

Steig, M. (1970) 'Defining the Grotesque: an Attempt at Synthesis', *Journal of Aesthetics and Art Criticism*, 29 (2): 253–260.

Steiner, G. (1971) *In Bluebeard's Castle*. London: Faber and Faber.

Strathern, M. (1991) *Partial Connections*. Savage, MD: Rowland and Littlewood.

Swingewood, A. (1977) *The Myth of Mass Culture*. London: Macmillan.

Talmon, Y. (1972) *Family and Community in the Kibbutz*. Cambridge, MA: Harvard University Press.

Tarrow, S. (1994) *Power in Movement*. Cambridge: Cambridge University Press.

Taylor, I., Evans, K. and Fraser, P. (eds) (1996) *A Tale of Two Cities: Global Change, Local Feeling and Everyday Life in the North of England: A Study of Manchester and Sheffield*. London: Routledge.

Teyssot, G. (1980) 'Heterotopias and the History of Spaces', *Architecture and Urbanism*, 121: 79–100.

Theory, Culture and Society (1988) 5 (2–3). [Special Issue on Postmodernism.]

Thompson, P. (1972) *The Grotesque*. London: Methuen.

Thornton, S. (1995) *Club Cultures*. Oxford: Polity.

Thrasher, F. (1927) *The Gang: a Study of 1,313 Gangs in Chicago*. Chicago: University of Chicago Press.

Thrift, N. (1983) 'On the Determination of Social Action in Space and Time', *Environment and Planning D: Society and Space*, 1 (1): 23–57.

Tipton, S. (1982) *Getting Saved from the Sixties*. Berkeley: University of California Press.

Todorov, T. (1995) *The Conquest of America*. New York: Harper.

Tomlinson, A. (1990) *Consumption, Identity and Style*. London: Routledge.

Tönnies, F. (1955) *Community and Association*. London: Routledge and Kegan Paul.

Touraine, A. (1981) *The Voice and the Eye: an Analysis of Social Movements*. Cambridge: Cambridge University Press.

Tuan, Y.-F. (1977) *Space and Place: the Perspective of Experience*. Minneapolis: University of Minnesota Press.

Tucker, K. (1991) 'How New are the New Social Movements?', *Theory, Culture and Society*, 8 (2): 75–98.

Turkle, S. (1995) *Life on the Screen*. London: Weidenfeld and Nicholson.

Turner, B. (1984) *The Body and Society*. London: Sage.

Turner, B. (1991) 'Recent Developments in the Theory of the Body', pp. 1–35 in M. Featherstone, M. Hepworth and B. Turner (eds), *The Body: Social Process and Cultural Theory*. London: Sage.

Turner, V. (1967) *The Forest of Symbols: Aspects of Ndembu Ritual*. Ithaca, NY: Cornell University Press.

Turner, V. (1969) *The Ritual Process: Structure and Anti-Structure*. London: Routledge and Kegan Paul.

Turner, V. (1973) 'The Center Out There: Pilgrim's Goal', *History of Religions*, 12 (3): 191–230.

Turner, V. (1974) *Drama, Fields and Metaphors: Symbolic Action in Human Societies*. Ithaca, NY: Cornell University Press.

Turner, V. (1976) 'Social Dramas and Ritual Metaphors', pp. 97–119 in R. Schechner and M. Schuman (eds), *Ritual, Play, and Performance: Readings in the Social Sciences/Theatre*. New York: The Seasbury Press.

Turner, V. (1977) 'Frame, Flow and Reflection: Ritual and Drama as Public Liminality', pp. 33–55 in M. Benamou and C. Caramello (eds), *Performance in Postmodern Culture*. Madison, WI: University of Wisconsin–Milwaukee/Coda Press.

Turner, V. (1982) *From Ritual to Theatre: the Human Seriousness of Play*. New York: Performing Arts Journal Publication.

Urry, J. (1990) *The Tourist Gaze: Leisure and Travel in Contemporary Societies*. London: Sage.

Urry, J. (1995) *Consuming Places*. London: Routledge.

Van Gennep, A. (1960) *The Rites of Passage*. Chicago: University of Chicago Press.

Vaniegem, R. (1983) *The Revolution of Everyday Life*. London: Left Bank Books/Rebel Press.

Von Stein, L. (1964) *The History of the Social Movement in France 1798–1850*. Toronto: Bedminster Press.

Walkowitz, J. (1992) *City of Dreadful Delight: Narratives of Sexual Danger in Late-Victorian London*. London: Virago.

Wallis, R. (ed.) (1979) *On the Margins of Science: the Social Construction of Rejected Knowledge*. Keele: University of Keele. (Sociological Review Monograph No. 27.)

Webb, J. (1974) *The Occult Underground*. La Salle, Illinois: Open Court.

Weber, M. (1965) *The Sociology of Religion*. London: Methuen.

Weber, M. (1968) *Economy and Society: an Outline of Interpretive Sociology, Volume 1*. G. Roth and C. Wittich (eds). New York: Bedminster Press.

Weber, M. (1970a) 'Science as a Vocation', pp. 129–156 in H. Gerth and C. Wright Mills (eds), *From Max Weber: Essays in Sociology*. London: Routledge and Kegan Paul.

Weber, M. (1970b) 'Politics as a Vocation', pp. 77–128 in H. Gerth and C. Wright Mills (eds), *From Max Weber: Essays in Sociology*. London: Routledge and Kegan Paul.

Weber, M. (1970c) 'The Sociology of Charismatic Authority,' pp. 245–252 in H. Gerth and C. Wright Mills (eds), *From Max Weber: Essays in Sociology*. London: Routledge and Kegan Paul.

Weber, M. (1985) *The Protestant Ethic and the Spirit of Capitalism*. London: Counterpoint/Unwin.

Webster, C. (1976) 'Communes: a Thematic Typology', pp. 127–134 in S. Hall and T. Jefferson (eds), *Resistance Through Rituals: Youth Subcultures in Post-War Britain*. London: Hutchinson/Centre for Contemporary Cultural Studies.

Werbner, R. (1989) *Ritual Passage Sacred Journey*. Manchester: Manchester University Press.

Werbner, P. and Modood, T. (eds) (1997) *Debating Cultural Hybridity*. London: Zed.

Williams, R. (1965) *The Long Revolution*. Harmondsworth: Penguin.

Williams, R. (1977) *Marxism and Literature*. Oxford: Oxford University Press.

Williams, R. (1979) *Politics and Letters*. London: New Left Books.

Willis, P. (1978) *Profane Culture*. London: Routledge and Kegan Paul.

Willis, P. (with Jones, S., Canaan, J. and Hurd, G.) (1991) *Common Culture: Symbolic Work and Play in the Everyday Cultures of the Young*. Milton Keynes: Open University Press.

Wilson, E. (1985) *Adorned in Dreams: Fashion and Modernity*. London: Virago.

Wilson, E. (1991) *The Sphinx in the City: Urban Life, the Control of Disorder and Women*. London: Virago.

Wirth, L. (1964) 'Urbanism as a Way of Life', pp. 60–83 in A. Riess (ed.), *On Cities and Social Life*. Chicago: University of Chicago Press.

Wouters, C. (1989) 'The Sociology of Emotions and Flight Attendants: Hochschild's *Managed Heart*', *Theory, Culture and Society*, 6 (1): 95–123.

Yearley, S. (1991) *The Green Case: a Sociology of Environmental Issues, Arguments and Politics*. London: HarperCollins.

Young, A. (1990) *Femininity in Dissent*. London: Routledge.

Young, M. and Wilmott, P. (1957) *Family and Kinship in East London*. Harmondsworth: Penguin.

Zald, M. and McCarthy, J. (eds) (1979) *The Dynamics of Social Movements*. Cambridge, MA: Winthrop.

Zukin, S. (1988) *Loft Living: Culture and Capital in Urban Change*. (Second Edition). London: Radius/Hutchinson.

Zukin, S. (1992) 'Postmodern Urban Landscapes: Mapping Culture and Power', pp. 221–247 in S. Lash and J. Friedman (eds), *Modernity and Identity*. Oxford: Basil Blackwell.

INDEX